Produced by Irving Thalberg

Produced by Irving Thalberg

Theory of Studio-Era Filmmaking

Ana Salzberg

EDINBURGH
University Press

Edinburgh University Press is one of the leading university presses in
the UK. We publish academic books and journals in our selected subject
areas across the humanities and social sciences, combining cutting-edge
scholarship with high editorial and production values to produce academic
works of lasting importance. For more information visit our website:
edinburghuniversitypress.com

Edinburgh University Press Ltd
The Tun – Holyrood Road
12(2f) Jackson's Entry
Edinburgh EH8 8PJ

First published in hardback by Edinburgh University Press 2020

Typeset in 11/13 Monotype Ehrhardt by
IDSUK (DataConnection) Ltd, and
printed and bound by CPI Group (UK) Ltd,
Croydon, CR0 4YY

A CIP record for this book is available from the British Library

ISBN 978 1 4744 5104 8 (hardback)
ISBN 978 1 4744 5105 5 (paperback)
ISBN 978 1 4744 5106 2 (webready PDF)
ISBN 978 1 4744 5107 9 (epub)

Contents

Acknowledgments

I would like to thank Gillian Leslie of Edinburgh University Press for her support of this project from its beginnings; Elizabeth Ezra, for her friendship and encouragement; and my colleagues in the School of Humanities, University of Dundee, for their camaraderie.

Many people have offered support at key points in the writing of this book. Kristine Krueger and Janet Lorenz of the Margaret Herrick Library, Academy of Motion Picture Arts and Sciences, have been very helpful over the past few years. Profound appreciation goes to Ned Comstock, of the USC Cinematic Arts Library, for sharing Thalberg treasures with me. My research on Thalberg's role in the development of the Production Code could not have been carried out without the gracious help of Professor Richard Maltby and the MPPDA Digital Archive of Flinders University; the latter is an extraordinary resource for film scholarship.

Cinema: Journal of Philosophy and the Moving Image kindly granted permission for me to reprint parts of "Seduction Incarnate: Pre-Production Code Hollywood and Possessive Spectatorship" (vol. 3, 2012).

Produced by Irving Thalberg is dedicated to my parents and husband; each is a wonder to me, and I could not love them more. Richard and Janice Salzberg are my greatest teachers: elegant, wise, and touched with grace. I am honored to be their daughter. Alex Thomson read this manuscript with his characteristic insight and generous spirit, and I am forever grateful to him. I cherish our story conferences and every moment together.

CHAPTER 1

Opening Credits

Hollywood lore has it that Irving Thalberg had a habit of tossing a coin in the air during story conferences. Writer Anita Loos describes him as "boyishly flip[ping] a big silver dollar" (1974: 36) while discussing the making of *Red-Headed Woman* (dir. Conway, 1932); film critic Bosley Crowther relates that Thalberg would "sit there flipping a gold coin [. . .] while his associates talked" (1957: 182); and in still another account, biographer Bob Thomas details meetings in which Thalberg would "flip [. . .] a twenty-dollar gold piece into the air, often letting it clatter on the top of his glass-covered desk" (1969: 111). As the head of production at Metro-Goldwyn-Mayer, Thalberg brought the studio to critical and commercial prestige in the 1920s and 1930s. He fostered the careers of legendary performers like Lon Chaney, Joan Crawford, Greta Garbo, John Gilbert, Jean Harlow, and his wife Norma Shearer, thus establishing MGM as the studio with (as their slogan went) "More stars than there are in the heavens." Thalberg also led a coterie of associate producers known as the "Thalberg men" (Marx 1975: 252), advising them as they refined their filmmaking style across a number of genres. Finally, Thalberg guided MGM through the production of era-defining films, from romantic dramas (including *Flesh and the Devil*, dir. Brown, 1927; *Grand Hotel*, dir. Goulding, 1932) and period epics (*Ben-Hur*, dir. Niblo, 1925; *Mutiny on the Bounty*, dir. Lloyd, 1935), horror films (*Freaks*, dir. Browning, 1932) and comedies (*A Night at the Opera*, dir. Wood, 1935). Yet in the chronicles of Thalberg's time at the studio, the grand scale of these accomplishments is juxtaposed with the minutiae of his idiosyncrasies—among these, of course, the continual flipping of the coin.

As New Hollywood producer Robert Evans would write in his 2013 memoir, "Thalberg's talent was mythical [. . .] [N]o one ever filled the immense void he left [. . .]" (210). His untimely death from pneumonia in 1936 at the age of 37 ended one of the most illustrious careers in Hollywood history. From the beginning of the 1920s, Thalberg occupied positions of authority in the film industry:

by the age of 20, he was general manager of Universal Pictures—four years before he and Louis B. Mayer founded MGM in 1924. Thalberg's fame was established early; in a 1926 profile, for instance, Dorothy Herzog described him as no less than "a combined Horatio Alger hero, Peter Pan, Napoleon, Falstaff and J. Pierpont Morgan" (66). According to Herzog, Thalberg "has a decisive mind, mellowed with imagination and fine sensibilities. He knows when a person is good or a picture is good. He gets a 'hunch' when he is right" (131). But Thalberg married intuition with pragmatism, a balance that would characterize his approach to production at MGM. When asked by story editor Samuel Marx to define "box office," the producer "thought for a moment, then said, 'A combination of a star and a title that the public wants to see' " (qtd. in Marx 1975: 217). As F. Scott Fitzgerald would write in his unfinished *roman à clef The Last Tycoon* (1941), Thalberg remains in the cultural imagination one of the few producers who could "keep the whole equation of pictures in their heads" (1993: 3).

Fitzgerald began work on *The Last Tycoon* after Thalberg's passing, inspired by the working relationship they had shared during the former's brief role as an MGM screenwriter (xxii, xxv). The experience was not a happy one— among other conflicts, Thalberg did not like Fitzgerald's script for *Red-Headed Woman*—but he would remember the fascination that the producer held. As Fitzgerald remarked, "[Thalberg's] final collapse is the death of an enemy for me, though I liked the guy enormously" (1993: xxii). Through the character of producer Monroe Stahr, Fitzgerald explored the creative impetus that drove Thalberg, as well as the allure of his personal presence: he was a figure who "had a long time ago run ahead through trackless wastes of perception into fields where very few men were able to follow him" (18). Since 1936, though, many have tried to "follow" Thalberg—not simply in relation to his cinematic success, but like Fitzgerald, in terms of making sense of his legacy. In the preface to his definitive biography, published in 2010, Mark A. Vieira makes explicit his aim to literally "follow" Thalberg:

> If you were to be transported from 2010 to 1930 [. . .] [w]hat insight would you gain about his production methods if you could go from the purchase of a play all the way to the premiere of the film he made from it? What would you learn by sitting next to him in a story conference? (2010: xv)

Indeed, factored into the whole equation of Thalberg scholarship across the decades is a kind of detective work, a piecing together of clues from personal accounts to make cohesive the mythical talent's short life. As Vieira points out, "The human being behind the legend has eluded most historians. How did he accomplish all he did in his short lifetime? Who was he?" (xv)

And so from Thalberg's single act of flipping a coin in the air—sometimes silver, sometimes gold—there emerge a number of interpretations. For Loos, it speaks to his youthful charm; for Crowther, it is a prelude to a story about Thalberg's "deference" to his colleagues (1957: 182). "[A] group of supervisors decided they'd had about enough of that nervous coin-flipping habit," relates Crowther, and in response, "Thalberg grinned and put his coin back" (182). For still another chronicler, the coin symbolizes the strain under which Thalberg functioned towards the end of his life:

> The tension showed; his hands shook, and he developed a habit of tossing a twenty-dollar gold piece up and down. He never stopped; he caught and tossed it again and again [. . .] It distracted everyone who worked with him. (Marx 1975: 243–244)

The variations on this single narrative speak to Vivian Sobchack's contention that the work of history itself defies authoritative objectivity, composed as it is of "the productive unreliability and partiality of lived and invested memories, murmurs, nostalgias, stories, myths, and dreams" (2000: 303, 313). This is especially true in the case of Hollywood history, in which the subject of a biographical narrative often becomes an object of cultish fascination. Thalberg himself is no exception to such a process, though it is widely associated with stars like Marilyn Monroe and James Dean—performers who died before their time and whose work continues to inspire ever-renewing waves of interest. Less overtly visible than his star counterparts, whose images appear on postcards, posters, and T-shirts, Thalberg's legacy is nonetheless an active element in a broader nostalgia for Hollywood's golden age. The Academy Awards continues to bestow the Irving G. Thalberg Memorial Award on "creative producers whose bodies of work reflect a consistently high quality of motion picture production";[1] Amazon Prime recently revived *The Last Tycoon* as a streaming soap opera (2016). This cultural memory is an unstable one, however; to recall the words of director and colleague George Cukor, speaking of an unidentified work on Thalberg in 1972, "I didn't read that recent book about him [. . .] That kind of book never seems to be about the person I knew" (qtd. in Lambert 1973: 106).[2]

Amid a constellation of media that seek to "know" Thalberg, paraphrasing Cukor's statement above, the flipping of the coin stands out as a metaphor for his cinematic legacy. The up-and-down of its motion, alternately compelling and frustrating, conceptually captures Thalberg's identity as a producer— the fluctuation between intuition and pragmatism, myth and materiality; his belonging equally to Hollywood legend and history; the flux between past success and modern-day influence; the existential interplay between the precocious "boy wonder" who died too soon and whose afterlife, conversely, endures in cultural perpetuity. In his lifetime, moreover, Thalberg managed to be both present and absent in the film industry: highly visible as a figure of power and both anonymous and ubiquitous in the productions themselves. For the numerous films that Thalberg oversaw at MGM until his death, not one bears his name.[3] Rather than announcing his influence, Thalberg neither sought nor received a screen credit for his *oeuvre*. He observed instead, "Credit you give yourself isn't worth having" (qtd. in Marx 1975: 30).

Both wry and insightful, this ethos helps to set Thalberg apart from equally famed producers—consider, for example, predecessor D. W. Griffith's embedding of his initials in the intertitles to his productions,[4] the fanfare around a David O. Selznick film, or even the generic signature of Freed Unit musicals. But aside from a resistance to effectively trademarking his work, the statement conveys Thalberg's authoritative equanimity. As biographer Vieira points out, "virtually no MGM film was made without Thalberg's imprint" (2010: xiv); there was little to prove when, as the word "imprint" suggests, the indexical traces of Thalberg's approach to production were always already evident. On an immediate level, such control encapsulates what, in their seminal history of classic Hollywood, David Bordwell, Janet Staiger, and Kristin Thompson identify as the "central producer" model of film production (1985: 320). They describe a process of "subdivision of supervision" at MGM, noting that while Thalberg would work with his various associate producers on the choice of performers, directors, and screenwriters, elements like script revisions, "cost estimates, sets, costumes [. . .] and so on were not final until approved by [him]" (320). Yet in turn, each of those production elements—as well as decisions relating to casting, editing, story composition, previews and retakes—generated from Thalberg's own concepts of what motion pictures could be. Thalberg would have needed to give himself credit not simply for the completion of the pictures themselves, but for the theories of filmmaking that guided their creation.

Like the mannerism of flipping a coin in the air, Thalberg's insights into producing have been well-documented in sources such as histories of MGM, story-conference notes, excerpts from personal papers, and press coverage of the day. Contemporaries recognized the historical and intellectual value of Thalberg's observations and recorded them for posterity after his passing; Fitzgerald's notes for *The Last Tycoon* included detailed reminiscences of conversations with Thalberg, for example, while Marx would begin to set down the producer's words in a 1942 *Hollywood Reporter* article entitled "Dialogue by Thalberg." Easily quotable and often witty, the directness of Thalberg's commentary belies its complexity. For example, his description of typecasting as "slow death for actors" (qtd. in Marx 1975: 156), or the abiding question "[w]hat can we do to make the picture better?" (qtd. in Thomas 1969: 140) as he called for retakes of key scenes, endure as more than aphorisms or good "dialogue." Indeed, the first comment speaks to Thalberg's commitment to "oblique casting" (Marx 1975: 156), which called for stars to move between different kinds of roles and so gain dimensionality in their performance styles and public personas; the second conveys his ethos of maximizing every film's potential for greatness. Thalberg's words offer not only a historical record of how he made films, but also more abstract reflections on the potential of the medium.

With this in mind, *Produced by Irving Thalberg* will argue for his significance as a theorist of studio-era filmmaking, as well as a legendary producer and executive. A wealth of biographical and film-historical resources has preceded this work, documenting Thalberg's contributions to the development of the studio era. The following presents a critical intervention in this scholarship, positing that his *oeuvre* from the founding of MGM in 1924 to his death in 1936 is as much conceptual as it is cinematic. Each chapter offers a reading of Thalberg's films through his own theoretical lens, thus highlighting his insights into production and introducing new ways of considering his classic pictures. The latter helped to define an entire era in Hollywood; how, in turn, did his work as a theorist help to shape those films? Thalberg made in-depth observations on nearly every facet of the production process, and each is dispersed across a number of sources: from comments to colleagues (as above), story conference notes, interviews, lectures, articles in magazines, and meetings with fellow executives. Indeed, this study will draw from a range of historical and archival sources to identify and collate Thalberg's key theories of filmmaking and explore their expression in works that he produced. Vieira set out to "[go] beyond the legend of Thalberg to find the human being" (xvii); in parallel terms, this work will go beyond the legendary producer to find the film theorist.

This book does not aim to be a work of history or biography. It builds upon the canon of existing Thalberg scholarship to propose a new understanding of his importance—not only for film history, but for film theory. As Thomas Elsaesser and Malte Hagener set out, film theory emerged concurrently with motion pictures themselves, and generated from a desire to understand "the essence of" the new medium (2015: 1). Along with the "inventors, manufacturers, artists, intellectuals, educators, and scientists" cited by Elsaesser and Hagener in that original wave of contemplation (1), Thalberg himself considered the unique potential of film both as an aesthetic form and a cultural phenomenon. Given Thalberg's executive oversight as well as his film-by-film presence as a producer, he perceived the medium from a particularly complex vantage point. In his daily life at the studio, this duality translated into a striking fluency in matters creative and logistical; Thomas notes that "Thalberg could leap from an intricate plot situation of a film to the contractual demands of a star in an instant, without sacrificing the complexities of either one" (111). In theoretical terms, this helped him develop a capacious set of propositions that reflected on an entire spectrum of concerns: from the responsibility of the studio to its public and the divisive question of morality in filmmaking, to the importance of a single scene in the arc of an entire production.

This study will adopt a methodology that draws from historical events to illuminate the dialogue between the specificities of the film-industrial context and Thalberg's theoretical explorations of the medium itself. Taking a chronological structure that follows his career from the founding of MGM, each chapter will establish the conditions of his productions—whether these relate to technological changes, shifts in corporate structures, or industry-wide concerns such as the Production Code—before exploring how those conditions influenced, and often *were* influenced by, Thalberg's evolving insights into filmmaking. The book will conclude by assessing his resonance in popular culture, tracing the mythology of Thalberg as it evolved after his death in 1936. The conclusion will also reflect on how modern-day viewing and production practices affect our understanding of his abiding cinematic influence. Inverting Vieira's idea of "transporting" (2010: xv) the reader from the present to Thalberg's past, the conclusion will trace his journey from the 1920s/1930s to contemporary Hollywood.

Connecting each of these analyses are, of course, Thalberg's own words. Key historical accounts have preserved his observations, including foundational works written by critics Bosley Crowther, Bob Thomas, and Samuel Marx, the latter of whom was an MGM story editor who had known Thalberg since their youth working for Universal Pictures. In Crowther's chronicle of MGM's heyday in *The Lion's Share* (1957) and Mayer biography *Hollywood Rajah* (1960), Thalberg appears as a major player; but it is in Marx's *Mayer and Thalberg: The Make-Believe Saints* (1975) and Thomas's *Thalberg: Life and Legend* (1969) that the producer's character and accomplishments are profiled extensively. Published only a few decades after Thalberg's death, and recording the reminiscences of his colleagues and contemporaries, these popular histories take on the gravity of primary sources. Yet just as these and other accounts present variations on the narrative of Thalberg flipping a coin, there are also variations on the wording of certain comments. The implications of this are twofold: first, such iterations of a single theory speak to Thalberg's prevalence in Hollywood histories; which, in turn, speaks to the importance of consolidating and exploring in-depth what these observations mean for film theory. That is, the chapters will examine what he was saying—in both the literal and figurative sense of the phrase.

To paraphrase Sobchack, such "productive"—and relative—"unreliability" renders the Thalberg-authored texts all the more impactful, with their sustained and comprehensive consideration of a given topic. Compared to counterpart David O. Selznick, whose prodigious memo-writing documented an entire career's worth of observations on the role of the producer,[5] Thalberg's own output was fairly modest. It includes, among other pieces, a 1929 speech at the University of Southern California, a 1933 article in the *Saturday Evening Post*, and a personal letter to Loew's, Inc. president Nicholas Schenck. Especially enlightening are story conference notes relating to particular films (as explored extensively in Schatz 1996, Vieira, and Spadoni), as well as the transcript of Thalberg's extemporaneous statements at a 1930 meeting discussing the strictures of the Production Code. Certain of these texts have featured in other biographical or historical works as a detailed record of Thalberg's contributions to the studio system; what each chapter will do here, however, is argue that these ideas belong to an entire theoretical model of film production. In so engaging with these diffuse sources, the following will draw together Thalberg's conceptual contributions and explore both their relationship to historical context and their cinematic expression. *Produced by Irving Thalberg*, therefore, chronicles not the life of the man but the direction of his thoughts; the ways that his aesthetic and industrial concerns developed as steadily as the studio that he helped to found. Putting in the title the credit that he never took, this study proposes that what Thalberg produced was a unified theoretical understanding of studio-era filmmaking.

PRODUCER STUDIES

Thalberg stated in 1930, "Your purpose as producers in this industry is to comply with the wishes of the great public and give the people that which the public is demanding, up to a certain point, with a modicum of discretion."[6] The context is particularly interesting here, considering that Thalberg was speaking to a room full of fellow producers and representatives from the Motion Picture Producers and Distributors of America (MPPDA) about the parameters of regulation in the industry. Equally fascinating is the fact that decades later, film scholars still explore what the "purpose" of the producer was and is—an existential question as much as an industrial one. Certainly the producer as such has attracted both popular and academic interest, seen, for example, in scholarly studies of figures like Val Lewton (Nemerov 2005), David O. Selznick (Vertrees 1997; Platte 2017), Walter Wanger (Bernstein 1994), and Darryl F. Zanuck (Lev 2013). Yet where Film Studies has long embraced the director as *auteur*, producer studies still represents a relatively new territory for analysis. As Andrew Spicer, A. T. McKenna, and Christopher Meir note, this field takes as its subject a "largely misunderstood and under-analysed [industry] figure [. . .] The producer is easy to caricature but the role is difficult to define" (2014: 1). These critics explore the implications of that caricature, identifying a fundamental "dichotomy between art and commerce" (3) that has generated dismissive and / or unsympathetic readings of the producer and the associated "grubbiness of bottom-line concerns" (1).

Accordingly, producer studies seeks to map out the complexities of the role across national traditions and eras of filmmaking, as well as across the more specific disciplinary divides between "economic film history" and formalist studies (2014: 1, 8). Spicer et al. highlight the impact of *auteur* studies on the relative neglect of the producer in film scholarship, inasmuch as the emphasis on authorship sustains that schism between "art and commerce" referenced above; the director embodies the former, the producer the latter (4). Thalberg figures in such art-and-commerce conflicts, notably in one of several troubled encounters with Erich von Stroheim: this time, over the making of *Greed* (1924). After firing the director at Universal, Thalberg once again asserted his control over von Stroheim's process by editing the hours-long *Greed* to a standard length (Marx 1975: 58). Though it is now legendary as a film that might have been, Thalberg defended his decision: "We took no chances in cutting it. We took it around to different theatres in the suburbs, ran it at its enormous length, and then we took note of the places at which interest seemed to droop" (qtd. in Vieira 2010: 47). Using the preview process to establish the "wishes of the great public," to recall his words above, Thalberg placed the audience—and the interests of the studio—above the wishes of the *auteur*.

Aside from such retroactive interventions, Thalberg was willing to work behind the camera. Thomas notes that "[i]t was not unusual for the director [of a given film] to step aside and allow Thalberg to stage the scene himself" (111), a statement supported by archival material. In a 1930 memo, the head of the Studio Relations Committee, Jason S. Joy, recounted the following about the making of Garbo vehicle *Romance* (dir. Brown, 1930):

> Irving Thalberg is a little disappointed with the last sequence between the clergyman and the singer. They "reshot" the thing any number of times with Thalberg himself finally directing it; and Thalberg is positive that he has gotten out of that particular actor all that he had to give.[7]

Striking here is the way that Thalberg's broader emphasis on retakes ("reshots") translates into an immediate, personal engagement with the filmmaking process. More than signaling his attentiveness to audience responses at previews or even his authority in ordering the retakes, the anecdote captures the balance between executive oversight and creative ability that helped define Thalberg's career. Marx's retrospective description of Thalberg's style of working with directors underscores his embeddedness in the day-to-day of production. According to Marx, Thalberg had a "set speech" for directors:

> I consider the director is on the set to communicate what *I expect of my actors*. It's my experience that many directors only realize seventy-five percent of our scenarios, and while audiences never know how much they missed, I do. You gentlemen have individualistic styles and I respect them. It's one of the principal reasons we want you here. But if you can't conform to *my system*, it would be wiser not to start your film at all. (Qtd. in Marx 1975: 96–97; emphasis added)

Such accounts place Thalberg not on either side of the art–commerce divide, but in a position of versatility that directly impacted both. Thalberg's authority as head of production at MGM, then, emerged from an intersection between front-office knowledge and artistic awareness—each one informing the other. This insight defined Thalberg's theories of production, imbuing more abstract notions of storytelling and dramatic impact with the concrete understanding of how to bring them to the screen.

Certainly the notion of an intense affinity between producer and camera is not new. Selznick "was always looking for ways to control camera work and editing" (1996: 272), according to Thomas Schatz; Zanuck spent mornings and evenings going over rushes of Fox's films, as well as making decisions as to the way films should be cut (Lev 45). And in his memoir *The Kid Stays in the Picture*, New Hollywood producer Evans—who played Thalberg in *The Man of a Thousand Faces* (dir. Pevney, 1958)—ascribes the success of *The Godfather* (dir. Coppola, 1972) to his work in the editing room (2003: 233–236). Such engagement with the filmmaking process has, in part, led to attempts to position the producer within the *auteur*-ist framework set out by Andrew Sarris (despite the latter's "almost evangelical zeal" in dismissing the producer, as Spicer et al. phrase it [4]). Matthew Bernstein, whose landmark work on Walter Wanger helped pioneer producer studies, has written of the challenges of attributing authorship to the producer in these terms. Though Bernstein discusses the authorial gravitas of figures like Lewton and Selznick, in that they supervised virtually every element of their films, Bernstein concludes that "the producer as auteur was clearly an exception" (2008: 186) to the streamlined production style of the studio system.

Yet the very act of transposing the producer into the *auteur*-ist model leads to more problematic conclusions. Bernstein compares Zanuck's significance as a near-*auteur* executive to Thalberg's influence at MGM, finding that the former's "creativity informed an entire studio's output"—as opposed to the latter merely "establishing MGM's high gloss, high quality production values" (185–186). Given Thalberg's extensive conceptual and logistical authority at MGM from its very inception, such an assessment needs to be interrogated further. What it reflects more broadly, however, is the difficulty of the authorship discourse itself. In a compare / contrast framework, one figure will always have more credibility as an *auteur* than another; and such valuations risk distorting the distinctive role played by each producer across their executive and creative contexts.

Rather than debate Thalberg's authorship, this book will highlight a dialogue more defining to his legacy: that one between film history and theory. Certainly, the idea of the producer-as-theorist might warrant some provisional defense—an acknowledgment, that is, of the challenges inherent in negotiating between various foci such as industrial conditions, the collaborative nature of filmmaking, and Thalberg's conceptual singularity. As Schatz has pointed out, "[I]solating the producer or anyone else as artist or visionary gets us nowhere" (1996: 8); but identifying the producer as a theorist does introduce new ways of understanding his or her contributions to the filmmaking process. Beyond the financial concerns of the bottom line, to paraphrase the title of Spicer et al.'s anthology, or even day-to-day creative interventions, producers like Thalberg adopted a holistic view of how motion pictures could fulfill their aesthetic potential. Tracing such concerns reveals that the role of the producer extends from the film set and front office to more elemental questions of how film audiences—and film scholars—think about the nature of entertainment itself. This theoretical model would be equally (or perhaps especially) appropriate for a figure like Selznick, whose extensive memos represent a stunning primary source for such a critical intervention.

In so arguing for Thalberg as a theorist of studio-era production, this study contributes both to producer studies and Thalberg scholarship: offering, in the former case, another perspective from which to consider the multi-faceted role of the producer as such; and drawing out, in the latter case, the critical significance of Thalberg's insights into film production. These have been recorded across a variety of sources. In Tino Balio's *Grand Design: Hollywood as a Modern Business Enterprise* (1993), Thalberg is "the prototypical central producer" (74) as well as the architect of MGM's prestige pictures in the early 1930s (184–189); Jerome Christensen's "studio authorship thesis," which argues for an understanding of the "corporate studio" itself as collective author (2011: 13), acknowledges Thalberg as central in establishing MGM's identity; and Schatz's illuminating exploration of early MGM identifies Thalberg as a figure of authority "poised [. . .] between capitalization and production, between conception and execution" (1996: 47). For Schatz, Thalberg's fluency in all facets of the studio process—from the logistical and financial to the conceptual and creative—pioneered the "role of studio production chief" (47). Yet just as the figure of the producer has inspired caricatures so too has Thalberg the individual generated—virtually from the beginning of his career, as noted earlier—a kaleidoscope of facts and lore, personal remembrances and romanticizing impulses. As Vieira points out, sources often refer to Thalberg as a "'genius,' and some stop [. . .] just short of calling [him] a saint" (2010: xv).

Where Crowther's, Marx's, and Thomas's books remain canonical in Thalberg scholarship, more recent works have addressed his legacy. Roland Flamini's *Thalberg: The Last Tycoon and the World of MGM* (1994) offers a sensitive, but at times sensationalized, account of Thalberg as innovator and individual. Vieira has been most instrumental in preserving Thalberg's life and times for the contemporary age. His definitive biography *Irving Thalberg: Boy Wonder to Producer Prince* (2010) is a highly illuminating work that incorporates extensive archival materials (including story-conference notes and a draft of Shearer's unpublished memoir) to offer a complete portrait of Thalberg's life and career. In another work of film history, Vieira published *Hollywood Dreams Made Real: Irving Thalberg and the Rise of MGM* (2008). Surveying the producer's films in a format suitable for the mass market, the volume features large photographs illustrating Vieira's enlightening historical commentary. Here, he cites the importance of film stills in capturing the impact of Thalberg's productions; in the preface, Vieira also points out how the producer's films live on in contemporary visual culture, citing Turner Classic Movies as a primary source for new generations of audiences (2008: 7).

Thalberg endures as one of the most complex individuals of the studio era, moving fluidly between art and commerce, myth and biography, past and present. *Produced by Irving Thalberg* reveals still another dimension of this historical figure, claiming the value of his sustained and unified set of theoretical propositions as recorded in archival and historical sources, and revealed in the films he produced. But before encountering his theories, it is important to know his story—at least the beginning of it. For the early days of Thalberg's career provide insight into both the foundations of his concepts and, more broadly, the origins of studio-era Hollywood itself. That is: Thalberg and Hollywood effectively grew up together.

"A 'PRESENCE' HE IS"

Thalberg was born in Brooklyn, New York, in 1899. From childhood, his health represented what Vieira calls a "ticking time bomb" (2010: xiv): suffering from a congenital heart defect, Thalberg was vulnerable to a number of illnesses which marred his school years. A year-long period of recovery from rheumatic fever meant that he could not complete high school (4); but as Marx explains, Thalberg's "conviction that he would die before thirty [led him to decide that] he had no time for college" (1975: 10) in any event. In his late teens, Thalberg took evening courses in administrative skills like typing and shorthand (Vieira 2010: 4–5). Complementing this practical training were Thalberg's own interests in literature and philosophy—both of which he had studied independently, and intensively, during his recuperation (4). This dual focus on the conceptual and the concrete would go on to define his tenure at MGM, but not before it caught the attention of Carl Laemmle, head of Universal Film Manufacturing Company (5–6).

After Thalberg took a job in Universal's New York office as a secretary to Laemmle's assistant, the studio head found the young man's opinions on film projects to be particularly insightful (5). Thalberg became Laemmle's personal secretary and relished the job, particularly the time he spent in the screening room viewing the works in development (Thomas 43). In reading Laemmle's correspondence and watching films with him, however, Thalberg soon realized that Universal's Hollywood lot was both disorganized and producing mediocre material (Thomas 43; Vieira 2010: 5–6). As Marx would recall of his youthful conversations with Thalberg, he already understood the responsibility of the film studio to its public: "The people have to take what we give them. It seems to me they deserve better" (qtd. in Marx 1975: 18). This instinct for filmmaking developed even further after Thalberg accompanied Laemmle on a trip to the Hollywood studio in 1919. Here, Thalberg shared his thoughts on how the running of the lot could be improved; as one Universal executive recalled, "He had a good business mind as well as an artist's mind" (qtd. in Vieira 2010: 7). By April 1920, Thalberg had earned the role of general manager (8), and as Marx related, "News about his knowledge for stories and his instinct for moviemaking spread swiftly through Hollywood" (1975: 28). He was not even 21 years old.

Thalberg's own accelerated success matched that of Hollywood itself. Laemmle had founded Universal in 1914 on 230 acres of land, making it one of the first "permanent installations" for film production (Koszarski 1990: 5, 102) in a pastoral environment. Within only eight years, Hollywood had drawn studios such as Vitagraph, Metro, and Goldwyn from the East Coast and was responsible for 84 percent of productions in the country (102, 104). Richard Koszarski notes that the head offices of the studios maintained their presence in the East and describes Hollywood as a "factory town" (100) of filmmaking rather than a corporate epicenter; but the industrialization of filmmaking, however divorced from executive oversight, had irrevocably altered the landscape. By 1927, Grace Kinglsey mused in *Photoplay* about the time "When Hollywood was a Pasture," recalling the Edenic landscape "before the Midas of the Movies came in to turn everything to hard and glittering gold":

> What visions of shady glens picked off with cheerful red berries, of vistas of purple hills, of peaceful, tree-lined streets, cottages smothered in roses, little quaint churches, that name Hollywood conjures up!
>
> Surely there dwelt the fairy godmothers in the golden orange orchards, the dew-covered lawns, the rose bushes that bloomed along Hollywood and Sunset Boulevards, where now the granite buildings loom and the traffic cops' whistles have replaced the song of the mocking birds [. . .] The Hollywood hills were clad in all their virginal mesquite and live oaks [. . .] Santa Monica Boulevard and environs were prairies with an occasional cottage [. . .] (Kingsley 1927: 32)

Here, Kingsley plays out a nostalgia for a once-upon-a-time environment, the date of which is never quite defined in the piece. Bucolic and free from corruption, the Hollywood of Kingsley's description represents a fairy tale idyll in which the stars themselves figure as benign human counterparts to the "fairy godmothers" in the orange groves. The celebrities hold dances every Thursday evening at the Hollywood Hotel, with its "wide verandahs" and "lovely court filled with flowers, fountains and ferns" (140), or run from cows who have wandered over to D. W. Griffith's studio from a nearby field (33). As the "Midas of the movies" phrasing suggests, the entrenchment of the film industry introduced still another mode of mythology—luxe, pleasure-seeking, artificial.

Thalberg, however, arrived at a threshold point between the Midas of mechanization and the charm of a bygone age: his pragmatism and precocious leadership belonging to the former, his personal charisma recalling the romance of the latter. Such a juxtaposition reveals much about the development of Thalberg's public persona, highlighting the existential interplay between the individual and his environment. From this perspective, it is worth returning to Herzog's 1926 profile of Thalberg, which established him as a lead in Hollywood's own emerging cast of characters. As that "combined Horatio Alger hero, Peter Pan, Napoleon, Falstaff and J. Pierpont Morgan" (66), Thalberg exists as both executive (not to say tactician) and storybook protagonist. Herzog would expand on this later in the piece, noting that " 'they'—the picture folk—[have] pointed to him as the 'boy wonder,' 'the Miracle Man,' a genius of motion pictures" (66). With such monikers placing him between adolescence and maturity, the Thalberg of the popular imagination shared a liminal space with an industry that was itself both precocious and established.

The idea of the Boy Wonder as such would follow Thalberg for the rest of his life. It speaks, though, to still other preoccupations in early Hollywood. As Koszarski points out, a fascination with mysticism emerged in the film industry in the 1920s. He cites the observations of screenwriter Perley Poore Sheehan, who perceived "[t]he rise of Hollywood and [. . .] Los Angeles [as] the culmination of ages of preparatory struggle, physical, mental and spiritual" (qtd. in Koszarski 100). Crowther would recall the era in similar terms:

Rococo buildings and oil wells, Aimee Semple McPherson holding forth with steamy evangelism in her Angelus Temple, movie stars in high-powered foreign cars racing in flashy ostentation along palm-fringed boulevards [. . .] Those were the years when Hollywood was truly the Great Phenomenon, the newly established capital of the fables that were girdling the world. (1960: 123)

Though Koszarski notes that this mysticism "faded from fashion" (100), Sheehan and Crowther's rhetoric resonates in the terms used to describe Thalberg. Boy Wonder, Miracle Man, even Peter Pan—each of these attributes to Thalberg a supernatural power that complements, if not totally belies, his intellectual labor as a producer.

This is not to frame Thalberg in a kind of *Day of the Locust* occult spectacle, but rather to contextualize the culture in which his own star ascended. Indeed, descriptions of his physical affect emphasize its mesmeric quality. Herzog declared, "[A] 'presence' he is, despite the fact he is a human being—modest, brilliant, blessed with the rare gifts of humor, human insight, and brains" (131); author Edna Ferber recalled of an early meeting, "[T]his young man whose word seemed so final at Universal City turned out to be a wisp of a boy, twenty-one, so slight as to appear actually frail. Something about this boy impressed me deeply" (qtd. in Marx 1975: 40). The compelling union of youthfulness and age-old sagacity would endure—as producer Walter Wanger wrote of the 33-year-old Thalberg, "He could cast a spell on anybody [. . .] His very appearance was impressive. Although he was quite slight, he carried himself in a most effective manner. It was amazing what he got people to do for him" (qtd. in Vieira 2010: 171).

Thalberg drew upon those personal and intellectual powers in a defining conflict at Universal: the firing of director von Stroheim from the production *Merry-Go-Round* (1922). In a memo outlining the decision, Thalberg cited the director's "disloyalty to our company [. . . and] flagrant disregard for the principles of censorship" (qtd. in Vieira 2010: 14). In addition to anticipating the questions of corporate loyalty that would shade his later days at MGM, as well as hinting at his future role in drafting the Production Code, Thalberg's actions highlighted the resolve that underlay his charisma. As Selznick would later recall, "This was the first time a director had been fired. It took guts and courage. Thalberg was only twenty-two" (qtd. in Vieira 14). Decades later, Spicer et al. would discuss the significance of this event, characterizing it as a "David and Goliath struggle" that established the authority of the producer in the studio era (2014: 2). As noted earlier, von Stroheim and Thalberg would again clash during the making of *Greed* in 1924, so the drama had hardly concluded; but what emerges here is the intertwining of executive power and creative vision that would define Thalberg's tenure at MGM.

Indeed, it is fascinating to see how Thalberg's years at Universal established the foundation for his future *modus operandi* at MGM: gaining confidence in his critical voice as he viewed Universal's works-in-progress; learning how best to resolve conflicts, either with difficult directors like von Stroheim or, as Thomas notes, challenging actors (43); and even testing the retake process that Thalberg would go on to perfect at his own studio. In 1923, he produced *The Hunchback of Notre Dame* (dir. Worsley) and began a running collaboration with star Lon Chaney. Realizing the significance of the film but also seeing where it could be improved, Thalberg arranged for the filming of more crowd scenes (Thomas 54). The cost was high—$150,000— but the decision helped heighten the dramatic and visual impact of the film, which would be a massive success for Universal (54). As Chapters 3 and 7 will explore respectively, Thalberg's focus on maximizing on-screen scale and the process of retakes would become characteristic of his aesthetic vision and mode of production at MGM.

But in 1923, such creative autonomy appeared distant to Thalberg. When Laemmle did not offer Thalberg a raise, even after the success of *Hunchback* (Thomas 54), he grew dissatisfied with his role at Universal. Seeking opportunities elsewhere and following his own principle to "never remain in a job when you have everything from it you can get" (Herzog 60), Thalberg began negotiations with Mayer. The latter had a comprehensive understanding of the film industry: Mayer had bought his first theater in Massachusetts in 1907; and as he added more theaters over time, he also learned more about what kind of films audiences enjoyed the most—and would pay the most to see (Marx 1975: 12). After cementing his success as an exhibitor with the 1915 showings of *The Birth of a Nation*, Mayer decided to enter film production (Marx 1975: 12–13; Thomas 63). In 1918, he found his first star in Anita Stewart and cast her in the hit *Virtuous Wives* (dir. Tucker); that same year, Mayer moved his small production company to California (Thomas 63). His films were released by First National Exhibitors' Circuit and, in a hint of things to come, Metro Pictures Corporation (Crowther 1960: 79).

Mayer and Thalberg's 1923 negotiations represent, then, an encounter between various elements of the burgeoning industry: the former had extensive experience both in the movie theaters and behind the scenes, therefore understanding exhibition as well as production; the latter had the creative drive and effective approach to leadership to match the industry's own accelerated advancements. What both shared at this defining moment was a focus on crafting the finest entertainment. Thalberg would have certainly agreed with Mayer's ethos in founding his production company—"My unchanging policy will be great star, great director, great play, great cast" (qtd. in Vieira 18). Mayer and Thalberg also shared a personal regard; as Mayer's daughter Irene described it, "My father got a son without having to raise one—wise, loving, filial" (qtd. in Vieira 2010: 20). The following chapters will pick up the threads of this Mayer–Thalberg relationship, exploring in detail the development of their partnership and the running of the studio.

Indeed, the collaborative nature of studio-era filmmaking itself demands a consideration of Thalberg's host of working relationships at MGM. Nicholas Schenck emerges as a key player through his role as the president of Loew's, Inc, the theater chain that would control MGM following a 1924 merger between Louis B. Mayer Productions, Metro Pictures, and the Goldwyn Company. The MGM producers known as the "Thalberg men" (Marx 1975: 252), including associate producers Paul Bern, Bernard Hyman, Albert Lewin, Hunt Stromberg, and Lawrence Weingarten, also feature here. Stars like Chaney, John Gilbert, and Greta Garbo have recurring roles in this historical narrative—with no star as important as Norma Shearer, Thalberg's wife, who was instrumental in cementing his cinematic legacy. Each of these figures, among many others, compose a cast of characters that helped to generate and sustain Thalberg's theories of filmmaking.

THE CHAPTERS

For all of his impact, Thalberg was, of course, not alone in his contemplations on the development of the medium. A loose chronology that traces his work in the film industry would span from about 1918–19 through to his death in 1936, accounting for both his time as Laemmle's secretary and the extraordinary authority he would have at MGM by the time of his passing. Running roughly parallel to Thalberg's career is another timeline: that of early film theory.[8] As Elsaesser and Hagener outline, this era of theory interrogated "the specificity and nature of film as a medium, as well as [. . .] cinema's legitimacy as an art form" (3). Notable works included Vachel Lindsay's *The Art of the Moving Picture* (1915), Hugo Munsterberg's *The Photoplay: A Psychological Study* (1916; see Langdale 2002), Siegfried Kracauer's essays on film in Weimar Germany (later collected in 1963), and Rudolf Arnheim's *Film as Art* (1933). Across the 1920s and 1930s in Soviet Russia, theorist-filmmakers like Sergei Eisenstein and Vsevolod Pudovkin reflected on the significance of the editing process for both ideological and narrative impact. A voracious reader of any number of literary and philosophical works (Thomas 61; Vieira 2010: 4), as well as a reflective practitioner of the motion picture craft, Thalberg would undoubtedly have pursued texts such as these—had they all been readily available to him. Allan Langdale notes that Munsterberg's *The Photoplay* had gone out of print by 1930 (1),[9] and Jay Leyda comments upon the "inadequate English renderings" of Eisenstein's essays (Eisenstein 1977: x).

Difficulties in accessibility aside, a retrospective glance suggests some interesting connections. For instance, Lindsay championed screenwriter Anita Loos's talents before she would go on to collaborate extensively with Thalberg;[10] Munsterberg was friends and colleagues with William James, the pragmatist philosopher so admired by Thalberg (Langdale 2002: 4; Vieira 2010: 4); Arnheim discusses Garbo film *The Mysterious Lady* (dir. Niblo, 1928), produced under Thalberg, as an example of effective use of depth and perspective (51–53); and years later, Vieira would specifically connect the editing style of Thalberg's 1935 film *Mutiny on the Bounty* to Eisenstein's theory of montage (2010: 326)—certainly key scenes bear a striking resemblance to sequences in *Battleship Potemkin* (1925).

From a contemporary perspective, reading these works alongside Thalberg's own reveals further shared concerns between his industrial context and the aesthetic, technological, and cognitive interests of his counterparts. Certain points in particular draw attention: Lindsay would discuss the "Picture of Crowd Splendor" (43), noting how cinema can "convey [. . .] the passions of masses of men" (43) in such a way that anticipates Thalberg's call for "great scenes" (qtd. in Vieira 2010: 37) in epic productions of *Ben-Hur* and *The Big Parade* (dir. Vidor, 1925) (not to mention the crowd scenes in *Hunchback*). Munsterberg's analysis of the interplay between film and the viewer's subjectivity, or "acts of attention" (qtd. in Langdale 88), parallels Thalberg's sensitivity to an audience's response to a film in previews. Kracauer's explorations of how cinema reflected modern life[11] presage Thalberg's own emphasis on the importance of "currency—the immediate fitting in with current thought" (1977: 119); later, Kracauer's analysis of "run-of-the-mill film productions" (1995: 308) from German studios[12] would anticipate Thalberg's own frustrations with the lowering of MGM's production standards in the mid-1930s. Finally, Arnheim's valorization of silent cinema, even in a talkie age (107),[13] recalls Thalberg's 1929 statement that "talking pictures are merely a broadened field" (qtd. in Manners 94) for the medium which did not need to exclude silent filmmaking.

Equally intriguing are the links between Eisenstein and Pudovkin's respective theories of editing and Thalberg's own conception of that technique. For Eisenstein, each shot represented "a montage cell (or molecule)" that, when placed in thematic, graphic, or rhythmic conflict with another shot, could construct an entire thought process (1977: 53–62); for Pudovkin, the sequencing of shots could "excite or soothe the spectator" with its heightened narrative impact and by "concentrat[ing] the attention of the spectator only on that element important to the action" (2016: 8). Thalberg would also explore the capacities of editing for dramatic effect; for example, after viewing an unsuccessful rough cut of *He Who Gets Slapped* (dir. Sjostrom, 1924), due to be MGM's first release, he " 'disappeared into the cutting room and didn't come out for two days and a night.' But when he had finished, they had a successful picture" (Day 1960: 214). In its completed form, *He Who Gets Slapped* evokes an atmosphere both perverse and mournful through associative editing—reminiscent of Eisenstein's model—while maintaining a gripping narrative pace in sympathy with Pudovkin.

Any such glossing of complex critical works is, by definition, reductive. But what the above does set out are constellations of shared aesthetic concerns. Each of these theorists, in their varied contexts, focuses on the effects of cinema on the audience, trying to define or—as in the case of the Soviet theorists and Thalberg himself—create that unique impact. Each acknowledges, or indeed revels in, the mechanical processes that awaken an emotional response or direction of thought; and each thinks critically about the radical (in every sense of the term) nature of a medium that was rapidly taken for granted in popular culture. Interestingly, one of the most famous journalistic pieces on Thalberg would adopt a quasi-abstract tone that uncannily recalls Dziga Vertov's in describing the camera's "mechanical eye." In 1932, an anonymous article in *Fortune* recognized Thalberg's authority at the studio and his overseeing of the story development, casting, and editing of virtually every film the studio released. At various points, the unknown author writes of Thalberg:

> His brain is the camera which photographs dozens of scripts in a week and decides which of them, if any, shall be turned over to MGM's twenty-seven departments to be made into a moving picture. It is also the recording apparatus which converts the squealing friction of 2,200 erratic underlings into the more than normally coherent chatter of an MGM talkie. ("Metro-Goldwyn-Mayer" 258)
>
> The kind of pictures that MGM makes and the ways it makes them are Irving Thalberg's problems. He is what Hollywood means by MGM (257)
>
> MGM's associate producers [. . .] are the principal cogs through which Irving Thalberg causes MGM's wheels to spin. [. . .] All the Associates [. . .] are professionally just so many extensions of Irving Thalberg's personality. (261)

Explicitly positing an existential affinity between Thalberg, MGM, and the filmic form itself, the article owes much (however unknowingly) to Vertov's own declaration of cinematic identity:

> I am eye. I am a mechanical eye.
>
> I, a machine, am showing you a world, the likes of which only I can see.
>
> [. . .] In aid to the eye-machine is the Kinok, the pilot, who not only steers the apparatus, but also trusts it in experiments in space and in whatever may follow. (1978: 4–5)

This is not to suggest that the anonymous *Fortune* writer even had access to Vertov's radical theory-poetry of the 1920s, or indeed to argue for a direct relationship between the Kinoks of Soviet Russia and MGM in the 1930s. The striking parallels do, however, highlight how just as Thalberg and theorists of the day reflected on the cinematic experience, so too did the popular press try to understand Thalberg's own extraordinary success at MGM; one way to do that was by likening him to the medium itself. If the Boy Wonder discourse framed Thalberg within the mysticism of early Hollywood, then the *Fortune* piece sought a more visceral means of articulating his preternatural talents.

In 1940, Leo Rosten also wrote of the "personality" of the Hollywood movie studio, attributing "the sum total of [that] personality, the aggregate pattern of its choices and its tastes" to the producers (242–243). In the *Fortune* article, however, "personality" seems to translate into identity—that is, Thalberg's identity. As Christensen points out, in this article "the executive effectively *impersonated* the studio as a feedback mechanism that integrated production, distribution, and exhibition" (26). More than an executive responsible for the running of the studio, or a producer supervising a film—more, even, than a mortal man—the Thalberg of *Fortune*'s description exists as a literally multi-dimensional entity composed of scripts and departments, "associates," and functionaries. He is also, most strikingly, the camera and "recording appara-tus" themselves. Part studio, part filmmaking technology, Irving Thalberg is a cinematic body.

As Chapter 6 will discuss in detail, the *Fortune* article represents both a conceptual analysis of Thalberg's importance to the studio and a watershed moment in the deterioration of his and Mayer's relationship. But the recurring emphasis on Thalberg's affinity with the filmic form, both in the *Fortune* piece and across Thalberg scholarship more broadly, also anticipates modern-day directions in embodied visuality. Vivian Sobchack's study of cinematic subjec-tivity is particularly helpful here, inasmuch as it outlines the complex relation-ships between the filmmaker's vision and the film's own "address" (1992: 9) to the spectator. Exploring the subjectivity of the cinematic body, citing its ability to both perceive phenomena and convey the experience of those perceptions "visibly, audibly, haptically" (1992: 9, 11), Sobchack recognizes the film itself as possessing an intelligence beyond that of the filmmaker. Yet she also recon-ciles the autonomy of the film with the subjectivity of its viewer, who him/her-self experiences a "dialogical and dialectical engagement" with the film (1992: 9, 23). As Sobchack writes, "Both film and spectator are capable of viewing and of being viewed, both are embodied in the world as the subject of vision and object for vision" (1992: 23). In a constellation of subjective interplays, then, the film's own capacity for perception and expression (1992: 11) emerges independent of the filmmaker's original intention in creating the work, while the spectator relates to the film with a singular intelligence informed by his/her own relationship to the surrounding world.

Thalberg himself innately understood the sensory impact of cinema, as well as the necessity of dialogical engagement between spectator and screen. His focus on scale, both dramatic and visual, in the belief that "every great film must have one great scene" (qtd. in Vieira 2010: 37) aimed to heighten a given film's "address" to the viewer; and Thalberg's emphasis on preview screenings spoke to his abiding faith in the response of the audience. The intersubjective dialogue between film and viewer that, today, Sobchack out-lines as a model of spectatorship was for Thalberg a practical, real-world necessity in determining the success of a film. The accompanying process of retakes also signaled Thalberg's awareness of the cinematic form's metamor-phic potential: as an animate subject, per Sobchack's analysis, even a troubled film had the propensity for renewal and, as certain of Thalberg's colleagues would phrase it, "healing" (Lewis 1993: 81). Equally important was the star's embodiment of a variety of roles—"oblique casting" ensured a dynamic on-screen presence matching the animation of the filmic form, where typecasting suggested a stasis that could compromise its vitality.

With this in mind, the study will engage at points with embodied visuality to flesh out, as it were, Thalberg's own theories—especially those relating to the versatility of the performing body and the importance of visual impact on the screen. Throughout the book, the term "cinematic body" will be incorporated to help convey the holistic sense of the medium that he so valued. Sobchack's model is also key in helping to define Thalberg's function as a producer or, as she says above, "filmmaker." Elsewhere, she notes that the term "filmmaker" designates *all* of the personnel responsible for the production of a film (1992: 9)—thus resisting that problematic *auteur*-ist focus on the director. As Jennifer Barker cautions in related terms, "The film is more than a representation of the filmmaker's vision" (2009: 9). This point is central to the structure of this book, which does not argue that Thalberg himself was the sole creative force behind MGM's productions, or indeed that their existence was totally predicated on his vision. The focus on Thalberg in the analyses of key films does not intend to usurp the significance of the director, star, or associate producer (where relevant). Instead, the following chapters seek to identify Thalberg's theories of filmmaking and examine how they diffused through MGM and the wider industry, as well as giving rise to cinematic bodies that endure to the modern day.

Each chapter will explore one of Thalberg's central theories, situating it in a film-historical moment before discussing its relationship to representative films. Though certain concepts emerge from specific events—the rise of the talkies or the development of the Production Code—others are broader in their application. For example, Thalberg explored how best to execute his theory of oblique casting across his tenure at MGM, just as he refined the process of retakes through the years. In these instances, the given theory has been positioned in the most appropriate historical context to illuminate facets of Thalberg's filmmaking style at the time. In terms of the cinematic corpus, it is important to note that though the book will focus primarily on those films personally produced by Thalberg,[14] it will also engage with pictures that he oversaw while head of production at MGM. In this way, the work will capture the breadth of his impact and influence even when not personally supervising a production. The chapters will also seek to highlight relatively under-analysed works in the Thalberg canon. Where, for instance, Thalberg's work on *Grand Hotel* has featured heavily in Schatz (1996) and Spadoni (1995) as evidence of his authorship and mastery, this book will consider a number of lesser-known films.

The first two chapters will explore MGM's beginnings, analyzing the concepts that informed the studio's silent mode of production. Chapter 2 discusses Thalberg's theory of oblique casting, which, again, called for a given star to move fluidly between different kinds of roles and so avoid the stasis of typecasting (Marx 1975: 156). The chapter will look at the legendarily versatile Chaney's performance in the first film produced by MGM, *He Who Gets Slapped,* as well as highlighting the Thalberg-produced work of Marion Davies. Less acclaimed than Chaney but comparable in the fluidity of her characterizations—or, more specifically, impersonations of fellow stars—Davies's work in *The Patsy* and *Show People* (both dir. Vidor, 1928) speaks further to Thalberg's concern with the polymorphic potential of the human form. The analysis will also consider the formation of MGM itself, arguing that the versatility of oblique casting provides a conceptual parallel to the new studio's process of self-definition.

Chapter 3 will go on to consider Thalberg's conviction that "every great film must have one great scene" (qtd. in Vieira 2010: 37), exploring what this meant for the dramatic and visual scale of epic filmmaking of the day. The chapter will consider this theory in relation to *The Big Parade* and *La Bohème* (dir. Vidor, 1926), looking closely at the ways that "great scenes" played out on the big screens of early movie palaces like Grauman's Egyptian. Thalberg's role in enhancing the star presences of Gilbert and Lillian Gish also features here, providing case studies of the development of his star-making process. Indeed, inasmuch as Gilbert is the leading actor in and Vidor the director of both films, the chapter will also consider their significance to Thalberg's silent-era productions.

The next two chapters center on sea changes in the industry, looking first at the rise of sound and then the development of the Production Code to explore how these shifts impacted Thalberg's approach to the cinematic form. Though he would go on to contribute significantly to the burgeoning genre of musicals with *The Broadway Melody of 1929* (dir. Beaumont, 1929), Thalberg did not initially recognize the dominance of sound cinema. As he stated somewhat apocryphally, "Novelty is always welcome, but talking pictures are just a passing fad" (qtd. in Vieira 2010: 78). Yet in a 1929 lecture at the University of Southern California entitled "The Modern Photoplay," Thalberg frames his response to sound within a broader theory of "entertainment value" (1977: 123)—not rejecting the importance of the technology, but aligning it with a more fundamental imperative to provide meaningful and immersive productions for the public. This chapter will look at *Broadway Melody* alongside *The Unholy Three* (dir. Conway, 1930) and *Wild Orchids* (dir. Franklin, 1929) to consider this response to sound.

Chapter 5 will go on to examine Thalberg's role in crafting the Motion Picture Production Code in 1930 and its influence on cinematic sensuality in a post-talkie context. In 1929, Thalberg would write "General Principles to Cover the Preparation of a Revised Code of Ethics for Talking Pictures" on behalf of a three-person subcommittee, thus informing the industry's adoption of a formal Production Code in 1930. In response to pressure from the MPPDA and the new challenges posed by sound cinema, Thalberg's General Principles outline his more abstract understanding of how studios could engage with the issue of regulation. Primary among those tenets is an extension of Thalberg's concept of "entertainment value": "We have constantly to keep in mind that the sole purpose of the commercial motion picture is to entertain. *It cannot be considered as education or as a sermon or even indirectly as an essentially moral or immoral force.*"[15] The chapter will take these General Principles—and Thalberg's extemporaneous defense of them at a 1930 meeting of the Association of Motion Picture Producers—as a lens through which to consider early-Code films *The Divorcée* (dir. Leonard, 1930) and *Red-Headed Woman*.

Chapters 6 and 7 consider the impact of the 1933 studio restructuring that effectively demoted Thalberg from head of production to unit producer. As professional tensions began to overshadow personal relationships, Mayer and Schenck effected a change in leadership that, in part, aimed to defuse Thalberg's authority over the studio. In response, Thalberg would set out private and public affirmations of his production ethos: in the case of the former, Thalberg defended his contributions to MGM in a personal letter to Schenck; and in the case of the latter, Thalberg wrote an article for the *Saturday Evening Post* entitled "Why Motion Pictures Cost So Much." In this piece, Thalberg conceives of "the intelligent producer" (Thalberg and Weir 1933: 10) who spares no creative or monetary expense in crafting entertainment—and in this way, constructed an alternative to the Boy Wonder double that had shadowed his career since Universal. The chapter will argue that taken together, the personal letter and public article present a theoretical turning point at which Thalberg reflected—and expanded—upon established concepts and, at the same time, "visualize[d]" (84) a new future for production. The chapter will explore how this transitional era played out in Thalberg's films of the period, looking at *Strange Interlude* (dir. Leonard, 1932), *The Barretts of Wimpole Street* (dir. Franklin, 1934), and *The Merry Widow* (dir. Lubitsch, 1934).

Chapter 7 will continue to pursue the implications of this restructuring, specifically in relation to Thalberg's focus on retakes. Since his earliest productions at MGM, Thalberg had established the process to ensure the quality of a given film; this chapter, though, will consider his abiding question of "what can we do to make the picture better?" (qtd. in Thomas 140) as more than a function of Thalberg's overarching imperative to provide "entertainment value." In these last years of his life and career, Thalberg sought to improve upon his own cinematic *oeuvre*, effectively "retaking" his thematic concerns and visual style in historical epics *Mutiny on the Bounty* and *Romeo and Juliet* (dir. Cukor, 1936). The chapter will close by addressing wife Shearer's own challenges in carrying on Thalberg's legacy in his unfinished film *Marie Antoinette* (dir. Van Dyke, 1938). But the latter was only one of Thalberg's incomplete projects: at the time of his death in 1936, he had laid plans for his own production studio. In this way, Thalberg was looking ahead to a period of autonomy through which he could revise and reconsider the modes of production he had established at MGM.

Finally, the conclusion will consider Thalberg's observation, "Once a star, always a star. [. . .] When you're a champion in this business, you're always a champion" (qtd. in Marx 1975: 148–149). Though this insight clearly refers to the resilience of stars, it nonetheless resonates when considering his own fame over the decades. This final analysis will look at the evolution of the Thalberg myth across a variety of media—novels, films, and television series—to follow the arc of his enduring allure; it will also address Thalberg's importance in contemporary media, exploring how his theories of classical filmmaking persist today.

More than just uncovering Thalberg's work as a theorist, this study seeks to *re*cover that work and begin a dialogue through which his past contributions help scholars think through the present and future of narrative film. In so rigorously tracing Thalberg's perspective as a reflective practitioner of the cinematic medium, *Produced by Irving Thalberg* posits that he developed a comprehensive theoretical approach to filmmaking. As suggested earlier, this theoretical mode functions independently of the films that he produced; for all of the historical specificity of the development and execution of the theories, their value does not depend on that context. For example, the process of the retake, and an understanding of its importance, was adopted throughout the industry; the question of "one great scene" persists in blockbuster productions conscious of filling even bigger screens.

With this understanding of the significance of the theories, the chapters will aim to integrate concepts such as "entertainment value," "oblique casting," and "one great scene" wholly in the study: removing quotation marks from the terms once they have been defined, and so referencing these concepts throughout the work as meaningful in themselves, apart from their provenance as "dialogue by Thalberg" (to borrow from the title of Marx's 1942 article). This rhetorical strategy aims to evoke an awareness of the versatility of Thalberg's ideas—they do not belong only to his voice, as it were, but to broader critical explorations of narrative filmmaking and the cinematic experience. Ultimately, these analyses will not suggest infallibility on Thalberg's part, nor will they argue that he was a lone visionary in developing the classical film aesthetics and techniques that endure in contemporary filmmaking. What this book does aim to chronicle is the evolution of still another one of Thalberg's "equations"—the balance, that is, between theorist and producer. They are two sides of the same coin.

NOTES

1. Available at <http://www.oscars.org/governors/thalberg> (last accessed October 24, 2019).
2. Based on the date of the interview, it is likely that Cukor was referring to Bob Thomas's 1969 biography.
3. *The Good Earth* (dir. Franklin, 1937), a film personally produced by Thalberg at the time of his death, included a posthumous credit: "To the memory of Irving Grant Thalberg we dedicate this picture, his last great achievement." The only film that featured his name in his lifetime was the Universal production *The Dangerous Little Demon* (Badger, 1922); he was listed as writer "I. R. Irving" (Vieira 2010: 11).
4. As stated in the opening to *The Birth of a Nation* (1915), "This is the trademark of the Griffith feature films. All pictures made under the personal direction of D.W. Griffith have the name 'Griffith' in the border line, with the initials 'DG' at bottom of captions. There is *no exception* to this rule."
5. Please see Behlmer (2000 [1972]).
6. Association of Motion Picture Producers [AMPP], "Discussion of the Production Code in Its Draft Form." MPPDA Digital Archive, Flinders University Library Special Collections. MPPDA Record 671, Record of Meeting. 8-1985 to 8-2132. Available at <https://mppda.flinders.edu.au/records/671> (last accessed 24 October, 2019), p. 80.
7. Margaret Herrick Library, Academy of Motion Picture Arts and Sciences, Motion Picture Association of America. Production Code Administration records. *The Big Trail* file.
8. In 1929, theorist/director René Clair would also praise Thalberg production *Broadway Melody of 1929* as "a marvel," describing it as "neither theater nor cinema, but something altogether new" (1985: 93).
9. Langdale quotes critic Wilford Beaton's appraisal of the work: "Neither in the main Hollywood library nor in any of its branches can a copy of this book be found. It is not for sale in a Hollywood bookstore [. . .] The film industry is one of tremendous proportions, yet this great contribution to its mentality is out of print" (qtd. in 1).
10. Lindsay identifies Loos, alongside her husband John Emerson, as screenwriters "who are as brainy as people dare to be and still remain in the department store film business" (2000 [1915]: 23).
11. "The Little Shopgirls Go to the Movies" (1927), in Kracauer (1995).
12. "Film 1928," in Kracauer (1995).
13. "People who did not understand anything of the art of film used to cite silence as one of its most serious drawbacks. These people regard the introduction of sound as an improvement or completion of silent film. This opinion is just as senseless as if the invention of three-dimensional oil painting were hailed as an advance on the hitherto known principles of painting" (107).
14. Following the detailed appendix of Mark A. Vieira's 2010 biography.
15. Association of Motion Picture Producers, "Discussion of the Production Code in Its Draft Form," pp. 136–137; emphasis in original.

CHAPTER 2

Oblique Casting and Early MGM

In 1924, MGM released its first film. Directed by Victor Sjostrom and based on a play by Leonid Andreyev, *He Who Gets Slapped* (1924) starred Lon Chaney as Paul Beaumont, a scientist whose lifelong work is stolen by his patron, Baron Regnard (Marc McDermott)—aided by Beaumont's wife, with whom he is having an affair. Traumatized by the laughter of fellow scientists when the Baron contemptuously smacks his face, Beaumont joins the circus and assumes the identity of "He Who Gets Slapped," a masochistic circus clown famous for being hit countless times in a single performance. Decades later, the popular reference work *The MGM Story* would describe the work succinctly as "a risky choice for the studio's debut" (Eames 1975: 10), for obvious reasons. Yet even as the film appears as a curious counterpart to MGM's subsequent productions, so renowned for their glamor, it nonetheless establishes themes that Thalberg would explore for the rest of his career: the nature of spectacle and artistic identity; thwarted romance; the tension between private desires and public expression. *He Who Gets Slapped* also captures Thalberg's developing concerns as a producer. In addition to highlighting three stars who would thrive under his tenure—Chaney, Shearer, and Gilbert—the film introduced Thalberg's broader fascination with the capaciousness of the performing body itself; how it could transform or reinvent itself to suit the demands of a particular role or narrative situation. *He Who Gets Slapped* represents, then, not so much "a risky choice" as a declaration *of* the risks that this new studio was willing to take under Thalberg's guidance.

With its exploration of passion and creativity in a carnivalesque setting, the film illuminates much about the origins of MGM itself. When Thalberg first allied himself with Louis B. Mayer Productions in 1923, the studio shared its production lot with a zoo. The Mission Road compound was owned by Colonel William N. Selig, an entrepreneur of early films who had developed the Selig Polyscope Company to compete with Thomas Edison's productions

(Schulberg 1981: 117). When Mayer first began renting the space in 1919, Selig's Zoo and its environs provided, as Bosley Crowther would recall,

> a thoroughly equipped establishment for the making of outdoor and animal films. In mission-style concrete buildings [Selig] housed some seven hundred assorted beasts [. . .] There were runs for jungle scenes, caves for 'illusions,' African village sets, and a eucalyptus grove of several acres to be used for sylvan scenes. (1960: 69)

Compounded with its relative isolation from Los Angeles proper (Vieira 2010: 19), the premises of Crowther's description bear traces of the otherworldly; an exoticism, however manufactured, that tempers accounts of Louis B. Mayer Productions with a fairy-tale sensibility. Budd Schulberg—whose father, producer B. P. Schulberg, also rented space on Mission Road—would reminisce about childhood days riding a tame alligator and ostrich (1981: 115), as well as petting Leo, the journeyman lion who had featured in a number of Selig's African-themed films (119). Even Mayer's performers had to compete with their animal neighbors: when preparing for her screen test, a nervous Norma Shearer decided to "be as brave as the lions in the zoo next door. I could hear them roaring through the walls of my dressing room. I decided to roar too—as loud as they did" (qtd. in Vieira 2010: 28). Replete with a ringmaster in the form of Selig, a "ruddy-faced hail-fellow with a Falstaffian figure" (Schulberg 1981: 117), there was certainly what Crowther termed "a strong circus flavor about" (1960: 68) Louis B. Mayer Productions.

This was the environment that Thalberg occupied as vice-president and production assistant (Crowther 1960: 88) at the earliest point of his partnership with Mayer. Given the later tensions between them, it is tempting to ascribe a storybook quality—if not quite a prelapsarian ideality—to that time and place. Irene Selznick, Mayer's daughter, remembered that "the growing bond between [Thalberg and Mayer] was evident. There was confidence, enthusiasm, and affection—all of it mutual" (qtd. in Vieira 2010: 27). The studio benefited from this bonhomie, though Crowther notes that "[i]t would be a surrender to fancy to encourage the happy thought that it was all sunshine and profits [. . .] during those embryonic days" (1960: 88). Even after signing talents like Shearer, Renée Adorée, Barbara LaMarr, and Wallace Beery, as well as directors Fred Niblo and John Stahl, Mayer and Thalberg found that "the business [of film production] was always a gamble" (88–90).

Louis B. Mayer Productions was not alone in taking this gamble, however. Theater-chain owner Marcus Loew himself had a struggling studio: Metro. Only two years earlier, Metro had had a huge success with Rudolph Valentino spectacle *The Four Horsemen of the Apocalypse* (dir. Ingram, 1921); but the hits had stalled, and Loew began to explore options for minimizing his losses

(Thomas 1969: 68). He joined forces with the head of the Goldwyn Company, Frank Joseph Godsol, in order to merge the Metro and Goldwyn companies—though both soon realized that this new studio would need to be run by more experienced industry figures (Crowther 1960: 93–94; Thomas 68). With the help of Robert Rubin, one of Loew's legal advisors as well as an old friend of Mayer's, the latter's production company caught the interest of Loew and Godsol (Crowther 1960: 94; Vieira 2010: 29–30). Though not hugely profitable, the studio was striking enough in its "intelligence, economy and efficiency" (Crowther 1960: 92) to suggest future success.

In April 1924, Metro, Goldwyn, and Mayer Studios were officially merged (Crowther 1960: 96). Also aligned were Mayer, Thalberg, and Rubin in a unit known as "the Mayer group" (96): Mayer as first vice-president and general manager of the studio; Rubin as secretary; and Thalberg—at the age of 24—taking the role of second vice-president and supervisor of production (94–96). In return for running the studio, the Mayer group would receive 20 percent of the profits (95)—an agreement that would, over the next ten years, introduce acrimony between the men rather than cement their solidarity. Yet in 1924, the possibility of such future conflicts was secondary to the excitement of the merger.

With Harry Rapf as a fellow supervisor of more routine productions (Rapf 2016: 40), Thalberg began developing projects for the impressive personnel who had come from the Goldwyn studios. Stars like Eleanor Boardman, John Gilbert, and Mae Murray; directors such as Frank Borzage, Robert Leonard, and former Universal foil Erich von Stroheim—each of these figures, among others, presented Thalberg with enormous possibilities for quality filmmaking. Equally promising were MGM's new Culver City premises, the site on which the studio (or rather Sony Pictures Studios) still stands. Thomas Ince had purchased the original 16-acre lot in 1915 and established an impressive compound in the midst of the Los Angeles wilderness (Crowther 1957: 66); following Ince's financial troubles, the Goldwyn studio bought and further developed the land. At the point at which MGM moved there, Culver City featured a "Corinthian-columned, eight-hundred-foot façade [behind which were] six glass-walled stages, dozens of outdoor sets, a swimming pool," and numerous other administrative offices and set-design workshops (Vieira 2010: 23).

As head of production, Thalberg controlled the casting process at MGM (Thomas 196). His decisions aimed to cultivate a given performer's singular appeal, which he considered a necessity for any star. As Dorothy Herzog wrote in her 1926 profile, "Mr. Thalberg points out that a screen hopeful should have something to GIVE before she can GET anything from this business" (131). Rejecting the stasis of typecasting—what he called "slow death for actors"—in favor of "oblique casting," Thalberg pursued roles that would develop alternate facets of, rather than simply reinforce, a star's public image (qtd. in Marx 1975:

156). The word "oblique" here is an intriguing one, inasmuch as it has both abstract and concrete connotations. Casting the performer from an unexpected angle, as it were, ensured that the public would "see" the star in a different way—not only in terms of characterization, but also within the scope of different cinematic worlds. With this in mind, Thalberg's approach to casting exceeded questions of strategy or marketing; it represented a conceptual understanding of how versatility, the ability to evolve, sustained a performer's career.

Of MGM's earliest stars, Chaney had a particular genius for embodying characters whose variety made impossible the formation of a set persona, and whose qualities diverged from the conventions of film protagonists. Celebrating his own obliquity, he remarked in a 1925 interview with *Photoplay*, "I have never played a part completely straight in my life" (qtd. in Denbo 100). Still another performer explored her own oblique characterizations in a manner far less intense, but perhaps more unexpected: Marion Davies. Admittedly, the two stars constitute an unlikely pairing—Chaney, "The Man of a Thousand Faces," and Davies, now acknowledged as a great comedic actress, but for a time best remembered as William Randolph Hearst's companion and the inspiration for Susan Alexander in Orson Welles's *Citizen Kane* (1941). Under Thalberg's guidance, Davies expanded her range in films that actively called upon her metamorphic capacities. In comedies *The Patsy* and *Show People* (both dir. Vidor, 1928), Davies impersonates various stars of the day in extended sequences—the fluidity of her characterizations here capturing the iconography of early Hollywood femininity itself.

These stars represent a case of extremes in Thalberg's canon of oblique castings: Chaney, who "never played a part completely straight," and Davies, a figure whose gifts for self-reflexive comedy belied her struggles to establish a star persona in her own right. Their challenges and successes provide a historical context within which to consider Thalberg's concerns with the evolution of a star presence, particularly at this fundamental point in his leadership at MGM. On one level, Thalberg's theory of oblique casting translates into an emphasis on the lived-body, which Sobchack has described as "excessive and ambiguous in its materiality, its polymorphism, and its production of existential meaning" (1992: 144). Such questions of expansion/limitation, dynamism/stasis, also suggest a related fascination with how a role would match, alter, or otherwise shape a player's public identity. This chapter will argue that Chaney and Davies's respective performances in the above films speak to Thalberg's overarching awareness of the versatility of the human form; but even more than this, his fostering of their metamorphic talents parallels the dynamism of the developing studio itself. Certainly Thalberg's focus on oblique casting played out through any number of his performers, but his role in the story of Chaney and Davies's careers introduces, fittingly, a variety of angles on the issue.

"UNUSUAL ASSIGNMENTS HELP OUR PEOPLE EXPAND"

At the time of MGM's formation in the early 1920s, the exhibition and viewing practices that came to define the studio era were hardly long cemented. Indeed, just as MGM itself was born in a circus-like atmosphere, so too were the historical screens on which audiences would have first encountered motion pictures. As Jennifer Barker points out, "the medium first emerged in the context of the amusement park, fairground, and penny arcade"—introducing a "kinetic thrill" kindred to that of the often-adjacent rollercoasters and park rides (2009: 132). She proposes that the mechanics of early viewing machines, in which audiences would turn a handle in order to propel images forward and pause them at will, parallel cinema's broader "titillating and terrifying" interplay between motion and stillness (135). This dynamic spectatorship emerged from even the most basic act: "Without the motion of the viewer depositing the coin [into the viewing machine], there could be no 'motion pictures' " (134).

The spectator of early cinematic works also contributed to a foundational revolution in literally *social* media. According to Janet Staiger's study of sexuality in early cinema, the diverse range of ethnicities and classes attending motion-picture venues (including amusement parks and vaudeville houses) introduced "an element of social danger" to the very act of cinema-going (1995: 8). The sensual nature of many early moving pictures imbued this spectatorship with a further sensationalism. As Tom Gunning has commented, erotic and exhibitionist tendencies characterized much of what he famously termed "the cinema of attractions," featuring images that highlighted the body and actors that deliberately returned the viewer's gaze (1990: 57).[1] In the early 1910s, however, exhibition spaces began to shift from these more transient environs to "increasingly grandiose, purpose-built theaters" (Maltby 2003: 118). Mayer was himself a part of that transition as an owner-manager of theaters in the northeast (Crowther 1960: 29, 33)—though it was his future business partner, Marcus Loew, who found the greatest success with an entire chain of theaters (Crowther 1957: 32, 42).

In this era of redefinition—replete with the industry's move to the West Coast, as discussed in the Introduction—the public's engagement with performers also evolved. Richard deCordova's seminal study of early stardom, or "picture personalities," traces the ways in which the anonymity of on-screen performers at the beginning of the 1900s gradually ceded to a marketing of their personal identities. Identities that were, at first, aligned with their respective studios: for example, Florence Lawrence was known only as "the Biograph Girl" before she joined Carl Laemmle's pre-Universal studio, Imp, in 1909; her name was hardly mentioned in promotional materials for either studio, though her face was highly recognizable (2001: 55–56). By the early 1910s, stars like Mary Pickford had become picture personalities—famous for roles that perpetuated a stable identity in serials or in films with a similar narrative tone. As deCordova notes, the extra-diegetic persona functioned "merely as an extension" of the diegetic character; fan magazine articles, for instance, only sustained the identification between actor and role (87). It was when the popular press began to explore the "private lives of the players" in the mid-1910s that the classic conception of the star—as opposed to a picture personality—emerged (98). By the time of the star scandals in the early 1920s, featuring Fatty Arbuckle and Wallace Reid, the over-determined private lives of the players had become a topic of public concern (117–119).

Such changes across the production and exhibition process provided the context for Thalberg's own theory of oblique casting. In an industry that was still evolving, why should a performer him- / herself be condemned to the stasis of typecasting? Only about a decade removed from a standard by which, to quote deCordova, a "tautological loop" united character, performer, and "extrafilmic discourse" (91), Thalberg explored the possibilities for variation; the star could not stand still, as it were, within a single type of role or film, because the cinematic form itself was so mutable. Where the norms of early stardom had represented a series of polarizing categories—the pendulum sweeping from anonymity to over-exposure; from the conflating of character and personality to the fixation on an extra-diegetic private life—the notion of oblique casting called for a radical multiplicity. The various roles would inform the complexity of the persona, which would in turn expand the collective identity of MGM. For a studio that would go on to proclaim that it featured "More Stars Than There are in the Heavens!", the idea of oblique casting suggests that MGM's stars held within themselves entire constellations of characters. Thalberg summed up his approach in a statement to his colleagues, whom he also expected to demonstrate adaptability in their work: "It's discipline. Unusual assignments help our people expand, and that helps us" (qtd. in Marx 1975: 82).

Thalberg's concern with casting was a defining element in the division of authority between him and Mayer. Where Thalberg shaped the careers of MGM stars with no interest in their personal lives, Mayer had control over the latter; in related terms, he himself had little interest in the nuances of films-in-production, choosing instead "to wait for the finished product" (Marx 1975: 89, 139) that Thalberg had overseen from its inception. In exploring how best to produce a given film, Thalberg was, as George Cukor would describe it, "one of the few who really tried to make his stars do surprising things, try different kinds of parts" (qtd. in Lambert 1973: 151). Though Thalberg himself did not extensively record his observations on the importance of oblique casting, the decisions he made provide case studies of this approach in action. One of the most famous examples is Thalberg's casting of Clark Gable in

Mutiny on the Bounty, in spite of the actor's objections to the period costuming. Thalberg persuaded him: "Do this one for me. If it isn't one of your greatest successes, I'll never ask you again to play a part that you don't want to do" (qtd. in Marx 1975: 243). Gable would go on to be nominated for a Best Actor Academy Award, and the film would win for Best Picture. This was not the only instance of oblique casting for Gable; in 1932, Thalberg would give him the role of gentleman psychiatrist Ned Darrell in *Strange Interlude*. This lead in the adaptation of Eugene O'Neill's play diverged from the amoral gangster types that Gable had played to such success in films like *A Free Soul* (dir. Brown, 1931)—and, in turn, made his subsequent leading role as the rugged owner of a rubber plantation in *Red Dust* (dir. Fleming, 1932) all the more striking.

In his discussion of Thalberg's theory, Samuel Marx references Wallace Beery and Marie Dressler as two further cases in point. As successful as the two stars would be together in *Min and Bill* (dir. Hill, 1930) and *Tugboat Annie* (dir. LeRoy, 1933), Thalberg did not exhaust their partnership. Dressler was also teamed up with Polly Moran in *Caught Short* (dir. Reisner, 1930), for example, and Beery starred in drama *The Big House* (dir. Hill, 1930) (1975: 156). A look at Thalberg's strategy with wife Shearer's career also neatly encapsulates his theory of oblique casting. According to Marx, "many in [Thalberg's] studio family [called her] his greatest production" (69); and as such, she starred in sensational dramas (*A Free Soul*) and sophisticated comedies (*Private Lives*, dir. Franklin, 1931), contemporary works (*Strange Interlude*) and classical/ historical pieces (*Romeo and Juliet*; *The Barretts of Wimpole Street*). As Marx elucidates,

> Thalberg planned to steer his wife through a carefully selected change of tempo in each succeeding character she portrayed, alternating comedies with drama, modern backgrounds with the past, melodramas with sophistication. He had moved her from silk to gingham to velvet. She never filmed two movies in a row that had similar themes: her producer-husband showed interest in material for her future only if it fit into this pattern. (156)

In more concise commentary from a 1936 interview with *Motion Picture*, the actress declared: "Most of my decisions are made for me. Which is pleasant, because I trust the *decider* so completely. But he *is* the decider" (qtd. in Zeitlin 1936: 33). When cultivating the various facets of MGM's stars, Thalberg's vision itself remained an abiding constant.

This is not to say that Thalberg insisted on oblique casting for the sake of it. Mark A. Vieira suggests that Thalberg hit on a "Garbo formula" (2005: 39) that cast the star in a number of—but not all of—her films as "an ageless, mysterious beauty encountered in a picturesque setting by an idealistic young man who soon discovers that she is married to [. . .] an older man." Even taking the existence of this narrative formula into account, Thalberg crafted an oblique *type* in Garbo herself: a romantic original with the sensuality of a vamp but the pathos of a melodramatic heroine, or what Christian Viviani has termed a "sanctified sinner" (2006: 96). Under Thalberg's direction, Garbo's range of roles included Eugene O'Neill's world-weary prostitute *Anna Christie* (dir. Brown, 1930) and the prima ballerina Grusinskaya in *Grand Hotel*; the sensual spy *Mata Hari* (dir. Fitzmaurice, 1931) and doomed *Camille* (dir. Cukor, 1936). Each of these roles played upon a central facet of Garbo's public appeal—her evocation of conflicted passion, for example—while heightening its impact through a variety of different narrative contexts.

Even as Thalberg oversaw the oblique casting of key stars, accounts vary as to his own flexibility. Bob Thomas relates that Thalberg would reason with an actor if he/she did not want to play a role, rather than threaten suspension— "I have never forced an actor to play a role against his will" (qtd. in Thomas 196). Edward G. Robinson, however, recalled that when negotiating his contract with Thalberg, the producer "put me in an icy rage, daring to suggest that I allow myself to be packaged and merchandised by him. It was his way or no way" (qtd. in Marx 1975: 119). The vagaries of balancing executive privilege and artistic sensitivities notwithstanding, Thalberg understood that the value of a performer's gift was measured by the audience themselves. As Marx offered in a revealing commentary,

> [Thalberg's] system of star making was to be obedient to the wishes of the customers. "The public makes the stars [. . .] I show actors to their best and watch for the response." [. . .] Out of this, Thalberg evolved a steady policy. He put ingénues and juveniles in front of every turning camera, holding only those who won audience approbation. The others were always expendable. (Marx 1975: 69)

Given Thalberg's focus on versatility in casting, the idea of "every turning camera" can arguably extend into every possible role: suggesting that it was a multi-faceted exposure to audiences that tested a potential star, with the screen as the mediator between audience and performer.

In so highlighting, testing, the range of a performer's abilities, Thalberg's approach to casting certainly underscored the versatility of the human figure; yet this approach also highlights his sensitivity to the dynamic conditions of the cinematic experience itself. Those "six glass-walled stages [and] dozens of outdoor sets" (Vieira 2010: 23) that composed the Culver City plant offered a kaleidoscope of artistic opportunity, within which the "unusual assignments" and creative "expansion" of which Thalberg spoke could take place. Seeking to maximize the resources of his new studio, aware of the shifting conditions of exhibition, and attentive to the perceptions of the spectator, Thalberg sought to make material the promise of a new era of filmmaking.

THE HEART OF THE MATTER

Lon Chaney—"The Man of a Thousand Faces"—represents the *ne plus ultra* of mutability. Famed for the complex make-up and prosthetic techniques that enabled his myriad characterizations, Chaney's starring roles included a sergeant in *Tell It to the Marines* (dir. Hill, 1926), a knife-throwing circus performer in *The Unknown* (dir. Browning, 1927), and an avenging magician in *West of Zanzibar* (dir. Browning, 1928)—each of these hits personally produced by Thalberg himself. He had fostered the performer's career since the early days at Universal, where he produced Chaney's star-turn in the spectacle *The Hunchback of Notre Dame*. Though Chaney would star in the post-Thalberg Universal picture *The Phantom of the Opera* (dir. Julian and Chaney, 1925), the breadth of his interpretations expanded at MGM where, as Chaney biographer Michael F. Blake describes it, Thalberg was an "ally" cultivating the actor's creativity (1995: 6).

Chaney, of course, was hardly an untried amateur when Thalberg produced *Hunchback*.[2] From Chaney's teenage years onward, he worked in the theater—first as a prop boy, and then as a performer in musical comedy, where he learned the art of applying make-up (Blake 15–19, 28). He began as a character actor at Universal Pictures in the early 1910s, when he met director Tod Browning. The latter would go on to direct Chaney in *The Miracle Man* (1919), a breakthrough role and one of ten films they made together (42, 45). Following the 1923 success of *Hunchback*, and Thalberg's subsequent exit from Universal, the latter offered Chaney the leading role in *He Who Gets Slapped*—the first film produced by the newly formed MGM. Chaney's deal was a one-picture prelude to a long-term contract subject to the success of the film; he would sign the latter contract in 1925 (149, 153). Only five years later, though, Thalberg would eulogize Chaney following his death from lung cancer. In Thalberg's words, the actor was "[g]reat not only because of his God-given talent, but also because he used that talent to illuminate certain dark corners of the human spirit. He showed the world the souls of those people who were born different than us" (qtd. in Vieira 2010: 127).

The very fluidity of Chaney's performances represents, paradoxically, a unifying element in his *oeuvre*. If audiences expected him to play, effectively, an *un*expected part, just how oblique were his characterizations? What Thalberg valued in Chaney was, however, more than his ability to "illuminate certain dark corners of the human spirit" in a variety of roles; for Chaney's very presence on the screen also illuminated the capacity of the human form to reincarnate itself, changing shape with the changing of a character. As one of the first actors that Thalberg had worked with during his early years at Universal, Chaney's influence on the producer was profound. Consider how Chaney's fluent use of prostheses and make-up in a film like *Hunchback*, or his radical metamorphosis in *The Phantom of the Opera*, would have impacted Thalberg at a point when he was just establishing MGM's own singular style of filmmaking. Before testing Gable in period films or O'Neill plays, before cultivating Shearer's versatility across genres, Thalberg would have encountered Chaney's own extraordinary transfigurations. The theory of oblique casting does not emerge *sui generis* from Thalberg, then, but rather from his collaborations with Chaney at this pivotal point in both of their careers.

Chaney's evocation of the monstrous has, however, greater implications beyond Thalberg and MGM. Gaylyn Studlar and Karen Randell have considered Chaney's place within specific historical contexts: the former argues that he transposed the 1920s freak-show phenomenon to the cinema (1996: 200), pointing to "sequences of [. . .] display [in his films] centered on their star-as-freak exhibition" (223). Randell, on the other hand, interprets Chaney's deformed characters as part of "trauma narratives" surrounding World War I veterans who themselves returned from battle transformed, disfigured (2003: 218). Noting that Chaney's famous metamorphoses "both alert[ed]" the viewers to and "distract[ed]" them from this historical event, Randell remarks that "there is a duality here that allows for the deformity to be displayed as a marketing tool [. . .] and as a fantasy spectacle within the film itself" (218). But as Chaney would himself remark in an interview, "I want to be to the public the material ghost of an idea, with no man, Lon Chaney, to be seen through the make-up" (qtd. in Denbo 1925: 100). What Chaney sought was a total merging of artificial and embodied form—emerging at the synthesis of which were his range of characters.

In the early 1920s, critics and audiences did not uniformly take to Chaney's style of performance. Before the release of *He Who Gets Slapped*, *Motion Picture* columnist Tamar Lane wrote, "As a character man, as a make-up artist, Chaney probably has no superior [. . .] But as an actor, as an expresser of subtle emotions, Chaney must take a seat at the foot of the class" (1924: 49). In *Picture-Play*[3] that same year, one spectator declared,

> If acting is the art of frightening old ladies, then Lon Chaney is undoubtedly the greatest actor in the world. But if acting means something more than wearing a rubber suit and disfiguring your face with putty, then Mr. Chaney cannot qualify. (Qtd. in Klumph 1924: 21)

In the same article, writer Helen Klumph would state that "the characterizations of Lon Chaney are usually too much concerned with externals" (21).

What these commentaries reveal is a distrust of—and discomfort with—the fusion of human form and special effects, with Chaney and his props ("externals") introducing a disquieting dissolution of boundaries between the human and the artificial, embodied form and inanimate device. Chaney understood that, as Sobchack has noted, the very act of engaging with inanimate objects evokes a "*sensual* and *sensible* expansion" of the lived-body itself; that is, "an enhanced awareness of what it is *to be material*" (2004: 290). In Chaney's case, however, props and prosthetics introduced a concrete expansion of an origin figure who was, by comparison, only the "ghost of an idea." Rejecting the stability of the prototypical "picture personality" who had dominated motion pictures only a few years before, and at the same time denying the exposure of self that had become a feature of the extra-diegetic discourse, Chaney and his numerous characterizations demanded an oblique identification between audience and star.

The attraction–repulsion of such identifications underlies the view of Chaney's many special effects as a collective crutch; there is a hesitation in approaching these uncanny transfigurations that represent extreme iterations of Thalberg's oblique casting. For even as the popularity of Chaney's various incarnations speaks to both a reluctant fascination with the monstrous and the unique socio-historical context of his performances, Thalberg's producing of this *oeuvre* attests to his own understanding of such a complex allure. As Shearer would later explain,

> Irving was a realist. He knew what lay behind man's weakness. He was fascinated by the unusual, the colorful—even the decadent and evil. He loved the impact of horror, but not merely for the sake of horror. These elements had to possess a reality, a logic, a meaning. There had to be sound ideas behind these ugly images to lend a story reason, to give the audience hope, and to impart some beauty—even if it was a sad beauty—to these visions of life. (Qtd. in Vieira 2010: 165)

Beyond outlining a strand in Thalberg's thematic concerns as a producer, the arc of Shearer's commentary is telling in itself. Her statement shifts from questions of the "decadent and evil" to notions of "reason," "hope," even "beauty"—highlighting Thalberg's perception of a continuum, rather than an opposition, between good and evil, heroism and villainy. Thalberg emerges as a figure who—like Chaney himself—sought to reveal to the audience that the "people who were born different than us" were, perhaps, not so alien after all.

Such duality—between self and other, the animate and inanimate—haunts *He Who Gets Slapped*. Sobchack has written of the relationship between subject and object, specifically in terms of experiencing pain. She remarks that "the passion of suffering" on the part of an individual awakens an understanding of "what it is to be treated *only* as an object" vulnerable to the will of another (2004: 287, 288). Certainly *He Who Gets Slapped* plays upon this dialogue, as Paul/HE subsumes his subjective identity into that of a passive object for abuse and entertainment; particularly evocative of this is the neon sign advertising his circus act, featuring a hand repeatedly smacking a clown's face in automated brutality. For the audience in the first performance sequence, HE is merely a multi-dimensional version of this sign: His face covered with grease paint, hair concealed by a skull cap, and body made amorphous by a voluminous costume, HE larks about the ring making pseudo-scientific statements and waits to be beaten by dozens of anonymous clowns. In a particularly violent part of the routine, the clowns bind and gag him and slap his face "to death"—then rip a cloth heart from his costume and bury it in the dirt of the ring before covering his body with funeral wreaths.

The grotesquerie of the sequence is not limited to the routine itself. Shots of the hysterical spectators, including the Baron, are intercut with the clowns' performance, and are frequently seen from the point of view of HE. In more images from his perspective, shots of the sadistic clowns dissolve into the scientists in front of whom he was first humiliated. For all his willing victimization, these point-of-view shots signal the prevailing of his subjectivity in spite of, or even in addition to, his reduction to an object—a point highlighted all the more by the focus on the cloth hearts worn on his costume. In the preceding scene, taking place backstage, HE watches Consuela, the woman he loves, as she stitches the larger of the hearts onto his costume and carefully secures a smaller one inside it. The latter is the "real" heart that will be ripped from the clown later in the routine, effectively killing him—a link between emotion, physical function, and stage prop seen also in the mourning clowns' act, as they shed tears by squeezing rubber bags filled with water.

Yet this exchange between Consuela and HE establishes the heart as not simply a prop or special effect, but also the exteriorization of his emotional center. Its material form enables HE to literally give Consuela his heart, and in turn allows her to literally hold it in her hands in a lingering close-up. Such a transaction between subject and object renders the end of his routine, with the burying of this heart, a death indeed. It is this union of subject and object that reaches its apotheosis in the final sequence of the film. When Consuela's father tries to force her to marry the Baron, HE takes revenge for both himself and the young woman he loves by letting a circus lion loose on the Baron—before dying from wounds received during their fight.[4] Staggering to the ring, HE receives a few slaps from his fellow clowns before pulling his quilted heart— now actually bleeding—from his wounded chest.

In this continuum between animate and inanimate, the passive object that is "he who gets slapped" has actively avenged both himself and Consuela, and the cloth heart reveals itself to be as vulnerable to loving, and bleeding, as flesh itself. The vivification of these objects brings to mind the criticism surrounding Chaney's use of make-up and prosthetics; the notion, that is, that his acting was less authentic for its use of synthetic properties. Yet in a film that itself engages with questions of identity and authenticity—Paul evolving into a nameless clown; the imposter Baron stealing Paul's work to claim it as his own—this affinity with the inanimate functions as an organic *synthesis* between individual and material world. That synthesis is, as the final scene conveys, the heart of the matter.

Doris Denbo in *Picture-Play* would describe Chaney's performance in *He Who Gets Slapped* as "a characterization of rare qualities and when he dies he pulls your heart strings until they nearly break" (88)—a commentary apropos not only to the film's imagery, but also to the pathos of the production itself. For underlying the hysteria of the performance sequences in the film is the "sad beauty" that, as Shearer wrote, was so compelling to Thalberg in both extra- and intra-diegetic terms. Commenting on Thalberg's affinity with actors, Bob Thomas notes that "[m]ost of them were beautiful people, and he had a deep admiration for beauty" (100); even more, "He understood [performers]. He recognized their follies, their outpourings of ego, their fickle nature, but he also realized they were unusual human beings" (100). By extension, then, Thalberg perceived the beauty in Chaney's depictions of the monstrous—in his power, that is, to transform himself through a merging of subjective animation and inanimate objects.

The film experienced a metamorphosis of its own before its release. After viewing the original, more sensational cut of the film, Thalberg spent two days re-editing the work (Vieira 2010: 42–43). This image of Thalberg devoting himself to recutting the film is compelling not only because it speaks to the excitement surrounding MGM's first production, but also because it conveys his ability to literally transform the body of the film itself. In shaping the inanimate material of the celluloid to evoke wholly human emotions, Thalberg paralleled Chaney's own fusion of object and artistry. And at this earliest point in MGM's history, Thalberg might well have been considering questions similar to those that would shade his relationship to performers: How should one scene and/or shot relate to another? How would *He Who Gets Slapped* meet or exceed audience expectations? And ultimately, how would the film work to define the studio's identity?

With such questions in mind, the story of Paul Beaumont and/as *He Who Gets Slapped* offers more than a sado-masochistic spectacle. It is a meta-commentary on Chaney's transformative powers through prosthetics and make-up, the *inanimate* tools that enabled him to animate his characters; it is also Thalberg's statement of intent, establishing MGM as a studio that would directly engage with existential issues of identity and performance. Even as he and Mayer were in the process of creating MGM, Thalberg foregrounded a concern with the creation of spectacle itself—exploring the underlying anxieties and pleasures of relating to the public. Indeed, in his study of Sjostrom's work in Hollywood, Bo Florin speaks to the allegorical complexities of the film, noting that *He Who Gets Slapped* "seems to aim at delivering a [. . .] philosophical statement on the conditions of life on the globe, using the clown as metaphor" (2013: 53). The film endures, then, as a quintessentially "unusual" production that, to borrow from Thalberg's own words, "helped [MGM] expand" both in terms of box-office success—it was a hit—and critical prestige.

He Who Gets Slapped also remains an origin story for MGM itself. On one level, it endures as a kind of prophetic allegory of Mayer and Thalberg's relationship, exploring as it does the competition over, and fragility of, professional and artistic identities, as well as the threat of betrayal. But even as its tone and thematic concerns arguably look to the end of Thalberg and Mayer's relationship, the film also captures the carnivalesque quality of their beginnings: the two professionals imagining and strategizing their future while lions roared and ostriches roamed in the Selig Zoo—the quasi-primal birthplace of a studio that would soon be renowned for its high glamor.

"I'M JUST FULL OF VIEW POINTS"

In addition to the Culver City lot and numerous personnel, MGM also inherited the small company Cosmopolitan Pictures. Formed in the late 1910s by Hearst, Cosmopolitan produced vehicles for Davies that included sentimental dramas (*Cecelia of the Pink Roses* [dir. Steger, 1918]) and period spectacles (*When Knighthood was in Flower* [dir. Vignola, 1922]); and by the early 1920s, the Goldwyn studio was distributing these films. Upon the merger, Mayer worked out a still more lucrative arrangement: according to Crowther, MGM agreed to produce Davies's pictures in exchange for "most favorable attention in the Hearst press" (1960: 122–123; Guiles 1973: 126). Crowther also notes that Hearst's sheer power, the "prestige and kudos" associated with him, attracted Mayer and helped him realize a vision of MGM as "the Versailles of the movies" (1960: 123–124). But the artistic conflicts between Cosmopolitan Pictures and MGM—or, more precisely, Hearst and Thalberg—at times offset the benefits of the vanity company for all parties concerned, including Davies herself.

In a 1928 interview promoting *Show People*, Davies expressed her delight in the film: "I know I'm a star *now*. I'm being supported by Jack Gilbert, Louis B. Mayer, Irving Thalberg, and Lon Chaney" (qtd. in Gebhart 52; emphasis added).[5] (Gilbert would appear in a cameo, while Thalberg personally produced the picture.) Beyond the felicitous naming of key figures in this chapter, Davies's statement resonates with its qualified assertion of stardom: at last, rather than as always. Ensconced in the protection of her independent production unit, Davies was, as Malcolm H. Oettinger of *Picture Play* wryly remarked, "deposited at the top" of the film colony (1930: 34). As he would point out, however, "it was [Davies's] task to justify that eminent position" in a skeptical industry: "Not unaware of the critical attitude toward her work, she made haste to improve [. . .] And now she is seriously considered as a screen actress, something that was denied her for years" (34). Indeed, in a *Screenland* article published a year earlier, Davies had been compared to Chaney (in admittedly hyperbolic phrasing) as "the cleverest character star the films have produced" (Jopp 1929: 72).

The studio's challenges in choosing appropriate projects for Davies had contributed to this "critical attitude toward her work." Oettinger stated that "no star has started more pictures and had them shelved after a week or two than has Marion Davies"; to which the actress herself responded, "I'm fortunate enough to have a special unit [. . .] and when we make a weak start, we simply call a halt and try for something better" (qtd. in Oettinger 106). Both pragmatic and cavalier, Davies's statement belies the difficulties of defining what that "something better" might be—especially given that both Hearst and Thalberg had different perspectives on the issue. In her posthumously published memoir, Davies recalled Hearst's great regard for Thalberg, quoting him as stating, "Ofttimes the word genius is misplaced, but in the case of Irving, it is a conceded fact" (qtd. in Davies 1975: 105). This admiration, though, did not inspire the magnate to cede control of his companion's career. In contrast to the vamps and flappers of the day, Hearst conceived of Davies as the heroine of sometimes ponderous period pictures like *Janice Meredith* (dir. Hopper, 1924) and *Yolanda* (dir. Vignola, 1925). As contemporary Louise Brooks would recall, Hearst's Davies was "a doll-sweetheart out of the eighteen-nineties, in the manner of the D.W. Griffith heroines, who had come to be totally rejected" (2000: 37).[6]

Thalberg, appropriately, saw Davies at an oblique angle. Diverging from the type of roles fostered by Hearst, Thalberg perceived Davies as a comedienne in the tradition of Mabel Normand (Guiles 150). This view of Davies was not simply a question of corporate strategy—that is, a desire to market her talents in comedy. Rather, Thalberg's emphasis on Davies's strengths derived from his perception of a conceptual break between the past and present industry. Representing the former was Hearst, with his conventional mode of typecasting; representing the latter was Thalberg, with his belief in a dynamic and fluid range of roles. Davies would ruefully recall his attempts to revitalize her image and his frustration with Hearst's myopia. According to Davies, Thalberg "was very kind," but "the only time that he got the hair up on his neck" (104) was in response to her patron's interference. As Thalberg told her,

> I'm trying to get you away from those namby-pamby pictures to do something with a little character. Mr. Hearst doesn't want you to do anything the slightest bit off-color, and I have no intention of doing that. I just want to strike a happy medium. I want you to do something that isn't entirely gutless, something that means something. And I don't want to be told about these things by another person. [. . .] If you leave it to me, I'll see you through. (Qtd. in Davies 104)

Stated simply, the conflict over the direction of Davies's career led to a *de facto* versatility born of instability. The theory of oblique casting as such called for the exploration of a number of roles, each carefully chosen to mine the star's depth; what Thalberg and Hearst's disagreements over Davies's performance style signaled was, by contrast, a vacillation between poles. Was Davies a contemporary comedienne "with a little character" or a "namby-pamby" sentimental figure? She could and would play both, but as a function of the inherent tension between Thalberg and Hearst rather than a celebration of her potential. This chapter in MGM's early history represents a situation in which Thalberg—the head of production, "the decider" of Shearer's description—found himself without total control.

These clashes over Davies's roles in individual films led, moreover, to a kind of public identity-in-limbo. Commentary of the day extended this lack of definition to include Davies's very physicality. In 1925, Adela Rogers St. Johns wrote "An Impression of Marion Davies," musing upon the star in flattering terms—after describing an initially indifferent response to her: "I [had] put her away in my mental cubby-hole under the label, 'Just another pretty blonde'" (59). Though she goes on to correct herself and comment at length on Davies's wholesome charm (and wax poetic about the star's stammer), St. Johns nonetheless addresses the vagueness of the actress's persona. "I realized how little the public had seen of the real Marion Davies [. . .] She has done so many costume pictures that Marion, just as she actually is, has been kept a good deal in the background" (104). If certain critics found Chaney's props to be a collective crutch, then St. Johns here speaks for critics who perceived Davies's very costumes as obstacles—objects that got in the way of an effective engagement between star and role, star and audience.

St. Johns's notion of a public image presenting a star "just as she actually is" is, of course, a fraught one; but the question here seems to be less about striving for authenticity than trying to combat amorphousness. In 1928, Myrtle Gebhart would even damn Davies's appearance with faint praise ("Though I know I have opponents, I don't think she is beautiful" [106]) but also give more outline to her personality by chronicling in detail her wit and propensity for practical jokes. The high spirits of these anecdotes give way, though, to Gebhart's description of a figure who "is neither haughty nor humble [. . .] She is not particularly reserved, nor does she gush in revelation of secrets" (106). Across St. Johns and Gebhart's commentaries, Davies appears as an utterly neutral performer with little traction for audience response one way or another. The period between 1927 and 1928 would represent, however, a turning point for Davies: she had had hits with contemporary films (*The Fair Coed* [dir. Wood, 1927] and *Tillie the Toiler* [dir. Henley, 1927]), but these were followed by the box-office disappointment of period piece *Quality Street* (dir. Franklin, 1927) (Guiles 203). Countering the sentimentality of the latter, Thalberg established a collaboration between Davies and King Vidor in thoroughly modern films that steered her towards "something with a little character."

The public responded favorably to these less "namby-pamby" roles; parts that were not, to borrow from Thalberg, "entirely gutless." Declaring her one of only a few "versatile" stars, a 1930 *Picture Play* article noted that though Davies spent her early career "march[ing] through pompous and pampered roles," she emerged as a "queen of high comedy" in contemporary pictures like *The Patsy* and *Show People* (Chamberlain 88). As Eirik Frisvold Hanssen remarks in his insightful article on these films, they represent "a genre transformation [for] Davies" more broadly even as they also play upon diegetic "themes of acting or performance, of adapting to social conventions and playing roles" (para. 2). *Show People* features Davies as Peggy Pepper, a young woman who becomes a star in comedies before abandoning her slapstick roots for high drama as "Patricia Pepoire." The foundation for Davies's role in this meta-Hollywood production, however, lies in *The Patsy* itself—specifically in the extended sequence in which Davies impersonates fellow stars Lillian Gish, Mae Murray, and Pola Negri.

A romantic comedy in a domestic setting, *The Patsy* is ostensibly an unlikely companion for *Show People*. Davies plays Pat, a put-upon but enterprising young woman bullied by her mother (the excellent Marie Dressler) and sister. When Pat falls in love with one of her sister's boyfriends, she gets his attention by telling him of her troubles with an imaginary suitor; the boyfriend's advice is to "cultivat[e] a personality." Hanssen has commented upon the self-reflexive quality of these two films, noting that the diegetic focus on "unstable identities and transformations" parallel the broader "aesthetic and technological transition" between silent and sound cinema (para. 2). This extra-diegetic resonance extends even further, as Pat's pursuit of "a personality" parallels Davies's own struggles to define her public identity. In wistful, and fitting, response to the above line of dialogue, Pat remarks, "I think I've got [a personality], but he's too slow to see it."

In the impersonation sequence—triggered by Pat's attempts to impress another young man—Davies indeed assumes the personalities of Gish, Murray, and Negri, simpering and vamping her way through these alternate identities with an uncanny precision. A shot of a framed photograph of each star precedes Davies's impressions, cementing the accuracy of her portrayals as she uses various props—a scarf, a sheet, some make-up—to help craft her metamorphoses. Where Chaney's performance in *He Who Gets Slapped* speaks to the affinity between actor and object, Davies's reliance on the props is minimal. Instead, the objects serve as material accents to her portrayals, underscoring her own nuances of gesture and expression. For her depiction of Murray, Davies sneers and raises her upper lip to capture the famous "bee-stung" visage; and Davies's wild-eyed and impassioned flailing capture the essence of vamp Negri even more than her exaggerated make-up and knife clenched roguishly between her teeth. Most impressive, perhaps, is Davies's moment as Gish (Figure 2.1): with only a kerchief around her head and sheet over her shoulders, Davies composes her face into an expression of wide-eyed, prim-mouthed innocence, fluttering about the room with wringing hands and tiny steps.[7]

It is a sequence that makes evident Davies's corporeal sensitivity to the Hollywood vogue, for which she was famed among friends. Myrtle Gebhart wrote, "You're absolutely nobody in Hollywood until Marion has mimicked you" (52); and biographer Fred Lawrence Guiles notes that she would often impersonate fellow MGM stars on the set of her films (228). But the scene also presents a collision between established types and Davies's more liminal public image. Because of the neutrality of Davies's persona, she could adopt the qualities of her more extreme contemporaries to comedic effect—highlighting the

Figure 2.1 Davies as Lillian Gish.

behavioral signatures that would have been instantly recognizable to audiences and are now cemented in the historical cinematic imagination. One interpretation could read the very act of impersonation as suggesting the comparative *a*morphousness of Davies's own star-image. But more than this, the polymorphous fluidity of these impressions—their quicksilver obliquity—capture the capaciousness of her talent. Playing on the geometric associations of oblique casting, the sequence has an almost cubist quality, revealing the many angles to Davies's comedic flair; she contains multitudes.

Show People would, however, go on to ask the same questions of its heroine that the industry asked of her interpreter, exploring the experience of an actress caught between comedy and drama. An inherently self-reflexive film—as Vidor noted, Gloria Swanson's career provided the inspiration for the narrative (1954: 110)—*Show People* explores the absurdity that often shaded the construction of Hollywood celebrity. Ingénue Peggy Pepper assumes the panache of leading lady Patricia Pepoire, who is herself an amalgam of, as one character describes it, "the temperament of Nazimova, the appeal of Garbo, the sweetness of Pickford, and the lure of Pola Negri." Patricia also attunes her physical appeal to that of the stars she admires; in a sequence featuring an interview with a magazine writer, Davies in a single take transforms from Murray to Gloria Swanson with subtle tilts of her lip. Singled out in *Motion Picture*'s review of the film, it is "a lightning transformation [. . .] that is miraculous" ("Current Pictures in Review" 1928: 62). Where *The Patsy* embeds Davies's impersonations within the wholesomeness of a romantic comedy, *Show People* incorporates them as one of many curious performances played out by Hollywood's inhabitants.

Among those performances were, as Hanssen remarks, celebrities "playing themselves" in cameos (para. 12). The film features appearances by a number of Hollywood figures, including Charlie Chaplin, director Vidor, and Douglas Fairbanks. Where the film makes a comedy of Peggy / Patricia's transformation, that very juxtaposition between real and ideal selves—or, as Hanssen terms it, "the sliding boundaries between real and fake" (para. 13)—extends to include several of the extra-diegetic stars. Laura Mulvey has commented on a scene in which Peggy fails to recognize Charlie Chaplin, citing this as illustrative of his ability "to move around publicly or socially without being recognized" (2017: 203) as his most famous character, the Little Tramp. This paradoxical condition of total fame and utter anonymity is mirrored later in the film—this time, using Davies as a foil. In a particularly striking scene, Davies makes a cameo as *herself*: dashing out of a car on the studio lot, tennis racket in hand, her presence hardly enchants Peggy Pepper. "Who is that?," she asks a colleague, shaking her head disparagingly when she hears the answer. For star-struck Peggy, "the real Marion Davies" does not impress (Figures 2.2 and 2.3).

Figure 2.2 Davies's cameo.

Figure 2.3 An unimpressed Peggy Pepper.

Thalberg and Hearst, fan magazines, even inside jokes from her own films—many sources puzzled over who Marion Davies was. But the relative neutrality of her image allowed for Davies to be not simply a performer in, but rather a commentator *on*, the productions of Hollywood's silent era. Hanssen has noted that "transformation and roleplaying [*sic*] are themes integral to Davies's screen characters" (para. 2), and her casting in several films about Hollywood and/or stardom—*Show People*, *Hollywood Revue of 1929* (dir. Reisner, 1929), *Blondie of the Follies* (dir. Goulding, 1932), *Going Hollywood* (dir. Walsh, 1933)—speaks to this greater awareness of her self-reflexive talents at Thalberg-era MGM. Indeed, Davies's performances endure as a chronicle of the early Hollywood mode with which she was so familiar. The impact of the impersonations lie both in their accuracy and, more importantly, their synthesis of the feminine types that Davies herself had explored: moving from the sentimental girlishness made so popular by Gish and Mary Pickford—and to which Hearst had resigned her—to the physical comedy of a Mabel Normand, the star to whom Thalberg perceived Davies as an heir. And through her impressions of Murray and Negri, Davies sketched the kind of vampish sensuality that neither Hearst nor Thalberg intended to test in her. As her Pat would remark in *The Patsy*, "I'm just full of view points."

Towards the end of the 1920s and beginning of the 1930s, certain of the difficulties in Davies's talkie career were blamed on Thalberg and Shearer's relationship. Though Davies's voice tested extremely well—in her account, Thalberg declared that she "stunned the other people" (qtd. in Davies 101)— her privileges at MGM diminished over time. Hedda Hopper noted that, as Thalberg's wife, Shearer "[n]aturally [. . .] got first whack at everything— stories, writers, directors, leading men" (1952: 135); and biographer Guiles blames the decline of Davies's career on Thalberg's focus on Shearer. Citing the producer's benign neglect, Guiles argues that Thalberg left Davies vulnerable to Hearst's dated tastes (250) while casting Shearer in dramatic leads that Davies wished to play—or that Hearst wanted her to: *Marie Antoinette, Romeo and Juliet*, and *The Barretts of Wimpole Street*. As Davies remarked in her memoir, "W.R. wanted me to do [*Marie Antoinette*], and I was going to try my best"; but to his appeals for Davies's casting in each of these films, "the studio said no [. . .] [T]hey said, 'Marion's too lively. She's got to do comedy" (253).

Such decisions attest to the continued struggle between Hearst's view of Davies as a classical actor and Thalberg's perception of her as a figure of wit and verve; it was not so much that Davies had to do comedy, but that Thalberg understood that some casting was just too oblique. Yet in considering the range of her self-reflexive performances, the 1929 description of Davies as "the cleverest character star the films have produced" (Jopp 72)—and its unlikely comparison of the actress with Chaney—reads as all the more apt. For where Chaney, to recall Thalberg's statements, "illuminate[d] certain dark corners of the human spirit," Davies too revealed her insight into still another unexpected character in all its facets: that of early Hollywood femininity, composed of vamps, ingenues, and comediennes.

FROM ANY ANGLE

In itself, Thalberg's theory of oblique casting illuminated the versatility of a given performer, exploring from all angles, as it were, his or her ability to evolve in terms of on-screen portrayals and public persona. With both Chaney and

Davies belonging to the first generation of MGM stars, their myriad characterizations—some more popular than others—provided a touchstone for Thalberg's subsequent iterations of oblique casting. Chaney's MGM roles composed an entire *oeuvre* of transformations that would establish Thalberg's fascination with the capaciousness of the performing body; and Davies's fluency in the Hollywood vogue reflected the variations of early studio-era celebrity, even as personal circumstances destabilized her own extra-diegetic persona.

Thalberg and the multiplicity of his own accomplishments also drew public commentary. In a 1927 article for *Vanity Fair*, Jim Tully mused upon Thalberg's "eighteen-hour day [which] involves editing, cutting, titling, casting, advising millionaire stars, giving fatherly advice to directors, script writers and authors [. . .] He is the big 'idea' man of his shadow world" (71). In summing up the producer's talents, Tully noted, "He can strike back from any angle" (98). In so casting himself from one role to another—editor, consigliere, creative "idea" man, and grounded strategist—Thalberg imbued his identity as head of production with a compelling dimensionality. This connection between Thalberg's theory of oblique casting and his own versatility highlights that, for him, change was a challenge to be welcomed; Thalberg perceived, that is, an evolutionary imperative in the entertainment industry.

Such an imperative underlies the quotations that introduced this chapter: "Unusual assignments help our people expand, and that helps us" (qtd. in Marx 1975: 82); "[Typecasting is] slow death for actors" (qtd. in Marx 1975: 156); and even, to Davies, "I'm trying to get you away from those namby-pamby pictures to do something with a little character" (qtd. in Davies 104). Returning to Cukor: Thalberg was "one of the few who really tried to make his stars do surprising things, try different kinds of parts" (qtd. in Lambert 1973: 151). The concept of oblique casting takes on all the more import when considered within the context of MGM's earliest days. For MGM was beginning to define its identity—the luxe "Versailles of the movies" (as cited by Crowther 1960: 123–124) that emerged from a Mission Road zoo; a studio that took aesthetic risks with material like *He Who Gets Slapped* but was also savvy enough to consider the construction of celebrity itself in *Show People*. To paraphrase Davies in *The Patsy*, the studio was full of viewpoints, and it was Thalberg's intention to maximize the impact of each.

NOTES

1. Portions of this discussion first appeared in Salzberg 2012.
2. Chaney biographer Michael F. Blake has drawn from archival materials to reveal that it was the actor himself who proposed the making of *Hunchback*—contrary to alternate accounts which attribute the idea to Thalberg (105–106). Blake does concede, however, that it was Thalberg who campaigned for the production and its expensive budget of $1, 250, 000 (ibid.).

3. Anthony Slide notes that in 1927, the hyphen "was mysteriously and without explanation removed from the title" of this publication; *Picture-Play* thus became *Picture Play* (2010: 29).

4. Studlar reads this narrative turn as part of a larger phenomenon in Chaney's films: A "family discourse of romantic sacrifice" (229), in which he plays an "oedipally tinged role as the sacrificial ideal father/impossible lover" (231).

5. This naming of Chaney among other figures involved in the production of *Show People* suggests that he may have been approached and/or considered for a cameo appearance in the film—which did not appear in the final cut.

6. As Louis Pizzitola remarks in *Hearst Over Hollywood*, the magnate would also offer extensive critiques on the direction and editing of Davies's films; during the making of *Zander the Great* (dir. Hill, 1925), for example, he demanded a "big [D. W.] Griffith effect" (qtd. in Pizzitola 219).

7. Davies's performance might have been heightened by her personal feelings towards Gish. Recalling an unpleasant exchange between them, Davies related, "[F]or a nice, sweet little girl she was very nasty" (Davies 53).

CHAPTER 3

One Great Scene: Thalberg's Silent Spectacles

One year after the merger that formed MGM, the studio released a short documentary. *Studio Tour 1925* offered viewers a tour of the premises, with an intertitle capturing their impressive dimensions: "The Studio embraces an area of 43 acres, and its 45 buildings, including 14 big stages, are connected by 3 miles of paved streets." Far from the Mission Road compound with its bucolic associations, the Culver City lot depicted here is effectively a city in itself: a site replete with its own laboratory that processed 40 million feet of film annually, a restaurant that fed "over 2,000 people a day," and power plants that generated enough energy "to light a city of 8,000 homes." The documentary presents a number of personnel, from directors, stars, and screenwriters to cameramen, publicists, and the head nurse of the studio hospital. It is only at the very end of the film that the audience is introduced to Mayer, Rapf, and Thalberg—"three executives responsible for [the studio's] progress, its success, its future—three men who pull the strings."

Given that MGM was only about a year old, the documentary is a fascinating record of not only the inhabitants of this enclave, but also of the way that the corporation wanted to present itself.[1] Even as the short film extols the up-to-the-minute, state-of-the-art technologies and amenities offered by the studio, there is an underlying sense of watching MGM write its own historical narrative—preserving, for posterity, the dawning of a new age of filmmaking. The studio emerges as a veritable society, governed by the "three men who pull the strings"; artistically minded but utterly efficient, already successful but still ambitious, MGM is a dream factory built on an epic scale.

What did "pulling the strings" mean in practice for Thalberg in 1925? The day-to-day running of the studio—and the responsibility, then shared with Rapf, for producing a slate of 48 films for Loew's theaters (Rapf 2016: 40)—would obviously have been even more dynamic than the documentary let on. Though in the coming years Thalberg would go on to devolve some of the more logistical responsibilities to associate producers, such a process of delegation was not yet in place. Instead, screenwriter Lenore Coffee recalled an intimate and intellectually-charged atmosphere in which colleagues discussed current and future films:

> The first thing Irving did after the merger was to inaugurate Saturday morning meetings. [. . .] We were a small group—only a handful of us; there was only one other producer besides Thalberg, Harry Rapf [. . .] Besides our group of writers and a director or two, there was Paul Bern, still Thalberg's assistant. (1973: 96)

Outside of this collegial idyll—"It was really like someone holding a seminar" (96)—things were far more fractured. Thalberg, Rapf, and Mayer spent the early days of MGM trying to synthesise the various filmmaking styles inherited from both Goldwyn Pictures and Metro. Bosley Crowther describes the black comedy of the "first few months of studio activities":

> Confusion and conflict were common. The organization of schedules and the handling of equipment were slow. Directors would hijack cameras and lights from the sets of other directors, who would hijack them back again. It took some months for the shakedown and smoothing out of operations to occur. (1957: 86)

Part of that "smoothing out of operations" was the instituting of Thalberg as central producer. As such, he was in control of "selecting the type of product, the type of production processes, level and integration of production, and maintenance of production performance" (Bordwell et al. 1988: 143) for MGM. This level of executive authority and creative oversight threatened several directors. Established successes such as Marshall Neilan, Rex Ingram, and Maurice Tourneur balked at the loss of autonomy and left MGM (Schatz 1996: 34); and Erich von Stroheim—who once again battled with Thalberg over what the latter called a "fetish for footage" (qtd. in Crowther 1957: 90)— also quit the studio after making *The Merry Widow* (1925).

More of a concern was a foundling project inherited from Goldwyn Pictures, described by Norma Shearer as "a baby, in its teething stage, and causing a lot of trouble" (qtd. in Vieira 2010: 48). It was an unwieldy Biblical epic, an adaptation of Lew Wallace's 1880 novel *Ben-Hur* being filmed in Italy with a $1.25 million-dollar budget. Dismayed by the mediocre footage and rising costs—as Thalberg wrote to Fred Niblo, "It is almost beyond my conception that such stuff could have been passed by people of even moderate intelligence" (qtd. in Vieira 2010: 49)—Thalberg and Mayer launched an intervention. They replaced director Charles Brabin and star George Walsh with Niblo and Ramon Navarro, respectively, and moved the production back to the Culver City lot (Vieira 2010: 48–49; Thomas 1969: 70–72). Even under Thalberg's direct supervision, aspects of the film still presented problems—namely, the chariot-race sequence. In the years to come at MGM, Thalberg would declare that "every great film must have one great scene" (qtd. in Vieira 2010: 37); but even before that concept had been articulated, it was clear that he had identified the chariot race as *Ben-Hur*'s key sequence.

Adding $300,000 to the already inflated budget, Thalberg instructed art director Cedric Gibbons to reconstruct the Circus Maximus with an eye to on-screen impact (Vieira 2010: 49; Thomas 72). "The audience is going to think the set is fake unless we prove to them it isn't," Thalberg explained. "What we need are some statues, huge statues we can place the extras beside so the audience will get a sense of the scale" (qtd. in Thomas 72). Gibbons accordingly designed statues that were twenty feet tall. On the day of the shoot, forty-two cameras captured these figures as they loomed over the charioteers; but while observing the filming, Thalberg wanted to heighten the intensity still further. As Bob Thomas relates,

> Thalberg eyed the crowd and called over J.J. Cohn of the production department.
> "How many people have you got, Joe?" Thalberg asked.
> "Thirty-nine hundred," Cohn replied.
> "Not enough. Get some more. [. . .] Pull them in off the street. The set needs more people." (Qtd. in Thomas 74)

In the final tally, a number of movie stars—including Marion Davies, Douglas Fairbanks, and Mary Pickford—were among over 4,000 extras who took part in the filming. But in contrast to the expansiveness of the production itself, the editing of the film was a nuanced process—made all the more cloistered by the fact that part of it took place in Thalberg's bedroom. Following a collapse brought on by the strain of the production, Thalberg was unable to sit up in bed, but he had the rushes projected onto his ceiling (Thomas 73–74, 76).

At first reading, these events speak to the duality of Thalberg's tenure at the studio, defined equally by his remarkable will and fragile health. But the account also illuminates the more theoretical concerns associated with the crafting of "one great scene"—the phrasing of which Samuel Marx records slightly differently:

> Thalberg repeated an analysis made by [playwright] Laurence Stallings [. . .] "Every film of major importance must have one great sequence from the standpoint of the camera, in acting and story, in light and shadow, in sound and fury." (Qtd. in Marx 1975: 247).

Though Marx here identifies Stallings as the inspiration for this approach, the making of the chariot-race scene reveals that such issues preoccupied Thalberg from the beginning of his career. The making of *Ben-Hur* is not simply a case study of MGM's own "teething stage," to paraphrase Shearer; it is a turning point that established Thalberg's fascination with scale in narrative and concrete terms. How could a film "prove to" the audience, following Thalberg's words, the value of suspending their disbelief? How could the dimensionality of a given set—in terms of both production design and human form—match the import of a diegetic climax? And how would that impact translate from the studio lot to the screen itself, whether it took shape on a bedroom ceiling or in a movie palace? Like the massive statues that gave a sense of proportion and perspective to MGM's Circus Maximus, this "one great scene" theorized by Thalberg stands as a structuring element alongside which the broader arc of a given film takes shape.

Thalberg's story conference notes reveal more about how he conceived of a "great scene" as a necessity. Consider, for instance, his discussion of a turning point in Garbo vehicle *Mata Hari*. Here, Thalberg outlines his vision for the sequence in relation to character development and thematic complexity. In terms of the former, he describes "the very thing I want to get in this scene. This is the only scene in the picture where it can happen"—thus highlighting the stakes of a single episode for the audience's understanding of the central relationship. Thalberg also argues for an unexpected interpretation of the love scene: "My objection [to] the scene [as it currently stands] is this: Whatever you expect to happen—happens."[2] As Chapter 7 will discuss in detail, such statements provide the foundation for Thalberg's oblique *interpretation* of defining events in a film. Just as he resisted typecasting his stars, he rejected playing dramatic scenes in a conventional or generic way.

Directors and writers alike responded to these insights, and would consult Thalberg on the development of action in a picture. As Clarence Brown, the director of films such as *Flesh and the Devil*, *Anna Christie*, and *A Free Soul*, recalled,

> You would be working with your writer, and you would come to this scene in the script. It didn't click. It just didn't jell [*sic*]. The scene was no goddam good. You would make a date with Irving, talk to him for thirty minutes, and you'd come away from his office with the best scene in the picture. (Qtd. in French 1969: 59)

In similar terms, Anita Loos recalled that after an indifferent preview of *Red-Headed Woman*, Thalberg asked her "to contrive a prologue that will tip the audience off that the movie's a comedy" (qtd. in Loos 1974: 43)—thus literally and figuratively setting the scene. Though arguably these types of concerns would be universal to any given script, Thalberg had a forensic fascination with the elemental significance of the scene as such. Irene Selznick pointed out that at the beginning of his time at MGM, "Thalberg was [. . .] concerned with the mastery of a single sequence in each film" (qtd. in Vieira 2010: 37).

Films made from 1917 to 1928 had a range of about nine to 18 scenes—and each of these had a duration of around four to eight minutes (Bordwell et al. 1988: 62). These statistics offer an objective account of what was a very immediate conceptual concern for Thalberg and the MGM screenwriters; as he would later write, "We deal in flesh and blood, not paper and ink. Ideas that register big on the typewritten page may not register at all on the screen" (Thalberg and Weir 1933: 85). Thalberg would explore the evolution from page to screen—as well as the dialogue between single sequence and entire production—in a 1925 interview with the *New York Times*. Published in the year in which, as Vidor noted, Thalberg was just "hit[ting] his stride" (1954: 69), the article details his process of adapting a play or novel. He discusses the importance of choosing a director and star, as well as the overarching issue of what types of properties appeal to which studios. ("[I]t should be remembered that different picture-making organizations are after different types of vehicles" ["Producing Executive" 1925: Section X, 7].) Especially fascinating, though, is the way that Thalberg connects more abstract questions of story arc to the material form of the film itself:

> This actual screen adaptation means [. . .] decisions as to the relative importance of each episode to the story as a whole, that is, whether the situation in the finished picture should be allowed 20 feet or 200 feet. [. . .] The tendency appears to be to register each point as quickly as possible, but sometimes this may be a great mistake, for it often happens that many situations that appear to be unnecessarily long in the scenario [script] again are lengthened by the director beyond all seeming reason and prove to be the most successful portions of a picture. [. . .] It's hard to know on paper how far one must go with the camera. (7)

Which is to say: in the translation from script to screen, how one scene or "situation" reads "on paper" does not always align with how much space it needs to take within the cinematic body ("whether the situation in the finished picture should be allowed 20 feet or 200 feet"). In order to fully realize the possibilities of those 9–18 sequences, the filmmakers had to reconcile the dual issues of pacing ("the tendency appears to be to register each point as quickly as possible") and dramatic impact. And in Thalberg's view, great scenes—"the most successful portions of a picture"—only reveal themselves as such when they appear on the screen. In geometric, almost geographic, terms, Thalberg perceives a central sequence as a fixed point, a kind of horizon line of 20 or 200 feet, that helps determine the scale of the remaining scenes—or as he says, "the relative importance of each episode to the story as a whole."

This concept has particular resonance in the context of epic filmmaking. Recalling Thalberg's own fundamental production practice in *Ben-Hur*, Sobchack has noted that historical epics represent the magnitude of their subjects "through *scale*: in the concretely 'big' presence of monumental sets and landscapes" (1990: 36). What Thalberg would establish in the 1920s, however, was the "big presence" of great scenes across epics both historical and melodramatic. Following the release of *Ben-Hur* in 1925, Thalberg produced two other spectacular projects: *The Big Parade* (1925) and *La Bohème* (1926), both directed by King Vidor and starring John Gilbert. From *The Big Parade*'s contemplation of World War I, a historical trauma barely completed, to the period drama of the Puccini adaptation, both films capture the early execution of a theory—"Every great film must have one great scene"—that would become established practice for Thalberg's prestige productions. The following analyses will not simply identify one great scene per se in these works, but rather explore the development of Thalberg's theory and its network of related concerns with exhibition and audience appeal. In the case of *The Big Parade*, Thalberg and Vidor would explore how the visual and narrative scope of a film could match the expansiveness of a movie palace screen. And in romance *La Bohème*, Thalberg emphasized the importance of love scenes in order to heighten what he termed "audience values" ("Producing Executive" Section X, 7) for a public seeking passion on a grand scale.

Given the constants of director and star, these films also illuminate much about the role of collaboration in Thalberg's producing style. As he would himself remark in 1929,

> I have discussed scenes with [Vidor] many times, and have advised him to do this or that to heighten the dramatic effect, and his greatest fear has always been to make any character do anything that was not natural for him to do. (1977: 120)

The making of these two films highlights the beginning of that discursive mode, through which Thalberg's intentionality as both theorist and producer would inform a given work while he remained sensitive to the singularity of the project. Thalberg and his methods would go on to exceed film history to become part of cultural legend, and *The Big Parade* and *La Bohème* preserve the beginning of that epic saga.

"FOR GRAUMAN'S EGYPTIAN"

The Big Parade, destined to endure as of the "biggest and best pictures" (Rittenhouse 1926: 74) of MGM's canon, emerged from two central motivations. As Vidor explained in his pitch to Thalberg, the director wanted to tell the story of

> a young American [. . .] who went to war and reacted normally to all the things that happened to him. It would be the story of the average man in whose hands does not lie the power to *create* the situations in which he finds himself but who nevertheless feels them emotionally. (Vidor 73)

This juxtaposition of individual and historical circumstance was, indeed, a recurring concern in Vidor's work, most famously seen in his 1928 film *The Crowd* and its exploration of one man's existence in contemporary society. But Vidor had still another motivation, which he also discussed with Thalberg: the director was frustrated with "making ephemeral films. They came to town, played a week or so, then went their way to comparative obscurity or complete oblivion" (Vidor 73). (More anecdotally, Loos recalled that "in those days MGM released a new picture every week: fifty-two movies a year, and every one a success" [1974: 42].) Vidor's were not idle concerns. Richard Koszarski points out that "constant changes of program" characterized motion picture exhibition, with weekly shifts in films designed to attract audiences (1990: 34). Where event films like *Ben-Hur* could be booked for months at a time, less spectacular films were expendable; Koszarski points out that "one quarter of exhibitors felt that the quality of the feature was of no importance to the box office" (35).

Loew's was, as it happened, a theater chain less sympathetic to this modus operandi. As Thomas Schatz has noted, Loew's at that time only owned around 100 theaters—focusing on first-run, prestige productions (1996: 39). In contrast to "expansion-oriented" studios such as Warners and Paramount, which owned 500 theaters that block-booked B-pictures as well as A-material, Loew's privileged "a steady output of first-class product for first-run theaters" (39). With this corporate backing, Thalberg's MGM developed a production style that rejected ephemeral films and cultivated instead comparatively permanent works: cinematic bodies that would be fully incarnated within the generous dimensions of a movie-palace screen, appealing to the greatest number of spectators for a sustained period of time. Such works established the model for the prestige film of the 1930s, which Tino Balio defines as "a big-budget special based on a presold property, often as not a 'classic,' and tailored for top stars" (1993: 179). Just as one great scene provided a focal point for the film itself, one great *screen* would provide both material and symbolic parameters for this caliber of motion picture.

A 1926 article from *Motion Picture Magazine* outlined parallel issues relating to the overarching question "What is an Epic Picture?" Filmmaker Elmer Clifton identifies *The Big Parade* as an "epic picture" as determined by a three-part process: "when (1) a great thought (2) is told in a simple and understandable way (3) by expert motion picture technicians" (qtd. in Rittenhouse 54). Clifton knew whereof he spoke: he had directed the whaling saga *Down to the Sea in Ships* (1922) after appearing in mentor D. W. Griffith's foundational epics *Birth of a Nation* (1915) and *Intolerance* (1916). Equally influential, of course, was Cecil B. DeMille, who directed *The Ten Commandments* in 1923. These *auteur*-ist productions established the epic genre in the terms subsequently used by Clifton; yet interestingly, he goes on to highlight the importance of the exhibition space itself in relation to *The Big Parade*:

> It was only after conferences between Irving Thalberg [. . .] (who was the first one to see [the film's] possibilities), Jack Gilbert, the star, and King Vidor, director, that enthusiasm was aroused about it. But once fired with vim, Vidor and Gilbert used to shakes hands daily, and repeat: "For Grauman's Egyptian." Which meant that they were going to make a tremendous effort to turn out a picture worthy of being shown in a theater which shows only the biggest and best pictures. (Qtd. in Rittenhouse 74)

On an immediate level, the mantra that defined the filming—"For Grauman's Egyptian"—conveys the bonhomie and artistic ambition of the collaborators,[3] as well as capturing the historic import of the movie palace itself. Built in 1922 and featuring a lush décor inspired by Ancient Egypt,[4] Grauman's Egyptian had hosted the premiere of *The Ten Commandments* in 1923 (Calhoun 1999: 34)—thus marking its symbolic weight for the makers of another epic film. Yet in more, or in fact less, abstract terms, the phrase "For Grauman's Egyptian" also identified a concrete site within which the film would take its ideal shape. For all of the conceptual and logistical investments in creating an epic film—a great picture requiring a great scene—where exactly would that scene be seen? Even as "For Grauman's Egyptian" emerges as a kind of incantation affirming the film's destiny, it also functions as a *destination* for the permanent film desired by Vidor—a site of projection and reception that would be claimed by the director and, indeed, the producer.

According to the terms set out in Clifton's three-part process, *The Big Parade*—from a screenplay written by famed playwright and World War I veteran Laurence Stallings, MGM staff writer Harry Behn, and Vidor himself (Vidor 74)—took the formidable subject of the recent war and made it relatable to the audience by expanding on Vidor's original "story of [an] average man" confronting a changing world. The film follows wealthy Jim Apperson (Gilbert) from enlistment to homecoming. He trains and becomes friends with two other soldiers from vastly different backgrounds, falls in love with a young French girl (Renée Adorée), and experiences the trauma of the trenches and a grievous wounding before reuniting with his sweetheart in France.

John Gilbert would credit Thalberg as "the man who first realized the immense possibilities in" the film ("Silent Director" 1925: X9). But he was also the man who first realized the possibility of Gilbert playing Jim. In a classic case of oblique casting, Thalberg chose Gilbert—then rising in popularity as the Great Lover—to play this "average man" and typical "young American" to remarkable effect.[5] Within a year of his success in a supporting role in *He Who Gets Slapped*, Gilbert was given the part of Jim Apperson—though Vidor admitted to initial reservations: "He was well on his way to being established as the 'Great Lover,' and it wasn't fair to change his character when his career [. . .] was finally in the ascendancy" (Vidor 75–76). Gilbert's daughter, Leatrice Gilbert Fountain, would describe it more succinctly: "Vidor hated the idea" (Fountain 1985: 111). Even Gilbert himself balked at first, but later he gave Thalberg the credit for encouraging him to take the role that made him a great star. "When we talked over my part [. . .] I said: 'Yes—nice part!' 'Why you're insane, man!' [Thalberg] returned. 'It's the biggest chance you ever had!' Twenty minutes later, I walked out of his office completely sold" (qtd. in Leslie 1926: 56).

Just as Thalberg pursued the oblique casting of Gilbert, he understood—as *Photoplay* noted—that "*The Big Parade* was a big thing—and he gambled on his theory" ("The Big Parade" 1926: 144). The picture was hailed as a classic upon its release. *Photoplay* named it the best film of 1925, praising it as "the first screen effort to present war without the usual saccharine romantic bunk" ("The Big Parade" 40). Decades later, historian Dario Vidojkovic identified the film as instrumental in changing both filmmakers' and audiences' views about productions dealing with the war; up to that point, he suggests, the subject was not a popular one (2017: 37). *The Big Parade*, then, is a "big picture from every angle" ("The Big Parade," 40): in terms of scale and subject, popularity and critical esteem, MGM's early success and contemporary cultural history.

From its very first sequence, *The Big Parade* frames its central male protagonists against a backdrop of industrial progress. At the same time, it introduces an environment in which, as Lea Jacobs has noted, "male friendship is underscored with the threat of loss and death" (2008: chapter 4).[6] The opening intertitle clearly sets the scene: "In the Spring of 1917, America was a nation occupied in peaceful progression." Moments later, we learn of "buildings climb[ing] skyward, monuments to commerce and profession." Images of mechanized landscapes—mills, smokestacks, skyscrapers under construction—illustrate these statements without the presence of a human form. The first character introduced is one of Jim's soon-to-be friends, "Just one of labor's millions, building a nation": Slim Jensen

(Karl Dane) appears sitting atop the steel beam of a skyscraper, a fade-in first focusing on his hands as he works a drill. Recalling Vidor's description of average men "in whose hands does not lie the power to *create* the situations in which" they find themselves (Vidor 73), Slim is building a nation that has effectively moved beyond the human touch.

This opening sequence introduces the three future soldiers in their respective class contexts, each of which bears an underlying trace of unease: Slim balances on a superstructure; bartender Bull O'Hara (Tom O'Brien) polishes glasses in the Bowery, framed in the center of a medium shot while two men loom in the foreground; and wealthy Jim is lying back with his face covered in shaving cream, tended to by an African-American barber. Jim obviously lives the life of the idle rich, but there is also an impotence to his position. As seen subsequently, his family home seems to belong to another time: it is a classical marble structure, the interior of which dwarfs its inhabitants—almost akin to a mausoleum, with its sweeping proportions and sense of grandeur. Jim emerges from this reliquary to meet the momentum of the industrial age; indeed, his decision to enlist derives in part from an actual big parade. Stopping traffic with a brass band playing, young men and women hanging out of motor cars, and flags waving, the long-shot spectacle appears as yet another instance of America's progression; a machine of patriotism, so seductive that it convinces Jim to join the army. The sequence ends, in fact, with Jim leaping into the parade and being literally carried away in a car.

The scene is mirrored later in the film, as Jim's sweetheart watches while his regiment is called to the front. Juxtaposing the "old world" innocence of the young village girl with the relentlessness of the army, Melisande stands still in a courtyard, gazing through a large archway as a convoy of lorries and men race past her. When she enters the fray and finally finds Jim, she too is carried away and dragged along behind his truck—unwilling to let him go, and as unable as he to resist the draw of the war. Beyond any romantic or sentimental attraction, this sequence establishes the existential affinity between Jim and Melisande: each is in thrall to the big parade of history (see Figures 3.1 and 3.2). In a variation on Clifton's tenets of epic filmmaking, the "great[ness]" of the war is rendered "understandable" through the experience of two individuals who are subject to it. What Melisande and Jim's personal suffering helps show, then, is the scale of the conflict. In related terms, both scenes illustrate Sobchack's concept of "cinematic onomatopoeia" in historical epics—that is, a process by which the "temporal *magnitude*" of the era is conveyed "by literal *quantity*" (1990: 36) of objects within the frame. Again recalling Thalberg's insistence on the excesses of the chariot scene—more people, higher statues—and even his early demand at Universal for larger crowds in *The Hunchback of Notre Dame*, Sobchack cites elements like the number of extras and details in the set design; here, in this more contemporary epic, we see the suffusion of trucks, men, and other matter related to modern warfare.

Figures 3.1 and 3.2 Jim (in foreground) and Melisande join the big parade.

Still other angles of the film preoccupied Thalberg. Given that, as Thomas notes, Thalberg "preferred films that dealt in human relationships, rather than crowd-filled spectacles" (70)—his talent for producing such spectacles notwithstanding—he valued the character-led nature of *The Big Parade*. What Thalberg wanted to see in the film, however, was an even greater sense of the conflict itself. As Thalberg would note in the *New York Times* article, "Sometimes [. . .] it is found that some individual thing which was most attractive in the original has been lost. Then that element must painfully be worked back in" ("Producing Executive" Section X, 7). Certainly the element that needed to be "worked back in" here was an essential one: as Thalberg told Mayer after watching a rough cut of the film, "It's a fine picture, but it isn't finished [. . .] It doesn't have the war in it" (qtd. in Thomas 84). Where Thomas matter-of-factly notes that Thalberg decided to "inject [. . .] battle scenes" (84), it is key to explore the nuances of what Thalberg meant by "the war" here.

Interestingly, Crowther frames this phase of the production in terms of scale: "[Thalberg] insisted that *more* money be budgeted to make it a *really big* film." Accordingly, the scenes of the Front itself "in the whole latter half of the film [. . .] [were] *greatly augmented* by Vidor and his crew" (1957: 105; emphases added). Vidor himself recounted the filming of scenes in Fort Sam Houston in Texas, in which "[w]e wanted two hundred trucks, three to four thousand men, a hundred aeroplanes, and any other equipment [the army] would let us use" to capture the mass movement towards the Front on "a long straight road" (79–80). Both Crowther and Vidor's terminology recalls the cinematic onomatopoeia theorized by Sobchack, with the excesses of the epic matching the expanse of history itself; their rhetoric also reveals much about Thalberg's own established sensitivity to on-screen impact. From the earliest films at MGM, Thalberg understood and supported the investments that such spectacular storytelling required. Indeed, writing later in another context on his practice of retakes, Thalberg would state, "we simply had to spend whatever might be needed to make that picture right" (Thalberg and Weir 1933: 11). When, accordingly, Vidor screened the Fort Sam Houston footage filmed by his assistant and found it disappointing, Thalberg authorized the reshoots. "That was typical of Thalberg," Vidor recalled. "He knew instinctively when someone presented a good idea or at least one which that person considered really important, and he didn't try to talk him out of it" (80).

But just as the success of the *Ben-Hur* chariot-race sequence was predicated on both the sensory and emotional investment of the spectator—"The audience is going to think the set is fake unless we prove to them it isn't"—the war in *The Big Parade* needed to be greater than the sum of its action imagery. It was not simply a case of offering more battles but rather, as with the device of framing Jim and Melisande against the big parades of history, illuminating their consequences for the individual. Indeed, Thomas inadvertently points to the means by which Thalberg heightened the presence of "the war" as such: "buil[ding] up" the opening and closing scenes of Jim in his family home (86). According to Thomas, the decision to develop the domestic sequences derived from Thalberg's desire to show Jim's personal evolution as well as to attract female audiences "who might find a war story unappealing" (86). Yet Thalberg would also have found that the crafting of a point-counterpoint structure—juxtaposing the home front with the battleground—served to intensify the impact of the war. Following the logic set out in the *New York Times* interview, in which he discusses "the relative importance of each episode to the story as a whole," here Thalberg underscored the importance of the war by exploring its relationship to the family home.

In the film's penultimate sequence, preceding Jim's return to France and reunion with Melisande, his family welcome him back home. Just as in the opening domestic scenes, Jim's love for his mother is highlighted—the bond between them made all the more poignant by the realization that her son has lost his leg. Timothy Barnard has discussed the significance of this scene to broader cinematic representations of amputees, tracing the number of shots focusing on Jim's legs throughout *The Big Parade* to suggest that this imagery subtly "precondition[s]" the devastating twist in the narrative (2010: 34).[7] In this concluding scene, though, the sight of Jim's dismemberment is inextricably linked to the *site* of its revelation; that is, the Apperson home. In a shot framed from the point of view of his family waiting expectantly in the foyer, Jim makes his way through the front door. Just as the scene thematically integrates the battlefront and the home front, Jim himself appears as both phantom and embodied form. The shadow of his crutch appears first, stretched out along the floor before Jim himself steps into the doorway; as he moves forward, the silhouette of his profile and doughboy hat materialize on the wall. In a film that continually explores the drama of one man's relationship to and role in history itself, represented through expansive landscapes and relentless, mechanized motion, this image of Jim's homecoming conveys his internalization of that proverbial "big parade." He is Jim Apperson, beloved son and sweetheart to Melisande, nonetheless carrying within him and casting the shadow of an everyman soldier. Not only is the war in the film, to paraphrase Thalberg, but it is also in Jim.

Where *The Big Parade* explores by turns the fragility and resilience "of the average man," following Vidor's characterization of Jim, the production itself was a wholly formidable success—the non-ephemeral, permanent film so desired by the director. For two years, it played at New York's Astor Theater; but most importantly, the film reached its intended screen and played at Grauman's Egyptian for six months (Vidor 83). The great scenes of the epic played out on the great screen of the movie palace, thus showing that in the studio's own history-in-the-making, Thalberg and MGM were (to paraphrase Vidor) hitting their stride.

"WHERE ARE THE LOVE SCENES?"

Sobchack has noted that Hollywood approaches its epics as both on- and off-screen spectacles, chronicling the production of a given film as assiduously as the event represented in the narrative. In press materials and making-of accounts, studios, cast, and crew may explore "the historic struggles under which it produced itself as a *mimetic imitation* of the historical events it is dramatizing" (1990: 35). Such a process played out in the discourse surrounding *The Big Parade*, though focusing less on "struggles" and more on the striking camaraderie between Vidor, Thalberg, and Gilbert. In this way, the three men stood as extra-diegetic, creative counterparts to the film's brothers-in-arms.

The next production featuring the three men, however, did not share that same sense of fraternity. Instead, the melodrama of *La Bohème* evoked a comparatively strained dialogue over how the film would be made. Star Gish viewed the work as an ethereal romance, a perspective at odds with Thalberg's understanding of where the public appeal, or "audience values" ("Producing Executive" Section X, 7), of the film lay—that is, in its love scenes. In a 1929 lecture at the University of Southern California, Thalberg would cite D. W. Griffith and Gish specifically in a point about the need for the industry to keep up with changing mores—suggesting a vivid memory of the making of *La Bohème*. As Thalberg explained, Griffith's "love scenes [. . .] were idealistic and things of beauty [. . .]; but his pictures are not successful today because modern ideas are changing. The idealistic love of a decade ago is not true today" (1977: 120). Such a retrospective account highlights the tension between these two conceptions of what would make a great scene: the star pursuing a more abstract representation of ill-fated love, drawing from the conventions of early Hollywood; the producer privileging a more passionate, modern aesthetic that would ensure both critical and commercial success.

Based on the Puccini opera (itself adapted from the 1851 novel by Henry Murger), *La Bohème* is a period romance that follows a group of impoverished artists in Paris. Central to the narrative is the tragic love affair between seamstress Mimi (Gish) and writer Rodolphe (Gilbert), who are driven apart by a misunderstanding before reuniting at Mimi's deathbed. In terms of MGM's own epic history, *La Bohème* ushered in an era of collaboration between the studio and Gish—short-lived at only three years, but marked by key works with Victor Sjostrom: *The Scarlet Letter* (1926) and *The Wind* (1928). Gish's contract offered her creative control over her films and directors (Koszarski

293), but in practice, she was still subject to MGM's demands. By Gish's own admission, her approach to filmmaking was not necessarily suited to the "front-office" values of the studio system (Gish 1969: 279); contemporary Louise Brooks would later describe Gish as a great talent resented by "movie moguls" for her "picture knowledge and business acumen" (87). Indeed, even in 1926, *Photoplay* editor James R. Quirk would offer an acerbic commentary on Gish's incompatibility with the Hollywood mode: "As a classic, [she] may be commercially successful, but as a regular commercial routine star, grinding on schedule with whatever material is at hand, her fate at the box-office would be [. . .] tragic" (1926: 129).[8]

Her tenure at MGM began auspiciously enough. Thalberg screened *The Big Parade* for Gish upon her arrival at the studio, and she was so struck by the film that she requested the same team—Vidor, Gilbert, and Adorée—for her own debut (Gish 278). *La Bohème* was Gish's choice of a project; the period piece suited the image of classical femininity that she had cultivated in Griffith dramas. Vidor would later reflect that "it seems strange [. . .] that a famous opera should be chosen as the story of a silent motion picture" (Vidor 85), but a certain musicality had already influenced his making of *The Big Parade*. While filming a sequence in which Jim's regiment marched through Belleau Wood, Vidor effectively choreographed each actor's step and gesture to match the "metronomic" beat of drums (77). When screening the film at Grauman's Egyptian, Vidor even asked that the orchestral accompaniment pause throughout the scene—in this way highlighting the rhythm inherent in the men's actions (77). This image of the corps moving in artful unison towards a final goal also resonated with the film's off-screen history. Reflecting on the making of *The Big Parade*, Gilbert would describe "an electrical current running between [Vidor's] mind and the players" ("Silent Director" X9), suggesting a preternatural connection between the director's vision and his cast. But again, where film history tells us that *The Big Parade* emerged from stimulating collaborations between director, producer, and actors, accounts of the making of *La Bohème* focus more on the respectful but decided conflict between key personnel.

As Annie Berke has argued, Gish was herself a theorist of screen acting who would later detail her critical observations in a cache of unpublished writings (2016: 176). With this strength of conceptual purpose, as it were, Gish began work on the film with as clear a view of its potential as Vidor and Thalberg. Her insights into how *La Bohème* should be made were extensive and greatly concerned with questions of authenticity, emotional impact, and the development of character. Gish outlined her role in the production at length in her 1969 memoir, in which she describes choosing and/or coordinating the cast and director, the story, the cinematographer, the film stock, the set design, the costumes, and (later in her time at MGM) all but discovering Greta Garbo

(277–278, 293).[9] In Gish's recollections of her time at the studio, Thalberg appears as a benign figure who is very much respected ("I knew he was my friend, so I listened [to him]" [294]) but who also respects *her* judgment. Indeed, Vidor would relate that the cast and crew (himself included) were fairly awed by Gish and her already legendary career—to the point where she became a guiding, not to say directorial, presence throughout the production.

Gish established herself as such very early. Vidor wrote a detailed account of the preproduction style that Gish had learned from Griffith, in which the entire film was rehearsed on a bare stage without any props (85–86). Though Vidor found the technique "too closely related to the theater and too far removed from photographic compositions" (86), he agreed to test it out:

> Miss Gish, as Mimi, moved in and out of her Parisian garret unlocking locks, turning knobs, and opening and closing doors that weren't there. Approaching a dresser that didn't exist, she would open drawers, remove an imaginary hairbrush, and brush her hair most beautifully before an imaginary mirror hung on the wall above an imaginary dresser. Her hair was real, but at times we began to wonder. (86)

This rehearsal process resonated thematically in the narrative itself: just as Gish acted *as if* she were concretely engaging with those objects and settings, the characters themselves act out grand desires—for fame, love, and artistic triumph—in the most minimal of circumstances. In both Gish's method and the diegetic world itself, the dream of fulfillment is, in effect, as compelling as its actuality. Though Vidor remained unconvinced by the rehearsal technique, a version of it nonetheless seems to appear in the film itself, when Mimi and Rodolphe act out ideas for scenes in his play—a performance-within-a-performance that incorporates a level of abstraction to the sequences.

In this way, Vidor's anecdote attests to that underlying tension between Gish's conceptual approach to the production—how she thought it *should* be in terms of preparation, costumes and set design (Gish 278–279)—and Thalberg's more pragmatic understanding of what it needed to be to fill the screen. Though not citing the producer specifically, Gish would remember "the front office" worrying, " 'How are we to get exhibitors to pay big prices for your pictures if they don't see production values?' [. . .] I couldn't accustom myself to their strange set of values" (Gish 279). What Thalberg in particular prioritized, however, were what he would term "*audience* values" ("Producing Executive" Section X, 7; emphasis added). Related to, but distinct from, front office "production values," the concept of audience values privileged the experience of the spectator paying to see a given film. Screenwriter Coffee would reflect that "Thalberg felt that [the writers'] sole aim in life was to find out why some films could 'tune into' the audience and why others could not" (96)—a question that certainly preoccupied the producer himself. As he explained to the *New York Times*, audience values were as elemental to a film's success as one great scene, and equally complex in their construction. They required

> the proper balancing of material [. . .] I might say that almost without exception every great picture has had definite audience values. And the few cases where great pictures have not been financial successes have been because some fundamental by-issue has been overlooked. I might cite 'The Last Laugh' in this connection, where all interest is concentrated in an old man with no romantic element at all.[10] ("Producing Executive" Section X, 7)

Given that *The Last Laugh* (dir. Murnau, 1925) was an UFA-produced *Kammerspiel* film—that is, an intimate exploration of middle-class life with Expressionist influences (Cook 2004: 101)—it seems incongruous for Thalberg to consider it within the context of Hollywood productions. Yet he draws implicit distinctions here between "great pictures" as a category and *financially-successful* great pictures.[11] *The Last Laugh* was not a romantic melodrama produced for box-office maximalism, but *La Bohème* was. The importance of "balancing material," then, necessitated the inclusion of a more sensational physicality meant to draw the audience.

This tension between the ethereal and the concrete, aesthetic ideals and audience values, would, appropriately, reach its climax in the filming of the romantic sequences. Gish conceived of the relationship between Mimi and Rodolphe as more spiritual than passionate: "It seemed to me that, if we avoided showing the lovers in a physical embrace, the scenes would build up suppressed emotion and be much more effective" (Gish 280). Or, as Vidor recalled, "She believed that the two lovers should *never* be shown in actual physical contact" (87; emphasis added). Considered in this way, the constant deferral of the lovers' embrace appears as an extension of Gish's rehearsal technique, gesturing to a concrete reality in order to reject it for a more poetic register. In forever keeping Mimi and Rodolphe's relationship on an abstract plane, Gish executed a kind of intellectual exercise in the crafting of a narrative arc; what this did not necessarily accomplish, though, was the creation of Thalbergian great scenes.

Vidor carried out Gish's ideas in the first cut of the film: "Throughout the entire action Mimi and Rodolphe never entered into physical embrace; each aggressive advance on [his] part was intercepted and turned into meanings more ethereal and poetic" (88). It was at this point that Thalberg asserted the authority of his own theoretical perspective. Upon viewing the first cut and its distinct lack of passion, he asked succinctly: "Where are the love scenes?"

(qtd. in Fountain 119). Just as Thalberg saw that the early cut of *The Big Parade* "[did not] have the war in it," he understood that the period melodrama lacked more earthly romance.

A related issue was the fact that, as Thalberg declared in the discussion of audience values, the spectator "expects certain things of the star, and those elements are usually worked in if they are not there originally" ("Producing Executive" Section X, 7). He goes on to cite Gish's virtuousness and Gilbert's persona as the Great Lover ("It is a fact that women go to the theatre to see him as a lover" [ibid.]) as examples of what audiences expect to see in their stars. Here emerge more facets to Thalberg's theory of oblique casting, the process of which could enhance the complexity of the very star image that (per Thalberg's words above) needed to be maintained. Gilbert as war hero Jim romanced his sweetheart in a battle-torn landscape depicted with realist sensibilities; as struggling artist Rodolphe, he pursues her in a storybook turn-of-the-century Paris. In each context, however, Gilbert is the Great Lover. To return to Thalberg's points concerning "the proper balancing of material" in a given film, he explored the proper balancing of a performer's known qualities and as-yet unknown possibilities.

The lack of passion in *La Bohème*'s love scenes compromised both of those factors: keeping the Great Lover from "do[ing] some great lovemaking" (Fountain 119) and thus deflating that aspect of his formidable charisma, and at the same time shifting Gish's luminous purity to a kind of prudishness. Indeed, she would recall that later in her time at the studio, Thalberg tried to orchestrate a scandal for her: "You see, you are way up there on a pedestal [. . .] and nobody cares. If you were knocked off the pedestal, everyone would care" (qtd. in Gish 294). Though Gish would demur at the invention of a scandal, the love scenes for *La Bohème* were retaken. These offered more than embraces; the sequences provided a means of gratifying the audience's expectations of the two great stars, as well as foregrounding the arc of Mimi and Rodolphe's pivotal connection—from shy admiration to devoted courtship, then to a parting before a deathbed reconciliation. This evolution is highlighted in a scene midway through the film, in which Rodolphe sits outside Mimi's window and tries to steal a kiss. They flirt and tease each other through the window that Mimi shuts in Rodolphe's face, only for him to kiss the pane of glass itself. The scene clearly builds on Gish's conception of the characters' interaction—in which, as Vidor described it, the pair would only "kiss with the cold barrier of a window-pane between them" (87)—but rather than an obstacle, the window-pane is an instrument of coquetry. It does not so much keep Mimi and Rodolphe apart as it promises their eventual union.

This takes place in the next sequence, in which the group of artists travel to the countryside for Easter. When the couple find themselves alone in a meadow, Mimi literally leads Rodolphe a merry dance before coyly running to a riverbank. Gilbert plays the scene with his trademark Great Lover intensity, but Gish brings a quicksilver sensuality: smiling knowingly while protesting her virtue, courting his touch before slipping away, and then shocking him by declaring her love in direct address to the camera, no less. It is, indeed, Gish-as-Mimi who first kisses Gilbert-as-Rodolphe—thus revealing vulnerability in the Great Lover and passion in Gish. Charles Affron cites this sequence as evidence of a collaboration between Gish and Vidor, noting the juxtaposition of both the former's "teasing standoffishness" and the latter's tendency in subsequent films to "keep [. . .] his lovers on the go" (1977: 68). But given that the character of the scene would have been defined through the Thalberg-ordered retakes, it could more precisely be said that the sequence brings together the vision of producer, star, and director. The best of both Gish's and Thalberg's values, as it were, emerges here with the "build[ing] up of suppressed emotion[s]" (Gish 280) and the impact of their physical expression.

Returning to Sobchack's points concerning the extra-diegetic "*mimetic imitation* of the historical events [a film] is dramatizing" (35), the production of the love scenes (and the recollections thereof) offer a charged exploration of a conflict between theoretical perspectives that parallels the drama of the film itself. Certainly Quirk's 1926 commentary on Gish's irreconcilable differences with the studio system represents part of that off-screen discourse, with the writer noting, "More than any other star Miss Gish must be her own producer. Whether or not she has the capacity remains to be seen, and whether or not she is permitted to be is still another matter" (129). With this in mind, *La Bohème* endures as a case study in tensions between stars and their studios—and, more specifically, between one mode of representing love stories and another. If the statues in the chariot race showed the grandeur of the Coliseum in *Ben-Hur*, and the domestic scenes heightened the devastation of the war in *The Big Parade*, then the love scenes in *La Bohème* highlight the extra-diegetic passage between early Hollywood poetry and Thalberg-era passion.

"A NEW ENTERPRISE ON A GRAND SCALE"

As one of the "three men who pull[ed] the strings" in MGM's earliest days, to return to the 1925 documentary, Thalberg helped define both the identity of the young studio and the epic storytelling practices of the era. The sophistication and industrial implications of his theoretical ambitions would evolve in the years to come—the emphasis on retakes, his authorship of the Production Code, the championing of "entertainment value" as an extension of audience values—but elemental to each future concept was the great scene itself.

With the success of hits like *The Big Parade* and *La Bohème*, Thalberg keenly understood that he actually held the "power to *create* the situations in which he [found] himself," to paraphrase Vidor's characterization of Jim Apperson (73). This granted him the ability to make decisions not simply in the interest of MGM's bottom-line, but in terms of its artistic integrity. When, for example, Vidor approached Thalberg with an idea in the late 1920s, the director described it as "a wonderful picture that will be praised wherever it is shown, but it probably won't make a dollar at the box office." Thalberg replied, "Don't worry about that. MGM can certainly afford a few experimental projects" (qtd. in Vidor 104).[12] In a variation on his theory of audience values, Thalberg remained mindful of maintaining the balance between commercial success and great pictures in themselves. The latter would not be sacrificed for the former.

For all of the significance of *The Big Parade* and *La Bohème* in aesthetic and theoretical terms, the box-office success of these films also translated into more concrete benefits for Thalberg and Mayer. As Schatz points out, their smooth running of the post-merger productions—and the rehabilitation of *Ben-Hur*—impressed the New York office (1996: 38). In 1925, Loew's and MGM negotiated a deal in which the studio would produce 44 films every year, and Thalberg and Mayer would receive a pay raise—the former moving from $650 weekly to $2,000 (39). About a year later, though, Thalberg assessed his role in the continued critical prestige and commercial rewards of MGM's productions and requested another raise. By the end of 1926, he was making $4,000 a week (Crowther 1957: 119). MGM/Loew's itself made $6.4 million in 1926, only two years after the merger (Schatz 1996: 39).

A compelling mental image, even a great scene, is of Thalberg himself at MGM in 1925 and 1926—occupying that "area of 43 acres, and its 45 buildings, including 14 big stages [. . .] connected by 3 miles of paved streets" cited in the documentary. In stark relief against this dream factory was a young man in his mid-twenties who admitted to Gish that he was "always being mistaken for his own office boy" (Gish 264). In this juxtaposition of individual and industrial endeavor, the Thalberg of 1926 seemed invincible—a Boy Wonder. Thalberg, however, saw himself somewhat differently. In Fitzgerald's notes for *The Last Tycoon*, he describes a 1927 exchange in which Thalberg confided,

[W]hen you're planning a new enterprise on a grand scale, the people under you mustn't ever know or guess that you're in any doubt because they've all got to have something to look up to and they mustn't ever dream that you're in doubt about any decision. Those things keep occurring. (Qtd. in Fitzgerald 1993: xviii)

One of the most significant of "those things" occurred within the next year. As the following chapter will explore, the rise of the talkies would test the supernatural and, in Gilbert's terms, "superstitious" faith (qtd. in Leslie 56) placed in Thalberg. MGM's hits in the mid-1920s left him poised to encounter that epic event, even as those triumphs also raised the stakes for any of his "new enterprise[s] on a grand scale."

In more abstract terms, the imagery that Thalberg used above distinctly recalls his words to Cedric Gibbons as he designed the statues for the chariot race:

> The audience is going to think the set is fake unless we prove to them it isn't. What we need are some [. . .] huge statues we can place the extras beside so the audience will get a sense of the scale. (Qtd. in Thomas 72)

As Fitzgerald's anecdote suggests, Thalberg understood that the running of MGM itself demanded a sense of spectacle. "[E]ven though you're utterly assailed by doubts at times as to the wisdom of your decision because all these other possible decisions keep echoing in your ear" (qtd. in Fitzgerald xviii), your audience must believe.

NOTES

1. Richard Koszarski identifies "stockholders or theater owners" as the intended audience (1990: 110).
2. "Conference Notes, 'Mata Hari'." December 4, 1931. MGM Collection, University of Southern California.
3. In her biography of John Gilbert, daughter Leatrice Gilbert Fountain recounts an episode in which "after one scene [. . .] Vidor shouted 'Cut!' and approached with his hand outstretched to Jack [Gilbert]. 'Grauman's Egyptian, baby,' he said, grinning. 'Grauman's Egyptian, Pops,' Jack said, nodding." (Fountain 1985: 112)
4. John Calhoun writes that it "featured a stucco and concrete block courtyard with friezes, murals, and carvings of Isis, Osiris, and other gods and pharaohs; a portico entrance supported by four towering columns; auditorium walls decorated with scenic representations of Egyptian royalty cruising the Nile; and a spectacular sunburst pattern, with scarabs, cobras, floodwaters, turquoise lotus plants, and six golden stars adorning the ceiling" (1999: 34).
5. As Vidor noted, Gilbert himself "was so sold on the down-to-earth characterization that he never used make-up again" (1954: 76) on the screen.
6. E-book available at<http://search.ebscohost.com.libezproxy.dundee.ac.uk/login.aspx?direct=true&db=nlebk&AN=295105&site=ehost-live&scope=site> (last accessed August 13, 2019).
7. Barnard's essay on the issue of amputation in the film makes compelling connections to writer Stallings' own experience losing his leg in World War I. The essay also cites Gilbert and Mayer's initial resistance to the depiction of Jim's dismemberment (24).

8. Louise Brooks discusses Quirk's antipathy towards Gish at length in her essay "Gish and Garbo" (2000: 89–90).
9. " 'She has such a lovely face,' I said to [cinematographer] Hendrick Sartov. 'Why don't you take some tests of her?' He did, with results that impressed the heads at M.G.M. for the first time" (Gish 1969: 293).
10. This 1925 film was directed by F. W. Murnau and starred Emil Jannings.
11. In a 1929 speech, Thalberg spoke at length about Murnau's "fine achievements, regardless of their commercial success" (1977: 120).
12. Though Vidor does not name the film, Vieira notes that this exchange refers to *Hallelujah!* (1929), "the first major studio film to be cast exclusively with African-Americans" (2010: 105).

CHAPTER 4

Entertainment Value and Sound Cinema

E ven in a film filled with notable cameos, John Gilbert's appearance in
Davies's vehicle *Show People* is striking. He first appears driving onto
the MGM lot before an astonished Peggy Pepper, and is then seated at what
an intertitle calls "the stars' table" in the studio commissary. In a pan around
the table, the shot takes in performers like Renée Adorée, Douglas Fairbanks,
William S. Hart, Rod La Rocque, Mae Murray, Norma Talmadge, and even gossip columnist Louella Parsons. Certain stars avoid the camera, while others offer
it an oblique glance; Gilbert, however, gazes at it directly and even encourages
his former wife, actress Leatrice Joy, to do the same. Utterly relaxed before the
camera and with his fellow performers, Gilbert strikes the eye as a star among
stars in this self-reflexive picture. The historical context, however, introduces
an element of poignancy to the scene, capturing as it does MGM on the cusp of
the talkies. Though it did not feature dialogue, *Show People* nonetheless utilized
synchronized sound in a gesture to the cinematic vogue; a gesture that renders
this lunch at the studio a kind of Last Supper for silent stars.

Where the previous chapter concluded with Gilbert at the height of his success and professional relationship with Thalberg, this chapter begins with the
star on the threshold of disaster. Following the poor audience response to his
sound debut in *His Glorious Night* (dir. Barrymore, 1929)—famously spoofed in
Singin' in the Rain (dir. Donen and Kelly, 1952)[1]—Gilbert faced a crisis that not
even Thalberg, "That Perfect Boss" (Leslie 1926: 56), could resolve. He tried:
Thalberg personally produced *Way for a Sailor* (dir. Wood, 1930), in which
Gilbert played a merchant marine; following its failure, Thalberg asked Samuel Marx to find a gangster "yarn" for Gilbert, and the result was the equally
unsuccessful *Gentlemen's Fate* (dir. LeRoy, 1931) (Marx 1975: 148). Caught
between loyalty to his friend and a pragmatic view of the bottom-line, Thalberg
would go on to cast and replace the alcoholic Gilbert in two A-pictures: *Grand
Hotel*, in which the role of the Baron was ultimately played by John Barrymore,

and Jean Harlow vehicle *Red Dust* (dir. Fleming, 1932), in which Gilbert was replaced by Clark Gable (Marx 188; Golden 2013: 244). In 1936, two years after his final film—and only 10 years after *The Big Parade* and *La Bohème*—Gilbert died at the age of 38 from a heart attack.

The collaboration between Gilbert, "The Great Lover of the Silver Screen," and the producer who helped construct that persona (Fountain 1985: 1) was one of the most successful of the silent era; it ended mournfully and prematurely. In the years to come, Norma Shearer would try to make sense of the dissolution of their relationship: "Irving was known for salvaging careers. [. . .] He held out his frail hand to many, and many found strength in it, but not John Gilbert" (qtd. in Golden 245). Gilbert's story reveals as much about Thalberg's response to sound cinema as it does about their personal friendship; certainly the pressures of being "the Boy Wonder" at a time of industrial and artistic redefinition were enormous for him. Though he could highlight the versatility of a star like Gilbert in any number of vehicles, Thalberg could not control the vagaries of a public attuned to what he called "the change, the looseness, the flexibility" (1977: 115) of a medium that was itself in transition. Gilbert's struggles helped set the scene for the talkies as one of the most significant "new enterprise[s] on a grand scale" (qtd. in Fitzgerald 1993: xviii) that Thalberg's MGM would face. For all of the personal pathos of Gilbert's crisis, his was a microcosm of the broader unsettling within Hollywood.

Not everyone recognized the sea change of talkies as such. As Donald Crafton notes, even the "legend" of *The Jazz Singer* (dir. Crosland, 1927) as an overnight phenomenon does not bear up under analysis of box-office statistics that show a "just above average" success (1997: 529). It is understandable, then, that Thalberg responded to news of the film in terms that read as near-apocryphal today: "Novelty is always welcome, but talking pictures are just a passing fad" (qtd. in Marx 1975: 100). Bosley Crowther cites another 1927 statement from Thalberg: "The talking motion picture has its place, as has color photography, but I do not believe [it] will ever replace the silent drama any more than I believe colored photography will replace entirely the present black-and-white" (qtd. in 1957: 145). Thalberg was not alone in such initial appraisals, with other major studios "hedging" by producing both silent and sound versions of their films (Crafton 165). His hesitation, however, has added another facet to the myth of the Boy Wonder; Otto Friedrich, for example, would later use this to mock Thalberg's claim to have had "[his] finger on the pulse of America" (2014: 24). As Richard Koszarski has stated in more measured terms, the reticence to commit to sound production showed that "Thalberg was not infallible" (1990: 253). In this way, the teleological narrative (and received wisdom) of sound's instant domination of the industry intersects with another narrative: that of Thalberg's alleged myopia at this crucial juncture. If talkies were always fated to be a success, then Thalberg's inability to recognize their importance endures as his inherent fatal flaw.

But on March 20, 1929, Thalberg delivered a speech at the University of Southern California that would offer more definitive—and conceptual—statements about the state of cinema than he would give to the mainstream press at the time. Bob Thomas points out that though Thalberg "seldom express[ed] his theories beyond the intimacy of the studio family," this lecture captured his comprehensive system of "earnest beliefs" in the significance of the medium (1969: 127). In an overarching analysis of "The Modern Photoplay," Thalberg declares that artistic endeavor and technological innovation are part of a broader context: what he terms "entertainment value" (1977: 114).

> We have seen that the foundation upon which the whole motion picture industry is built is the desire to provide entertainment. Therefore, when we are judging or criticizing what we see on the screen, we must first consider it from the standpoint of entertainment value. We can also judge it from an artistic or technical viewpoint as well, but its entertainment value must be the first criterion. (114)

In this opening argument, Thalberg establishes the ethos that informs his approach to filmmaking; it is a striking statement of purpose that synthesizes many of the conceptual threads outlined throughout his career as a whole. The importance of one great scene and oblique casting, the necessity of previews and the accompanying demand for retakes—all of these come together as part of what he identifies as a "foundation[al]" intention to attract and please the public. As Thalberg sets out, "Entertainment is the purpose and end of the photoplay" (114).

As the lecture continues, it is clear that he considered sound cinema as part of this imperative, rather than a priority in itself. At a time when the talkies dominated the cultural discourse, Thalberg instead viewed them at a remove; they were not paramount to his conception of contemporary film, but rather illustrative of what he considers to be the industry's primary impetus—to entertain the public. He remarks that "[sound] has distinctly proven its entertainment value [. . .] The range and variety of entertainment that can now be secured are infinitely greater" (123). Yet what audiences appreciate in sound, according to Thalberg, is not simply the enhancement of the medium but the excitement of change. "The great popularity and interest in talking pictures, which up to this time have been only fairly good and some quite bad, has been their novelty," he states. "Thus, we have a medium in which difference, in which change of form is in itself an entertainment asset" (115–116).

This 1929 lecture offers a theoretical lens through which to view Thalberg's complex relationship to the rise of the talkies. There are convincing historical readings to explain his reticence towards sound: for example, Mark A. Vieira has characterized Thalberg's initial resistance as "a combination of arrogance and incredulity" (2010: 90), and Scott Eyman perceives a parallel "class-based" snobbery on the part of Mayer and Thalberg towards minor studio Warner Bros. and their talkie preoccupations (1997: 243). Certain of Thalberg's own statements to the press—sound as "a passing fad"—suggest an outright dismissal of the new technology. In "The Modern Photoplay," however, Thalberg presents a sustained, conceptual critique of filmmaking of the day, in which he does not at all reject sound but instead perceives it as only part of an entire industrial and artistic endeavor. The following will draw from this comprehensive commentary and look closely at three films released in various stages of the talkie revolution—*Wild Orchids* (dir. Franklin, 1929), *Broadway Melody of 1929* (dir. Beaumont, 1929), and *The Unholy Three* (dir. Conway, 1930)—to consider Thalberg's response to sound as part of his broader conception of "entertainment value" rather than as an isolated historical episode.

"THE IMMEDIATE FITTING IN WITH CURRENT THOUGHT"

Thalberg uses the term "entertainment value" throughout his lecture, and in several different contexts. It applies to anything from the act of "break[ing] into song" in *Broadway Melody* (1977: 115) to Warner Baxter's voice in the film *In Old Arizona* (dir. Cummings, 1928); sound film itself (123) to the use of other "novel methods of presentation" in filmmaking (126). Ultimately, Thalberg perceives entertainment value in, or as, any element that heightens the public's engagement with the film, and so elevates that production from a passing diversion to an immersive experience. Thalberg draws the distinction between the former and the latter in a comment on early talkie productions: "In a thing that was developing as quickly as sound pictures, it was interesting to let water run just to hear it run" (126). Empty of purpose or meaning, the running water may be fleetingly entertaining—but it has no value. By contrast, Thalberg's description of the impact of Baxter's voice provides a succinct definition of entertainment value: "[It] possessed entertainment value without which the story would not have reached the success that the film did reach. His voice meant the difference between mediocrity and success" (115). Such commentary could apply equally well to the chariot race scene in *Ben-Hur*, the love scenes in *La Bohème*, or Davies's impersonations in *The Patsy*. Which is to say, entertainment value derives from those features that help a picture maximize its potential for "success," whether they relate to the narrative, cinematic techniques, or the abilities of the performer him/herself.

Creating that substantial entertainment value demanded, conversely, a commitment to the nuances of production. This margin of excellence—"the difference between mediocrity and success"—was a point of focus for Thalberg throughout his career. In discussing the value of retakes, for example, he would declare that "[t]he difference between something good and something bad is great, but the difference between something good and something superior is often very small" (qtd. in Crowther 1957: 181). In related terms, Thalberg's emphasis on oblique casting represents another instance of mining a production's potential for greatness: offering the audience a new way of seeing a familiar star, as well as introducing a sense of the unexpected to established genre pictures or character types. In effect, the concept of entertainment value as such holds within it myriad creative concerns, each yielding a heightened mode of engagement between spectator and screen.

In this way, entertainment value represents the evolution of Thalberg's 1925 conception of audience values. In the case of the latter, Thalberg exalted the importance of "the proper balancing of material," whether that referred to subject matter or the casting of a performer in a particular role. As he would note, "[T]he audience expects certain things of the star, and those elements are usually worked in if they are not there originally" ("Producing Executive" 1925: Section X, 7). By this reckoning, the meeting of audience expectations would itself provide entertainment value—just as the oblique casting of an *un*expected star would offer a sensational surprise. Where, however, Thalberg effectively measured audience values through the immediate response of the spectator, he attributed a more holistic quality to the concept of entertainment value. That is, the question of a film "reach[ing] [its full] success" (115) is as important for the work of art itself as it is for the enjoyment of the viewer. Entertainment value emphatically matters to the audience, but its very cultivation bespeaks a creative integrity on the part of the studio producing that film.

In explaining the abiding pursuit of entertainment value, Thalberg emphasizes the importance of "currency—the immediate fitting in with current thought" (119). He frames the shifting industrial and aesthetic norms within a broader context—a fascination with contemporary ways of living and thinking—and remarks that "one of [his] chief functions is to be an observer and sense and feel the moods of the public" (116). There are two distinct threads in his understanding of currency: the first is related to "topical[ity]," or "the necessity of having the subject matter of photoplays correspond closely to current thinking" (116); and the second implicitly relates to the indexical nature of the medium and its significance for future audiences. As Thalberg points out, "the motion picture [. . .] will be the most effective way of showing posterity how we live today" (119).

Equally compelling is an exploration of how MGM made films then. By 1929, movie studios had acknowledged the necessity of "fitting in with" the

Zeitgeist and adopting sound production—understanding that their "currency" in both monetary and temporal terms depended on technological fluency. Though Thalberg's tone in this speech is reflective, philosophical, it belies the strain of trying to maintain the studio's critical and commercial dominance over the previous two years. Later in the talk, Thalberg would implicitly address this point in response to a question from the audience concerning "competition within the industry" as a motivator in the talkie revolution: "Competition [. . .] was a factor in that it put one company in a condition where they were willing to take a chance" (123). This company was, of course, Warner Bros., who took their chances with *The Jazz Singer*—though, as Thomas Schatz points out, the "governing irony" in this narrative of innovation is that the studio was less concerned with changing the face (or voice) of filmmaking than with solidifying its own position (1996: 58). Warners was as of the mid-1920s a minor player among studios like MGM/Loew's, Paramount, and First National, and the company invested in the Vitaphone sound technology as a means of improving its standing in the industry (Crafton 68, 70–71). Fox had also explored the possibilities of sound cinema with Murnau's *Sunrise* (1927), which featured synchronized sound recorded through the Movietone process—and was released only two weeks before *The Jazz Singer* (525). These events put pressure on MGM to at least respond, though not necessarily commit fully, to the advancements of sound technology.

As part of a 1930 article entitled "Strange As It May Seem," *Motion Picture* recorded several of the earliest reactions to the idea of talkies. Sam Goldwyn, Paramount's Jesse Lasky, even Douglas Fairbanks and Cecil B. DeMille—all are quoted either dismissing or disparaging the advent of sound. Thalberg himself appears in the article: "[Talkies] just aren't as enjoyable as silent pictures. Color and sound are, at best, fads!" (qtd. in Ramsey 1930: 35). Nicholas Schenck, appointed the president of Loew's following Marcus Loew's death in 1927, was similarly disposed in the New York office: Samuel Marx recalled that Schenck refused to pay the cost of refitting the movie theaters for sound (estimated at $20,000 per venue [Thomas 122]) and that he only approved talkie production in early 1928, after theater managers reported that they were losing audiences (Marx 1975: 105). Even after allowing for this new technology, Schenck expressed reservations: "The novelty of sound has upset all reason. Sound has been applied indiscriminately whether it belonged or not" (qtd. in Crafton 206).

Crafton has identified Schenck and Thalberg's resistance to sound as part of a broader strategy to allow competitors to develop the technology that MGM would subsequently use (169). Even with this in mind, MGM's struggle to catch up with the acknowledged sophistication of Warners and Fox—as well as with Paramount's rapid acceleration of sound production (Vieira 2010: 90)—did not go unnoticed. This is conveyed rather dryly in an anecdote published by the *New York Times* in July 1928. Mordaunt Hall reports that at an industry event, Harry Rapf spoke about

> the close way in which certain secrets of the making of talking and sound pictures at [Warners and Fox] were guarded. At this Jack Warner arose [. . .] and said that any rivals were welcome to come to the Warner studio the following morning at 8:30. Then he added jokingly, "They will be thrown out at 8:31." (Hall 1928: Section X, 3)

Warner's imagery is striking in conveying the "inside" and "outside" of an industry hierarchy, which would almost certainly have been humbling for a major studio like MGM. But however belated, the latter's commitment to sound production was impressive. In the above article, Thalberg outlined plans for a "special studio [. . .] reinforced with concrete pillars that [go] down twenty feet [and] soundproof stage doors [that] will weigh about nine tons each" (Hall Section X, 3). By the time it was built in 1929, the soundstage was so vast that 12 scenes could be filmed at once (Crafton 207). Thalberg also assigned the task of building up MGM's sound capabilities to engineer (and brother-in-law) Douglas Shearer—the same special-effects man who had, in 1925, tried to convince the studio to explore talking trailers to promote their films (Crowther 1957: 138–139).

It was Shearer who engineered MGM's first sound effort, *White Shadows in the South Seas* (dir. Flaherty and van Dyke, 1928). This tropical drama featured a synchronized soundtrack of music and sound effects—and even Leo the Lion's first roar (Crowther 1957: 146). For all of the success of that film, Marx would recall the sound revolution on MGM's lot as, literally, an unwelcome shift in the landscape:

> The whole look of the studio changed. The need for more space obliterated the green lawns. The willows and magnolias were cut down. New and narrow alleyways of cement were paved between the gray workshops that were being bunched together like oversized packing cases. [. . .] Finally, cement stages stood in place. Soundproof booths for engineers were fitted inside [. . .] In these cells, men fiddled with futuristic-appearing consoles that would trap the sounds of actors [. . .] (1975: 107)

Just as the Mission Road site of Mayer and Thalberg's earliest collaborations lingered as a near-prelapsarian idyll, the Culver City studio of the silent era emerges here as a wholly natural environment corrupted by the mechanization of sound. Marx recalls Thalberg "glumly survey[ing] the boxlike tombs [. . .] It seemed that the shutting out of sunlight from the stages symbolized the coming of darker days" (108).

Darker days would soon come, as it happened. On March 3, 1929—only weeks before Thalberg's USC lecture—Schenck joined William Fox, head of Fox Film Corporation, to declare publicly that the latter had bought the controlling interest in Loew's after purchasing stocks from the family and estate of founder Marcus Loew (Thomas 153; Crowther 1957: 156). Schenck benefited personally from the deal, earning a $10-million commission on Fox's $50-million coup (Marx 1975: 116); and Thalberg and Mayer, who had both been completely unaware of the negotiations, learned that MGM was now subject to Fox. Mayer and Thalberg's primary concern, then, shifted from debating which studio would dominate in the sound market to the anxiety over who would control MGM itself. In an unpleasant turn of phrase, Schenck informed a furious Thalberg that the "Boy Wonder" was simply another commodity purchased by Fox: "My good friend Irving, Mr. William Fox considers your contract one of our most important assets" (qtd. in Marx 116).

The deal was dead by the end of the year, following the stock market crash in October and the government filing an anti-trust lawsuit against Fox[2]—crises further exacerbated by Fox's injuries in a serious car accident (Thomas 156; Crowther 1957: 161). The implications of the deal, however, were irreversible. Schenck had betrayed Mayer and Thalberg for what the latter called an "unprincipled sell-out" (qtd. in Marx 1975: 116), and the Loew's magnate offered them financial compensation for the troubles; but Thalberg did not feel that this was appropriate acknowledgment of his contributions to the studio. In a reworking of the "Mayer Group's" percentages in the company, Mayer ceded a portion of his share in the profits to Thalberg, leaving a split of Mayer at 43 percent, Thalberg at 30 percent, and Rubin at 27 percent (Thomas 158). MGM had been shaken both in its relationship to Loew's and within its internal structure, at a time when the industry itself was radically shifting.

As Thalberg stated in the USC lecture, "the very methods by which [film] tells its stories, the very change that each type of film brings about are in themselves of interest, and have distinct box office value" (115); by extension, how did his perspectives on filmmaking evolve with the changes taking place around him? The analyses of the following films highlight the ways in which Thalberg cultivated entertainment value—whether through producing appropriate transitional vehicles for performers moving from silents to talkies, or establishing new narrative modes through the musical.

"THE STYLE OF THE MOMENT"

In statements to the popular press, Thalberg expressed his concerns with maintaining the versatility of the medium: "You can't lay down wholesale rules and say that they will work in every case [. . .] If Hollywood only realized it, the talking pictures are merely a broadened field" (qtd. in Manners 1929: 94). He also maintained that unlike other studios, MGM would not be making-over its silent stars—or effectively trading them for stage actors with better voices—to fit with the talkie vogue:

> We aren't following the lead of many of the other producers and casting out the tried and true favorites. Nor are we considering the policy of producing only talkie pictures with stage stars. In the first place, I don't think the public will stand for the replacement of stars whom they have loved and admired for years for the mere sake of enunciation and the ability to read lines. At that, some of the stage stars I have seen in the talking films are poor in comparison to screen players who talk naturally. (Qtd. in Manners 40, 94)

Time would prove that this strategy was more idealistic than practical—as, for instance, Gilbert's career arc suggests. In this statement, though, Thalberg's approach to talkies as part of an entire "broadened field" of cinema intersects with his theory of oblique casting, in which he asserted the fluidity of the per-forming body. For Thalberg, film itself is an equally capacious form; it can be silent *or* sound, depending on the appropriateness of the material. Certainly studios were following the practice of creating dual versions of films, as part of the "hedging" strategy described by Crafton (165). For example, an April 1929 *New York Times* article reported that Fox Film Corporation had two years' worth of silent films in their vaults, "to tide the company over until [. . .] it will be making talking pictures exclusively" ("Plan Silent Versions" 1929: 32). What Thalberg would assert in the USC lecture, however, was a more radical approach: "I don't see why [silent and sound films] cannot develop side by side. Certain subjects are best interpreted through the silent form [. . .] A good silent picture will draw better than a poor talking picture" (126). Which is to say—where a studio like Fox held the films of the past to ensure its immediate future, Thalberg conceived of a parallel evolution in the two forms.

One of MGM's "good silent pictures" was *Wild Orchids*, which Thalberg would cite in an interview: "I would always want to make pictures like *Wild Orchids* [. . .] silently. There is nothing the people in those stories say that they cannot express without words" (qtd. in Vieira 2010: 98). This melodramatic nar-rative lends itself to the silent cinema: American couple Lillie and John Sterling (Garbo and Lewis Stone) visit Java, where Lillie enters into a torrid romance with hedonistic Prince de Gace (Nils Asther). At the end of the film, she returns to her elderly husband—who had to that point been strikingly immune to her charms. The dramatic setting would also have been a factor in Thalberg's deci-sion to keep the film silent; as he noted in the 1929 *New York Times* piece cited above, "pictures having a foreign locale and an exotic atmosphere" were likely to have been made in both silent and sound versions ("Plan Silent Versions" 32). *Wild Orchids* was produced with synchronized sound, however: a hybrid in which sound effects and a musical score matched the action, while the dialogue itself was noted in intertitles.

A *Motion Picture* review underscored the film's place in the broadened field of cinema. The critical verdict is itself favorable enough—closing with "see *Wild Orchids*"—but its context is the most striking. On a two-page layout of "Current Pictures—Silent and Sound—In Review," the film is identified as Synchronized, while still other films are denoted as All Talkie, Silent, and Part Talkie (1929: 62–63). Interestingly, the writers do not mention sound or the lack thereof in the reviews of synchronized or silent films; but they do take against poorly made part-talkie *The Redeeming Sin* (dir. Bretherton, 1929) and note the "wretched photography that seems a feature of the talkies" in *Weary River* (dir. Lloyd, 1929). Even as only a snapshot of the era, these "Current Reviews" capture what Thalberg had noted in his lecture: a mainstream acceptance of well-made silent and synchronized pictures, and an impatience with makeshift (part-)talkies.

This was a response that Thalberg had also acknowledged at the level of the star—to recall the observation cited earlier: "In the first place, I don't think the public will stand for the replacement of stars whom they have loved and admired for years for the mere sake of enunciation and the ability to read lines" (qtd. in Manners 40). Sound for the sake of sound, either in the films or from the stars themselves, was not a Thalberg strategy; nor did he view the audience's identification with popular performers as passing, and therefore expendable, attachments. Accordingly, star vehicles were produced relatively slowly and with mixed results. For example, Norma Shearer was the lead in MGM's first all-talkie drama, *The Trial of Mary Dugan* (dir. Veiller, 1929), which would receive positive reviews—but in preproduction, Thalberg had the cast perform live in front of an audience ("They'll be the jury; I'll be judge") (Crowther 1957: 153). Crowther points out that unexpected stars also emerged from the transition to talkies—including Lionel Barrymore in *Alias Jimmy Valentine* (dir. Conway, 1928) (147). As if further demonstrating the volatility of the era, popular leading man William Haines's dialogue was dubbed in the latter film, and he became a casualty of sound.

In certain respects, *Wild Orchids* was an ideal project for Garbo. As discussed in Chapter 2, Thalberg had conceived of a kind of "formula" for her films, in which she would play the center of a love triangle—caught between an older husband or paramour and a younger lover (Vieira 2005: 77). She had already starred in dramas such as *Flesh and the Devil* (dir. Brown, 1926), *Anna Karenina* adaptation *Love* (dir. Goulding, 1927), and *The Mysterious Lady* (dir. Niblo, 1928), and *Wild Orchids* transposed her continental allure to the far East. Yet Garbo's appeal at this time of transition exceeded the high melodrama of love triangles and "East meets West" exoticism; indeed, as *Picture Play* writer Walter Ramsey would note in 1930, she "suggests mystery, a mystery that has its being in silence. What, then, will the spoken, tangible thought have to do with this peculiar appeal?" (qtd. in Salzberg 2014: 23). Or, it could be asked, how did her "peculiar appeal" relate to the broader shifts taking place in the industry?

Such questions recall a statement in Thalberg's USC speech, highlighting the significance of a given performer's relationship to "currency":

> The various [. . .] stars are examples of style and we can very easily trace their popularity up and down on the style of the moment. For instance, it is no accident that Clara Bow with her representation of the flapper of today, is a star. If it hadn't been her, it would have been some other girl of exactly her type. (119–120)

Thalberg points to the cultural *Zeitgeist* as the source for both Bow's public identity and popularity; she is a star because she incarnates "the style of the moment." Taking his model of thought further, it could be said that Garbo embodied MGM's cinematic style of the moment: Thalberg's emphasis on versatility in a sound era paralleled the star's own complex appeal. Just as synchronized sound offered a mesmerizing hybridity—gesturing to a diegetic reality with perfectly timed musical accompaniment and sound effects, while suspending the physicality of the human voice—Garbo also offered her audiences an alluring duality.[3] She inspired dramatic action but was not wholly a *femme fatale*; she had what Christian Viviani termed an "aura of goodness" that shaded her sensuality (2006: 96). Thalberg himself cultivated what has been called her "magnetic passivity" (Salzberg 2014: 22): as he noted, "She is a fascinating artist, but she is limited. She must never create situations. She must be thrust into them; the drama comes in how she rides them out" (qtd. in Thomas 308).

In *Wild Orchids*, Garbo "rides out" an emotional conflict between loyalty to her uninterested husband and attraction to the dissolute prince. Prince de Gace's danger and appeal lie, as in the classic Orientalist paradigm, in his exoticism: he comes from what an intertitle calls "a land of magic beauty—cursed with heat—relentless heat."[4] Lucy Fischer notes that the Javanese setting speaks to a broader Art Deco context, signaling the movement's "championing of an Orientalist aesthetic" and its "infus[ing of] the staid Western world with the alleged carnality of the East" (2001: 92). The film also follows what Homay King has called the "lost girl" narrative, in which young women travel to the East and undergo "a traumatic encounter with otherness" (2010: 138). Lillie's first sight of the prince is, fittingly, a shocking one, as she comes upon him savagely beating his servant with a whip. The prince's physical violence immediately shifts to his predatory appraisal of Lillie's beauty—a moment that she later reimagines, with herself as the object of his sadistic sexuality.

This latter scene recalls Thalberg's description of *Wild Orchids* as a film in which "there is nothing the people [. . .] say that they cannot express without words" (qtd. in Vieira 2010: 98). Indeed, Lillie's realization of her attraction to the Prince plays out through purely formal means, with the synchronized musical soundtrack playing a key part in the storytelling. While husband and wife retire to their twin beds—John ignoring Lillie's advances—their light-hearted motif plays; but as Lillie sadly contemplates her marriage and gazes at the orchids to which the Prince compared her, the melody shifts to a more plaintive, minor tune. This motif had scored part of the Prince and Lillie's first encounter, and it foreshadows her subsequent dream of him. As she lies on her bed, tossing and turning, there is an overlapping image of the Prince—facing the camera—lashing out violently with the whip. The musical score further recaptures that initial meeting, as there is a reprise of the frantic string-based motif that played while the Prince beat his servant.

Where Thalberg referred to the broadened field of cinema through sound, here the film plays with sensorial density: the musical motifs shift into each other and explicitly recall the earlier sequence, even as the images of Lillie and the Prince themselves overlap in an overtly sexual way (see Figure 4.1). Ostensibly following to the extreme Thalberg's conception of Garbo as a performer who "must never create situations," she incarnates here the passive, masochistic partner in a torrid fantasy—though one that she herself imagines. The interlude ends with an affirmation of her ambiguous place in the world of the film: she wakes up screaming from the dream loudly enough to wake her husband, but the audience cannot hear her.

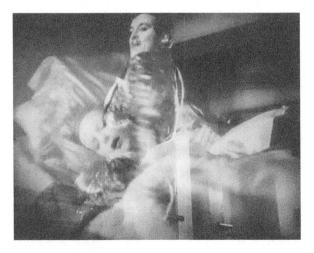

Figure 4.1 Lillie and the Prince.

Subsequent sequences at the Prince's plantation in Java further heighten the link between eroticism and sound, particularly in the dance numbers performed by the native servants for Lillie and John. Eyman describes the contrast between the musical number and the "surrounding silent film" as "uncomfortably stark" (246), but such oppositions underscore Lillie/Garbo's complex relationship to the sonic action. In the first part of the scene, a troupe of men dance and chant in synch with the soundtrack, then female dancers perform a sensual routine for the Prince's guests. The musical spectacle is foregrounded as such by eyeline matches between the seated audience and the dancers who face the camera, merging extra- and intra-diegetic viewership to highlight both the novelty of the number and Lillie/Garbo's relative alienation from it. Lillie is an interested observer—"What a fascinating costume!" she notes as the women dance—but distant from the proceedings until the Prince sends her a native costume of her own.

In narrative terms, the symbolic import is overdetermined. Wearing the dress, Lillie further explores her own frustrated desires by assuming the role of exotic, sexualized other to the exasperation of her husband ("Take off that junk and go to bed") and the titillation of the Prince. On a broader level, though, Garbo's donning of the costume speaks to her own ambivalent relationship to the soundscape of the film. The sequence closes with Lillie/Garbo walking to her balcony to follow the sound of the servants singing, at which point the camera zooms in to highlight her rapturous reaction. It is against this vocal backdrop of a cappella harmonies that the Prince joins Lillie in a passionate embrace—thus linking the newness of the synchronized soundtrack to an erotically charged exoticism. Garbo has adopted the iconography of the musical number, but has not entirely joined in, as it were.

Returning, then, to Thalberg's observation that stardom reflects "the style of the moment" (1977: 119–120), Garbo's role in *Wild Orchids* highlights not only her own continental allure but the greater mystique of sound in the cinema. Thalberg would produce Garbo's talkie debut in *Anna Christie* (dir. Brown) only a year later, to great commercial and critical success[5]; one reviewer described her voice as "disturbing, incongruous, its individuality [. . .] so pronounced that it would belong to no one less strongly individual than Garbo herself" (qtd. in Salzberg 2014: 29). It is interesting to note, however, that she would also go on to star in MGM's final synchronized-sound feature, *The Kiss* (dir. Feyder, 1929). Where *Wild Orchids* exalts the possibilities introduced by sound cinema, exploring synchronization while maintaining silence, *The Kiss* is less ambitious. There are sounds of a telephone ringing and a gunshot, but these emerge as a half-hearted echo of *Orchids'* acoustic fluency. Between the February release of *Wild Orchids* and November's *The Kiss*, the talkies had cemented their dominance at MGM—suggesting, on one hand, that the broadened field of the medium was leaving the silents behind and thus gradually narrowing. But at the same time, as indicated by *Broadway Melody*, that field was still expanding its capacities for sonic sophistication.

INTERRUPTIONS AND INNOVATIONS: *THE BROADWAY MELODY OF 1929*

Next to the *Motion Picture* review of *Wild Orchids* is a rave for another MGM film: All-Talkie production *Broadway Melody of 1929*.

> By far the most scintillating entertainment that has emanated from Hollywood since the advent of sound in cinema, "The Broadway Melody" indicates what may be expected from the studios once the intricacies of the new development are thoroughly mastered. It has made more converts to talkies than all of its predecessors. If every sound picture was warranted as fine as the "Melody," there would be no doubt as to public demand. Unfortunately there is bound to be many a dud before we get another like this one. ("Current Pictures – Silent and Sound – in Review" 62)

This review considers *Broadway Melody* within its industrial context, lauding the new production while observing the disappointments associated with the "advent of sound." For *Motion Picture*, the film is not so much a *sui generis* success, but a "scintillating entertainment" relative to the acknowledged vagaries of sound cinema. Where a publication like *Photoplay*, for example, focuses solely on the virtues of the film—"a credit to its makers and a joy to the fans [. . .] [T]he talkies find new speed and freedom" ("The Shadow Stage" 1929: 52)—the review above suggests a public cynicism and studio anxiety around the crafting of worthy talkies.

For all that MGM was "the most conservative studio" through the talkie wave (Crafton 290), Thalberg's production of *Broadway Melody* represented a turning point in the industry. The narrative itself established the tropes of the backstage musical: two sisters, Hank (Bessie Love) and Queenie (Anita Page), come to New York to make it on Broadway, and their struggles to succeed are paralleled by the drama of their shared affection for singer Eddie (Charles King). Queenie and Eddie eventually marry, and a lonely Hank goes back out on tour—ending the film with an acknowledgment of the conflict between love and fame. Bringing the story to the screen, though, was what Thalberg described as "an experiment; we don't know whether the audience will accept a musical on film" (qtd. in Thomas 124). As star Anita Page would recall, "We were doing the film, and [Thalberg] began coming onto the set [. . .] Pretty soon he began to see that it had great possibilities, and we began to get more and more [production] time" (qtd. in Eyman 309).

Over the three months of production, Thalberg oversaw innovations in the burgeoning genre and sound technology itself. Commissioning original songs, conceiving of a climactic musical number in color (titled "Wedding of the Painted Doll"), and approving the play-back process engineered by Douglas Shearer (Crowther 1957: 150–152)—each of these decisions would shape the musical form so associated with MGM. (Indeed, Arthur Freed, who would go on to lead the legendary Freed Unit of musical production, was the lyricist for the film's songs.) Rick Altman has noted that *Broadway Melody* "established the backstage musical as king of the Hollywood backlot" (1987: 140); and Eyman also points out that the roots of the MGM Music Department emerged from an argument between Douglas Shearer and Thalberg, in which the latter recognized that the studio needed a permanent staff of musicians and composers (310).

For all of the success of the film—it made over $1 million and won the Academy Award for Best Picture—the novelty of the musical form engendered some criticism. In his USC speech, Thalberg addresses the dismissal of *Broadway Melody*—his avowed "experiment" with the capacities of sound for storytelling and spectacle—as a "glorified vaudeville show":

> The very fact that [the film] didn't follow any pattern and that people break into song with orchestral accompaniment just out of nowhere, is only bad if the effect is bad. If the effect on the minds and sensibilities of the listeners is unpleasant, if it destroys the continuity of the story, then, of course, it is bad. I think it has distinct entertainment value. How can we tell when such an interruption will be entertainment or when it will be bad? [. . .] It is intuitive, instinctive—some do and others do not have it. (115)

In these opening passages of the lecture, Thalberg returns to his overarching argument: "entertainment is the purpose and end of the photoplay" (114). He places the film's "interruptions," or radical departure with narrative and sonic norms, within a pragmatic context relating to audience response. "If the effect" of such interruptions or innovations is "bad"—which is to say, if audiences do not understand the story or enjoy the visual and aural impact—then the film has failed on its own terms. If, however, *Broadway Melody* and its experiments prove both to immerse the spectators in the diegesis and provide a sensory charge (appealing to "minds and sensibilities"), then the picture is a success; it has "distinct entertainment value." Conceptual issues with the relationship between stage and screen notwithstanding (the critique of a "glorified vaudeville show"), Thalberg here highlights the importance of an "intuitive, instinctive" understanding of what the public wants to see—and hear.

Admittedly, the point regarding intuition and instinct introduces a more speculative note into the discussion—one that recalls, however inadvertently,

Dorothy Herzog's description of Thalberg as "know[ing] when a person is good or a picture is good. He gets a 'hunch' when he is right" (1926: 131). What, then, does the film itself show in terms of "entertainment value"? How did Thalberg's intuitive understanding of *Broadway Melody*'s success translate to the screen? The filming of "The Wedding of the Painted Doll" illuminates this process in part, capturing Thalberg's own awareness of the tensions between theater and cinema. After seeing the musical number in the rushes, Thalberg protested and ordered a retake:

> That's not a motion picture. It's not a movie at all; it's a stage presentation. [. . .] This time arrange the cameras so we can get some different angles, instead of making the audience look at it from the front, as if they were in a legitimate theater. (Qtd. in Thomas 126)

Rejecting the perspective of a static seat in a theater, Thalberg insisted on highlighting the cinematic nature of the sequence—using various angles on the action to bring the audience closer to the spectacle itself.

The sequence begins in a standard long shot that emphasizes the grandeur of the Broadway stage. Yet as more dancers appear, there is a cut to a tighter long shot—highlighting, in this way, not the vastness of the theater but the intricacies of the choreography and the expressivity of the chorus line. Where, by contrast, the dance numbers in *Wild Orchids* acquiesced to the sound phenomenon while conveying Garbo's reticence through static framings, here the shifting perspective of the camera is as dynamic as the performers themselves. The alternation between longer and closer shots—using deep space to convey the sense of dancers appearing almost magically—carries on throughout the scene, presenting the stage from the side as well as straight on. And with this perpetual movement is an invitation to the viewer to consider themselves part of the action, rather than removed from it as in a classical "stage presentation" (to borrow Thalberg's words). Though the sequence opens and closes with the trope of a curtain rising and falling, in this way framing the scene in a realistic context, the musical number itself presents the stage as a space shared between the on- and off-screen worlds. It is an "interruption" of theatrical conventions, as Thalberg described it, but also an affirmation of cinematic versatility.

In his *Variety* review of the film, Sid Silverman pointed out that such moments of immersion made *Broadway Melody* a threat to the very theatrical world it depicted:

> If the talker [*sic*] studios can top the production efforts of the stage and get the camera close enough to make the ensemble seem to be in the same theatre, what's going to happen in Boston between a musical comedy stage at $4.40 and screen at ℂ.75. (1929)

Figure 4.2 "You Were Meant for Me."

The film also introduced further, less quantifiable disruptions to both cinematic storytelling and theatrical conventions—especially in an earlier sequence, in which Eddie sings the ballad "You Were Meant for Me" to Queenie. Where "Wedding of the Painted Doll" is relatively grounded within the context of the Broadway stage, "You Were Meant for Me" eschews that traditional setting and instead takes place in a hotel room. This shift to a distinctly non-performative space highlights the possibility of integrating the theatrical and the quotidian; as Jane Feuer notes, "[W]hen performance [in a musical] is taken outside the theater, the proscenium is reborn out of ordinary space and the world is a stage" (1993: 24). Certainly this is what occurs between Queenie and Eddie, in which the latter, motivated by his desire to convince her of his love, performs a kind of musical soliloquy (see Figure 4.2).

Arguably a monologue would have been impressive enough, given that it was part of the new talkie style; but the fact that Eddie communicates his emotions through a musical solo is all the more striking. Moreover, the accompanying sense of naturalism within the number—the couple seated together in medium shot in the hotel living room; Eddie and Queenie breaking into dialogue as the score continues playing—renders it, conversely, one of the film's more stylized sequences. Thalberg addresses a criticism of that scene in the Q&A portion of the lecture, in which one audience member asked if it was not a mistake to have Eddie "suddenly burst [. . .] into song with the accompaniment of an orchestra, there being no orchestra in the room" (129). Thalberg responded by, again, pointing to the spectator's willingness to be entertained:

> We risked this novel method of presentation because we knew from experience how strong the play instinct [. . .] really is—how far the audience will really go, in adjusting itself. They had accepted the illusion of depth,

spoken titles, and many other things because they came to the theatre to play—to make believe. Entertain them and they will not be critical of details of technique [. . .] It was natural that the detail [. . .] should be picked up by experts in the industry [. . .] but the audiences have accepted it. (130)

Notable in this passage is Thalberg's privileging of the popular audience over the critical expert, thus aligning his own creative priorities with the experience of the viewer. In citing the "play instinct," Thalberg once again returns to the audience's primary desire for entertainment and MGM's inventive responsiveness to that demand. In a dialogue of mutual adaptability, the spectator "accepts" the "novel method[s] of presentation" set out in the film—even as those are put in place to maintain the currency (returning to Thalberg's earlier terms) of the production.

Intrinsic to this dialogue is the spectator's proactive engagement with the film itself: it is not simply a question of suspending disbelief, but of "how far the audience will [. . .] go" in effectively meeting the film on its own terms. Indeed, the concept of "playing" here conveys a key sense of the spectator's agency; they are fellow actors in, rather than passive recipients of, the construction of that entertainment. "Wedding of the Painted Doll" might alter accepted norms of theatrical presentation, and "You Were Meant for Me" may completely depart from those conventions; but just as the audience responded to the novelty of sound, they "accepted" the innovations engendered by that novelty—and, as Thalberg suggests above, offered their own evolving process of spectatorship.

"CHANGE IS THE LIFE-BLOOD OF THE ART":
THE UNHOLY THREE

As he concludes his lecture, Thalberg returns to the question of currency and the artist:

You have seen that change in form and change in subject matter are of great importance to the motion picture. Indeed, one may truthfully say that change is the life-blood of the art and this doesn't apply only to the form, but also to the people employed in the industry. The favorites of yesterday are gone and the favorites of tomorrow come up. (121)

At first reading, the above seems to contradict the statements that Thalberg would make only a few months later in *Motion Picture*—namely, "We aren't following the lead of many of the other producers and casting out the tried and true favorites" (qtd. in Manners 40). His acceptance of change as a necessity, however, diverges strikingly from what he condemns in the article as poor professional practice. Where the latter disposes of performers in the pursuit of novelty for its own sake, Thalberg understands "change" in organic terms: an evolutionary drive, that is, through which the medium and the industry ensure their future. The "life-blood" of both is their capacity to develop; and as with Thalberg's theory of oblique casting, it is this metamorphic property that ensures both the currency and future relevance of film.

It is fitting, then, to return to Lon Chaney and trace the adjustment of his own shifting form to the demands of the talkies. *He Who Gets Slapped*, MGM's first film, introduced Thalberg's fascination with performances of transformation; *The Unholy Three*, Chaney's final film, would raise the stakes of that process of redefinition to include the human voice. Chaney was both a favorite of yesterday and a contemporary success, to paraphrase Thalberg; like Garbo, Chaney was a popular star whose fate was not, at that point, linked inextricably to the talkies. Thalberg would even go on to connect Chaney in particular to the broader question of entertainment value, harkening back to earlier statements made at USC:

> [J]ust for the sake of argument, say that [Chaney] isn't a [talkie] sensation [. . .] If such should prove to be the case, we will make his pictures as silent features. He will continue in pantomime in the same way in which he has entertained the public for years. And his pictures will not be one whit less popular. [. . .] In this panic over the talking pictures, *we must not lose sight of the prime requisite of entertaining the public.* If Lon Chaney *entertains the public* as a pantomimist, then let him continue in his top-notch medium, the silent picture. (Qtd. in Manners 94; emphases added)

As it happened, Chaney would prove extremely popular with his first and only talkie. It was a canny choice for Chaney's sound debut: he had already starred as Professor Echo, a scheming ventriloquist carrying out robberies with two other circus performers, in Tod Browning's original silent version in 1925. Chaney had been hesitant to speak on film and, in his words, "spoil any illusion" (qtd. in Vieira 2010: 121); but he proved himself capable of, as *Photoplay* described it, "apply[ing] all the cleverness and ingenuity for which he's famous in an effort to do the same weird and awesome things with his talk that he has done with his face and body" (Lang 1930: 75).

Where the silent film could only signal the changing voices through intertitles and Chaney's corporeal fluency, this echo of his first Professor Echo allows him to shift between the voices of a mischievous dummy, a benevolent grandmother, and several other incidental characters (including two parrots). So polyphonic is Chaney's role that it requires something of an adjustment to recognize his natural speaking voice—though even that is left open to doubt.

Chaney explained, "I want to talk not as Lon Chaney would talk, but as the character he happens to be playing would talk. There is no sense in making up a face for a character, then using one's own voice" (qtd. in Nelson 1930: 117). Undermining the ostensible immediacy of the talkies by introducing this level of uncertainty, Chaney in *The Unholy Three* plays out a sustained, virtuosic vocal masquerade. If, as Thalberg stated, "Change is the life-blood of the art," then Chaney's foray into talkies provides a wry commentary on that dynamism: reflecting through this remake on just how far MGM had evolved in its modes of entertainment value, while using that sonic innovation to further distance the audience from an established star. As Thalberg himself advised Chaney, "Just use a couple of voices and let 'em guess" (qtd. in Nelson 33).

Certainly much of the success of the film relies on a parallel, diegetic evocation of the uncanny. After an establishing sequence in a sideshow, the Unholy Three themselves take on different identities so they can carry out robberies: Echo transforms himself into Mrs. O'Grady, the geriatric owner of a pet store; little person Tweedledee (Harry Earles) poses as her toddler grandson; and strongman Hercules (Ivan Linow) pretends to be the baby's father. In the silent version, the impact of these incongruities is dependent on costuming and the actors' changes in body language. The sound remake, however, introduces constantly shifting juxtapositions between voice and image: Tweedledee, dressed as a baby in booties and bonnet, can call a woman a "big tramp" as easily as he coos nonsensically; and a gray-haired and stooped-over "Mrs. O'Grady" alternately threatens her fellow criminals ("You're holding out on me, you dirty rat!") and prattles away with customers. This absurdity also plays out inversely, when Echo tries to distract his girlfriend (Lila Lee) from an admirer. Dressed in topcoat and bowler hat, hiding in another room, Echo must call to Rosie in Mrs. O'Grady's voice in order to maintain the charade for the unsuspecting visitor. Recalling Gaylyn Studlar's contention that Chaney often played men who were "inappropriate, inadequate match[es]" for their love interests (1996: 213), the intertwining of Echo's sexual jealousy and Mrs. O'Grady's maternal voice introduces a disquieting, quasi-incestuous element into the love triangle.

Playing upon the public's desire for what Thalberg called "the change, the looseness, the flexibility" (115) offered by cinema, *The Unholy Three* demands an accelerated spectatorship that keeps up with these continually distorted associations. The slippages foregrounded throughout the film were, in fact, already intrinsic to the extra-diegetic process of revealing the voices of silent stars; as Crafton notes, fans expressed a wide-ranging "concern [. . .] that there be a good match between a voice and a star's perceived image" (490). Again, Gilbert endures as a classic case in point of the anxiety surrounding any disjuncture between a performer's visual and sonic impact—as referenced by Chaney himself. Taking a less than sympathetic view of those silent performers who attempted to refine their voices, Chaney stated, "[Voice culture] ruins voices. That's what is the matter with John Gilbert!" (qtd. in Lang 141). To frame this observation in the context of Thalberg's lecture, Chaney highlights a moment of transition in which a favorite of today—Gilbert—was slipping away to become a "favorite of yesterday."

Drawing an implicit distinction between the affectations of "voice culture" and the cultivation of his own vocal masks, Chaney met the sound revolution on his own terms. In this volatile period, Chaney—like Thalberg—considered how the talkies could relate to his own artistry. Lang, for instance, tells his readers that Chaney "has been studying, studying, studying sound" (141) in order to understand the technology that had challenged so many performers. This level of control over the medium emerges in the trial sequence of *The Unholy Three*, when "Mrs. O'Grady" testifies to protect the young man whom Rosie loves. In the silent film, Echo throws his voice to testify "for" the innocent young man, a sonic superimposition signaled by the use of dissolving shots between the two men. In the talkie version, however, Mrs. O'Grady speaks for herself—for a time. Echo ably maintains the role of the kindly old woman while being questioned by the defense; it is only when the prosecutor's cross-examination turns aggressive that Echo breaks character. Holding a hand up to her head, Mrs. O'Grady cries, "Oh, I have *such a headache*"—only it is Echo's voice declaiming this last phrase. The dropping of this vocal mask raises the prosecutor's suspicions, and he carries out the literal unmasking of Echo by pulling of his wig and glasses (see Figures 4.3 and 4.4).

In thematic terms, Echo's mistake could be read as a Freudian slip, suggesting that he wants to be caught and punished, in this way fitting with Studlar's view of Chaney's "typical, oedipally tinged role as the sacrificial ideal father/impossible lover" (231). On an extra-diegetic level, though, the apparent

Figure 4.3 Mrs. O'Grady.

Figure 4.4 Professor Echo unmasked.

effortlessness with which Chaney shifts from one voice into another, like notes on a scale, highlights his virtuosity. At a turning point in the narrative in which Echo loses control, Chaney reaffirms his mastery over the sonic register. As if flouting the notion of a "good match" between voice and star, following Crafton, Chaney here makes a virtue of the uncertainty that had shadowed fellow performers' transition to talkies. Simultaneously playing a baffled old woman and a frustrated criminal, Chaney demonstrates that change—and instability—is the life-blood of his art.

Again, *The Unholy Three* was Chaney's first talkie and final film; it is therefore impossible to know what vocal characterizations he would have brought to the screen, had he lived. Yet Chaney's performance(s) here offer a metonymic exploration of the state of flux that dominated the industry at the time—the tension between sound and silence, novelty and familiarity, "now" and "then." Thalberg advised that in this changing industry, "The favorites of yesterday are gone and the favorites of tomorrow come up" (121); the question that Chaney poses, by extension, is how well audiences can ever know them.

PROVEN ENTERTAINMENT VALUE

Recording engineer Shearer would later recall that Thalberg perceived the essential benefits of the talkies: "[h]e saw sound as the completion of the medium. He believed it would bring reality to film" (qtd. in Vieira 2010: 88). This insight is no revisionist attempt to absolve Thalberg of his initial resistance. Indeed, like his fellow producers, Thalberg was immersed in all the possibilities and volatility of the sound drama as it unfolded; but by the time of his

USC lecture, he would have committed to—and helped establish—the techno-logical and aesthetic significance of the talkies. Thalberg declared that because of sound, "[t]he range and variety of entertainment that can now be secured are infinitely greater" (123). Revitalizing the pacing of narratives—"Hours which were formerly required to tell things are no longer needed" (123)—as well as introducing "speech and music and sound effects" (123), the talkies strengthened MGM's ability to deliver immersive productions. As Thalberg stated, sound "has distinctly proven its entertainment value" (123).

The following year, Thalberg would author a paper on behalf of the Pro-ducers-Technicians Committee of the Academy of Motion Picture Arts and Sciences, which he and Mayer had helped to found in 1927 (Vieira 2010: 73). In "Technical Activities of the Motion Picture Arts and Sciences," published in the *Journal of the Society of Motion Picture Engineers*, Thalberg outlines the purpose of that committee (of which he was chair) and its exploration of issues such as the humming of equipment (picked up by the recording tech-nology), screen illumination, and the standardization of release print quality (1930: 5). He also discusses the formation of the Academy School of Sound Recording, at which top engineers and scholars offered 900 studio employees "a technical training not confined to the methods of their own studios, nor to a few narrow principles of application, but embracing the entire known tech-nic of sound" (4). Acknowledging the "policy of competition and secrecy" (3) between studios that had characterized the sound revolution—recalling the *New York Times* anecdote featuring Rapf and Warner—Thalberg valorizes a more collaborative approach to the changes faced by the industry. Only two years after describing sound as a novelty, a fad, he emerges here as a figure in control of this new cinema—or at least an authority on how to solve the chal-lenges it introduced. Where once Thalberg's MGM had lagged behind in the talkie revolution, he ultimately took a place as arbiter of its innovations.

Written on behalf of the Producers-Technicians Committee and entirely impersonal in tone, this paper presents a kind of epilogue to the theoreti-cal vision set out in Thalberg's USC lecture. Solving problems with sound recording, sharing best practice, and standardizing technical knowledge—all of these present formal counterpoints to the issues that Thalberg addressed in 1929. If, as he then declared, a film's "entertainment value must be the first criterion" (114), then the "Technical Activities of the Motion Picture Arts and Sciences" provides the machinery for facilitating that engagement with the public. As Thalberg would remark in the lecture, "there is no medium of today that so universally must please as great a number of people" (119)—yet as the next chapter will explore, it was in response to this very imperative that the Motion Picture Production Code developed. Thalberg would soon learn that both in the movie theaters and the studio itself, it was impossible to please everyone.

NOTES

1. As Alexander Walker points out, the issue with Gilbert's debut had less to do with his voice than with its lack of restraint: "Audiences still relatively new to the talkies found it embarrassing to hear, to *overhear*, a man declare his passion for a woman" (1978: 169). That is, "the really fatal element was the matter of passion, not pitch" (1970: 185). Walker also considers the incongruity of Gilbert not taking a voice test, as countless other stars had done; the writer poses the theory that Gilbert's value to negotiations with producer William Fox for a (failed) deal distracted studio executives from the testing process (see Walker 1970: 185–186).
2. In a further dramatic twist, Mayer used his connections in the Hoover administration to ensure that the Justice Department filed the suit (Crowther 1957: 161).
3. Scholars have also commented on Garbo's androgynous appeal; see, for example, "'A Queer Feeling When I Look at You': Hollywood Stars and Lesbian Spectatorship in the 1930s" (Weiss 1991: 283–299).
4. Vieira notes that the original title of the film was, simply, *Heat* (2005: 77).
5. See, for example, Salzberg 2014 (Chapter I: "'Garbo talks!': Expectation and Realization").

CHAPTER 5

Love Stories and General Principles: The Development of the Production Code

One of the more famous anecdotes about Norma Shearer and Irving Thalberg's life together, both as a married couple and MGM professionals, concerns the making of *The Divorcée* (dir. Leonard, 1930). Shearer was convinced that she could star in this adaptation of the provocative 1929 Ursula Parrott novel *Ex-Wife*; Thalberg was equally certain that his wife was not right for the part of Jerry, a sexually liberated woman. As Shearer remarked, "Irving won't give me the part because he thinks I'm not glamorous enough" (qtd. in Lambert 1990: 130). But Shearer was single-minded in her pursuit of the role: she asked soon-to-be legendary photographer George Hurrell to take a series of sensual photographs which, when showed to Thalberg, convinced him that she could play the part (Lambert 1990: 129–130). As Hurrell recalled,

> That was the kind of determination that Norma had. Always the tenacity to follow a hunch. Thalberg had doubted she could be sexy enough to bring off the part, and my pictures proved she could. Of course, the way she brought it off was a commentary on the time and its approach to expressing sexuality. (Qtd. in Lambert 1990: 130)

This anecdote introduces several defining threads in Shearer and Thalberg's working relationship, which would in itself be considered one of his "greatest production[s]" (Marx 1975: 69). There are the negotiations over their shared vision for her career; the evidence of Shearer's characteristic "tenacity" which, in time, would be instrumental in cementing the Thalberg legend; and a tacit acknowledgment of the perception that Shearer received preferential treatment, and parts, from her husband. Indeed, Thalberg remained mindful of the need to maintain objectivity when considering his wife's roles. It was a sentiment he would later share with associate producer and trusted friend

Paul Bern, who pursued the leading role in another controversial adaptation, *Red-Headed Woman* (dir. Conway, 1932), for future wife Jean Harlow. "You're behaving like I did with Norma [. . .] It's a kind of romantic astigmatism that attacks producers when they fall for an actress" (qtd. in Vieira 2010: 201), Thalberg mused.

These questions of "romantic" perspectives and coveted roles are, to return to Hurrell's comments, also indicative of the industry's broader re-evaluation of how female stars "express[ed] sexuality." How could a single character—and, by extension, a single film—convey the evolution of cultural and cinematic mores? Thalberg was, at this point, central in defining Hollywood's response to those shifts. In 1930, MGM and its fellow studios in the Motion Picture Producers and Distributors of America (MPPDA) adopted the Production Code, a document meant to preserve and protect the moral tone of Hollywood films. The Code included the decree that crime "shall never be presented in such a way as to throw sympathy with the crime as against law and justice"; it also set forth that "scenes of passion should not be introduced when not essential to the plot." Ultimately, the Code intoned, "the sanctity of the institution of marriage and the home shall be upheld" (qtd. in Maltby 2003: 594–595). With its guidelines regarding the representation of sensitive or controversial material, the Code formalized best-practice techniques that had been circulated by the MPPDA throughout the 1920s in response to public dismay over Hollywood's alleged hedonism.

As Richard Maltby notes, the Code itself was a living document that would be revised over the years, and its authorship was collective: studio executives contributed to the tenets set out in the Code in dialogue with MPPDA head Will Hays, Catholic publisher Martin Quigley, and Daniel J. Lord, a Jesuit priest (2003: 62). But even in the complex history of the Production Code and its contributors, Thalberg himself remained a constant. He had taken an early and active role in determining the industry's stance on what should, or could, be represented on the screen: in 1927, Thalberg was one of a small group of executives responsible for drafting the Don'ts and Be Carefuls, a set of guidelines for the depiction of various sensitive issues. And in 1929, upon the realization that sound introduced still more controversial topics, Thalberg authored a key document. "General Principles to Cover the Preparation of a Revised Code of Ethics for Talking Pictures"—written by Thalberg on behalf of a three-person subcommittee[1]—would inform the adoption of a formal Production Code in 1930.

Released in 1930 and 1932, respectively, both *The Divorcée* and *Red-Headed Woman* endure as classic productions of the early Production Code era.[2] Dealing wryly with issues of infidelity, sexual liberation, and double standards of morality relating to men and women, these works provide, to borrow again from Hurrell, "a commentary on the time and its approach to expressing sexuality" (qtd. in Lambert 1990: 130). The pictures also appeared at a turning point in Thalberg's career, at which he no longer needed to prove the excellence of the studio but could instead reflect on his own artistic ambitions. Throughout the 1920s, he and Mayer had worked to establish MGM as one of the premier studios in the industry; by the end of the decade, Thalberg had mastered sound production and even maintained MGM's box-office clout in the midst of the Depression (Vieira 2010: 133). The year 1930 alone saw Thalberg personally produce 12 films, including *Anna Christie* and *The Unholy Three*, but that figure dropped by half between 1931 and 1932. Biographer Mark A. Vieira attributes this to "new directions" in Thalberg's personal life—he and Shearer had just had their first child, a son—and professional identity (131). Galvanized by the success of MGM's 1930 offerings, Thalberg explored new sources for material and performers; his fascination with Broadway, for example, yielded collaborations with Helen Hayes and couple Alfred Lunt and Lynne Fontanne (132, 147–148). Thalberg also continued to oversee the production of *Trader Horn* (dir. van Dyck, 1931), an epic adventure that began its troubled filming on location in Africa in 1929 and was not released until 1931 (133).

While he carried out these complex ventures, Thalberg relied on his associate producers, or the "Thalberg Men," to produce more quotidian features. Each associate appealed to a different genre or facet of film production: Bern and Lewin shared a more conventional academic background and had each led MGM's scenario department (Schatz 1996: 45); Rapf and Bernard Hyman worked on comedies and "middle- and low-budget" movies (Schatz 45); and Hunt Stromberg focused on "action and adventure films" (Vieira 2010: 68). But as Vieira notes, Thalberg continued to "shepherd [. . .] every film" (131) from script development to final production, even with the contributions of these producers. The making of *The Divorcée* and *Red-Headed Woman* helps to illustrate this process: Thalberg did not personally produce these films, and accounts of who did supervise the productions are somewhat ambiguous. Robert Z. Leonard directed and is credited with producing the former, while Lambert attributes the supervision of the film to Bern (1990: 132); Bern produced *Red-Headed Woman*, but novelist and screenwriter Anita Loos's account of writing the screenplay focuses on Thalberg and his associate Albert Lewin (1974: 37, 39). Thalberg endures as the constant amid these variables; the arbiter of executive and aesthetic elements like casting and story development, and the figure who established the conditions under which the films were made. Particularly significant at this time were Thalberg's negotiations with the Studio Relations Committee, "the division of the MPPDA responsible for the administration of censorship" (Jacobs 1997: 27). As the following will explore, Thalberg's complex relationship with the demands of the Code, as well as his understanding of great scenes and characterization, intimately informed the production of these works.

Loos would offer her own perspective on Thalberg's "shepherding" ethos. In recollections of her time at MGM, Loos explained that "one always wrote *with* [Thalberg]. You would take your material in and go over it with him, and his suggestions became part of your script" (qtd. in Vieira 2010: 172).[3] Loos offers a particularly illuminating account of Thalberg's creative process in the early 1930s, when she found herself working with him on the script for *Red-Headed Woman* (adapted from the 1931 Katherine Brush novel). Here, Thalberg shared with Loos some of the essential concerns that defined his *oeuvre* as a whole. In story conferences, Loos "learned in time that to Irving Thalberg every film had to be a love story"—regardless of genre or the age and gender of the characters (1974: 36). Rather than privilege the romantic love between heterosexual couples, according to Loos, Thalberg would mine the devotion and "mutual fascination" that could be found between men (*Mutiny on the Bounty*, dir. Lloyd, 1935) as well as parents and their children (*The Champ*, dir. Vidor, 1931; and *The Sin of Madelon Claudet*, dir. Selwyn 1931) (36–37). When Loos suggested that Thalberg would even try to make a love story out of *Frankenstein*, he replied, "Why not? That old yarn is about due for a new twist" (qtd. in Loos 38).

Such accounts of Thalberg's thematic focus recall an early film like *The Big Parade*, with its dual love stories between the brothers-in-arms and the wartime sweethearts; even Chaney's more eccentric, mournful attachments in *He Who Gets Slapped* and *The Unholy Three* fit here. If, as Loos goes on to remark, "Irving insisted that plots grow out of character" (38), then "love story" can be read as a capacious term meant to account for the complex relationships between lead characters. Thalberg's understanding of the love story as such, however, assumes still more significance within the context of the Production Code. For example, when working on the screenplays for films that did feature more conventional romances, Loos found that

> Irving's films never dealt in pornography; his chief requirement was to show two lovers in some sort of a guileless romp with all their clothes on. Even in the script Irving prepared for *Camille* [dir. Cukor, 1936], which was to be graced with the steaming presence of Greta Garbo, the love scenes featured tenderness, not passion. (38)

This focus on the emotional tenor of the relationship rather than overt physicality certainly relates to Thalberg's broad definition of love stories. Loos's description of a blanket guilelessness is less convincing, especially when thinking back, for example, to the Thalberg-mandated love scenes in *La Bohème* or the sado-masochistic undercurrents of *Wild Orchids*. As Loos herself would remark, "Irving could spot sublimated sex in any human relationship" (37). Indeed, though Thalberg "never dealt in pornography," frissons of sensuality are themselves defining elements in his films. At once cultivating charged relationships and moderate in how he envisioned their expression, the Thalberg of Loos's description negotiated a delicate balance of desire. What these variations in her accounts of working with Thalberg in 1931 reveal, then, are both his thematic preoccupations and, implicitly, his understanding of industrial pressures in the representation of sexuality and vice—inasmuch as he had been considering the latter since his work with the MPPDA began in the late 1920s.

Thalberg's General Principles represented the culmination of this years-long contemplation of what studios could present on the screen. In this document, Thalberg returns to similar questions as the ones defining his University of Southern California lecture—entertainment as the primary intention of the industry, the dialogic engagement between a film and its viewer. Though the work concludes with a list of the various subjects that films must treat sensitively or not show at all, it is Thalberg's preamble that provides his statement of purpose: "We have constantly to keep in mind that the sole purpose of the commercial motion picture is to entertain. *It cannot be considered as education or as a sermon or even indirectly as an essentially moral or immoral force.*"[4] Maltby has connected such statements from Thalberg to producers' broader attempts to "deny authorial responsibility" for the public's response to a film, highlighting here a kind of *caveat emptor* mentality that would absolve the studios from any pastoral obligation (2003: 61, 63). Yet when reframed within the context of Thalberg's theoretical concerns, the General Principles offer an extension of his abiding focus on entertainment value—and his resistance to the intrusion of a moral imperative.

Taken together, the General Principles and anecdotal accounts of the day (such as Loos's) reveal Thalberg's complex relationship to the question of regulation in Hollywood. Loos highlights his focus on the intensity of human relationships, though she also alludes to his negotiations of the limitations under which such themes could be explored—limitations which Thalberg himself had engaged with from their inception. Where, ultimately, the 1930 formalization of the Production Code provided a set of guidelines to govern the *practice* of making films, Thalberg's General Principles are just that: his *conception* of how studios should approach the question of censorship itself. In this way, MGM films of the early Code era reveal the tension between Thalberg's theoretical model and the more stringent and specific mandates set out in the Code. The following analyses will explore this further by taking the General Principles, and Thalberg's defense of them at a 1930 meeting with Lord, as a framework through which to consider *The Divorcée* and *Red-Headed Woman*. Both of these films emerged from the intersection between Thalberg's theory of the industry's moral responsibilities and the sometimes vexed execution of Code mandates.

With this in mind, the following will trace the conceptual evolution of Thalberg's approach to industry regulation; the arc, that is, from his early investment in the Don'ts and Be Carefuls to his 1930 reticence towards what he called a "far reaching"[5] code of conduct. Both *The Divorcée* and *Red-Headed Woman* are, ultimately, sensual love stories that demonstrate Thalberg's privileging of entertainment value above the imposition of moral values. Even as he identified the risk of "romantic astigmatism" both in himself and his colleagues, Thalberg remained clear-sighted in his understanding of the film industry's role in bringing such love stories to the screen. As he wrote in the General Principles, "There is one field in which the motion picture is directly responsible for spiritual and moral progress. That is its own—entertainment. The picture industry should constantly be endeavoring to present better entertainment to a larger audience."[6]

"THE AUDIENCE OUGHT TO HAVE GOOD ENTERTAINMENT"

Though the Hays-era Production Code is considered the cultural touchstone for film censorship, questions of morality and representation had been prevalent since the beginning of the motion picture industry. In 1909, theater owners founded the National Board of Review in an effort to prevent government-imposed censorship. The Board allowed the inclusion of sensational material provided that it was a realist element essential to the plot, motivated by the demands of the narrative, and/or introduced an educational component (Staiger 1995: 106). A series of star-scandals in the early 1920s proved that titillation and pleasure-seeking were not confined to diegetic worlds, however. The Fatty Arbuckle trial (1922), the deaths of Olive Thomas (1920) and Wallace Reid (1923), the murder of Thomas Ince (1924) and William Desmond Taylor (and the accompanying incrimination of stars Mary Miles Minter and Mabel Normand in 1922)—each generated attempts to redeem the reputation of the industry. In light of this, it is intriguing to recall Thalberg's offer to engineer a scandal for Lillian Gish—suggesting that such controversies were not always detrimental to the success of a studio.

As early as 1922, Thalberg had shown an intolerance of figures and films that overtly breached codes of good practice. Leslie Kreiner Wilson has pointed out that issues of morality and censorship were key factors in Thalberg's decision to fire Erich von Stroheim from the problematic production of *Merry-Go-Round* at Universal. As Thalberg wrote in the letter terminating von Stroheim's contract:

> Among other difficulties with which we have had to contend has been your flagrant disregard for the principles of censorship and your repeated [. . .] attempts to include scenes photographed by you, situations and incidents so reprehensible that they could not [. . .] be expected to meet with the approval of censorship boards. (Qtd. in Wilson 2014: 125)

Though, as noted in the Introduction, Thalberg's firing of von Stroheim is often interpreted as the moment when his executive power as a producer emerged, this event also speaks to Thalberg's aligning of aesthetic and logistical issues. Von Stroheim's filming of controversial images was not simply "reprehensible" in moral terms; it was also an affront to the studio that would, in turn, not be able to sell the picture successfully.

That same year, Hays was appointed president of the MPPDA in an effort to rehabilitate Hollywood's reputation (Koszarksi 1990: 206). Between 1922 and 1924, Hays established a "formula" of thirteen points for good conduct in filmmaking, advising against the depiction of sex and criminal activity, among other vices. He asked that studios submit their developing stories for review by the MPPDA (Koszarski 206–207). But as Richard Koszarski notes, studios' engagement with these processes was "voluntary" (207)—clearly a point of frustration for Hays. In 1926, he sent Thalberg a memo outlining the MPPDA's concerns over what could not be shown onscreen: drinking, nudity, and contempt for the law were covered in broad terms. Hays also makes clear that Thalberg should disseminate these guidelines to the directors—an expectation which highlights the producer's authority over a given director's vision for a film.[7]

While the guidelines here are fairly broad, Thalberg himself would be instrumental in constructing a more specific set of rules. On May 24, 1927, Thalberg and a subcommittee of MPPDA members (including Hays, Paul Bern, and Jason S. Joy) agreed to the Don'ts and Be Carefuls, a code of practice that would later inform the Production Code. The document, authored by Thalberg and producers Sol Wurtzel and E. H. Allen, specified two categories of sensitive issues. The Don'ts featured topics that would "*not* appear in pictures, irrespective of the manner in which they are treated" (1; emphasis added), and included the same elements outlined in Hays' 1926 memo with the addition of (among other things) "excessive, lustful kissing," "ridicule of the clergy," and "any inference of sex perversion."[8] There were also a series of Be Carefuls, topics that required "great care" in their representation. These included the depiction of criminal behavior and sexual/romantic situations ("man and woman in bed together"; "First night scenes"; "Deliberate seduction of girls").[9]

Interestingly, the May 24, 1927 document outlining the rationale for the Don'ts and Be Carefuls appeals not to the industry's moral obligation—an element that would shade the 1930 iteration of the Code—but rather to the strategic value of such guidelines. After noting that censorship boards across the country have protested against sensational films, the committee argues:

> By eliminating these scenes and titles we not only save footage and the possibility of a mutilated picture when they are eliminated [by state censors] but also effectively forestall the demand for further censorship and further develop the ground work [sic] for the repeal of such censorship as now exists.[10]

The language is compelling in its very pragmatism, outlining ways to thwart the pressures of external censorship boards. This approach also anticipates a more formal process of self-regulation that began in the late 1920s, per historian Lea Jacobs's analysis. Through self-regulation, studios would negotiate with "industry censors"—originally the Studio Relations Committee, "reconstituted" in 1934 as the Production Code Administration—to make pre-emptive alterations to plots, as well as cut images and/or dialogue that may have been considered offensive (1997: ix–x, 19, 20–21).

Transposed to a theoretical context, the above rationale for the Don'ts and Be Carefuls speaks to a frustration with the greater violations done to the cinematic body. The image of "a mutilated picture" suggests a particular violence, especially given Thalberg's view of the holistic impact of a film as emerging from discrete elements of scene construction and casting. There is, then, an attempt to maintain control of the filmmaking process while offering a performative acquiescence to the demands of censorship. Indeed, for all of Thalberg's contributions to the authorship of the restrictions, he did not follow them blindly. As with Hays's original thirteen points, studios only needed to follow the Don'ts and Be Carefuls at their discretion (Koszarski 208), and MGM appears not to have always prioritized them. A 1928 memo to Hays, for instance, tallies up nine studios and their violations of the Don'ts and Be Carefuls; MGM tied with Fox for the second-highest number of total violations and scored the greatest number of "pictures listed as probable sources of criticism."[11] Thalberg's qualified commitment to these guidelines foreshadowed the ambiguities that would characterize his engagement with the Production Code at the beginning of the 1930s: he privileged, and was an authority on, aesthetic concerns rather than moral issues.

The rise of the talkies introduced still more challenges than those anticipated by the Don'ts and Be Carefuls. As Donald Crafton notes, sound allowed for "new and unregulated utterances" (1997: 445) that were harder to monitor than silent-era intertitles, for instance. He also points out that accommodating state censor boards was more complex in sound production, as their demands could entail the resynchronization of a soundtrack (447). Where, returning to the Don'ts and Be Carefuls, a "mutilated" silent film lost scenes and titles, a talkie also risked losing its voice. Accordingly, Hays sought an industrial view of such problems from a subcommittee composed of Jack Warner, Sol Wurtzel, and Thalberg. The latter drafted the General Principles; but as Hays noted, Warner and Wurtzel "had the opportunity to present their ideas quite fully, very exhaustively"[12] in the document.

Admittedly, Thalberg's perception of what sound allowed for was far more optimistic than certain of his colleagues'. His discussion in the General Principles expands upon his view of the talkies as a broadened field, as outlined in the previous chapter. Thalberg perceives it as facilitating "wider latitude in subject and treatment"[13] rather than necessarily introducing new dangers. In fact, he seems to identify absolutism as the real threat to filmmaking. As he writes in the opening paragraph, "There is a very general tendency to over-emphasize the moral and educational influence of motion pictures. This tendency has developed until the motion picture is held wholly or in part responsible for every trend in manners and morals."[14] Throughout the document, Thalberg seeks to establish not so much the industry's lack of responsibility but rather the limits of its moral obligations.

If the rationale for the Don'ts and Be Carefuls took a proactive stance against the influence of censors, the General Principles document adopts a theoretical tone that both reflects on the institution of cinema and *de*flects a moral imperative. At the heart of the piece is a belief that "artificial standards" of virtue or conduct cannot be enforced by the studio and should not be "forced" upon the audience:

A crowd cannot be told to enjoy good music or fine acting or better stories. These must be presented so entertainingly that there is no escape from enjoyment. It would be small social service to raise the moral or spiritual standard of entertainment at a rate which caused the crowd to walk out.[15]

Retaining the focus of his USC speech, Thalberg here emphasizes the importance of entertainment value—above, that is, the imposition of moral values. But even more emphatically, Thalberg argues that the latter has no traction in the audience without the former. Just as a well-made and engaging film offers "no escape from enjoyment," it would offer no escape from an edifying tone. But that tone must, as Thalberg cautions, be reasonable in its expectations; to paraphrase his words, it would be a small service to the film industry itself if the concerns over appropriate content and imagery stifled the production of entertaining works and, in turn, discouraged audiences from buying tickets.

There is a great deal of rhetorical force in Thalberg's writing. He incorporates bold imagery comparing cinema to media encountered on a daily basis—"It is one vast reflection of every image in the stream of contemporary life. It is as contemporary as a newspaper or a comic strip"[16]—and literally underlines several key passages. Such an emphatic style would be necessary at the February 10, 1930 meeting of the Association of Motion Picture Producers (AMPP), at which Thalberg defended these General Principles in a debate with Father Daniel Lord. As Maltby remarks in his illuminating analysis of this meeting, the transcript of the exchange between Thalberg and Lord reveals a conceptual impasse between not simply what could or should be shown on screen, but between broader definitions of industrial responsibility and the experience of spectatorship (1995: 20). At this meeting, Lord discussed in point-by-point detail the tenets of the Production Code and called for the industry to accept "the great responsibility and opportunity of putting right ideas before [the audience]; the opportunity of setting before them right moral principles."[17] In his model of cinema-going, Lord conceives of a mass of spectators that "go to the theatres—sit there passively—ACCEPT and RECEIVE; with the result that they go out from that entertainment either very much improved or very much deteriorated [. . .]"[18]

Thalberg's General Principles, by contrast, highlighted the dialogue between spectator and film:

> People influence pictures far more than pictures influence people. The motion picture does not present the audience with tastes and manners and views and morals; it *reflects* those they already have [. . .] The motion picture is literally bound to the mental and moral level of its vast audience.[19]

Maltby points out that in taking this line of argument, Thalberg characterizes producers as "transparent agents of transmission, simply mediating between writers and" the audience (1995: 19); from this perspective, the producers are effectively "passiv[e] [. . .] in the selection of subject matter" (19). Transposing Thalberg's statement to his related theory of entertainment value, however, reveals a parallel concern with the issue of currency: "[T]here is no medium of today that so universally must please as great a number of people, and to do this it must be current in its thinking and in the processes by which its heroes and heroines do things" (1977: 119). Which is to say, character motivations and diegetic subject matter must not emerge from abstract notions of what cultural mores *should* be, but rather in accord with the concerns of the public. In both of the above excerpts, Thalberg highlights still another process of regulation more elemental to the medium itself: the producer's continual awareness of and attunement to his viewers.

Thalberg's word choice of "reflect," then, signals a process of affirmative engagement instead of a disavowal of responsibility. Viewed in this way, his conception of a reflective filmmaking does not argue for a passive producer but rather one who is responsive to and aware of the desires of the audience. Where Lord regards the audience as recipients of cinematic, moral matter, Thalberg argues for an intersubjective exchange between industry and spectator. "The audience ought to have good entertainment," he writes in the General Principles, playing on the dual meanings of good. "But if there is to be an audience there must first be entertainment."[20]

"CLEANING UP" *THE DIVORCÉE*

If, as Loos maintained, Thalberg "insisted that plots grow out of character" (38), then the historical narrative of regulation reveals much about his own professional identity at this time. Thalberg's undeniable influence in the industry meant that his views would always be sought at such key junctures as the development of the Production Code, but it was as an aesthetic authority, rather than a moral authority, that he shared his conception of what the role of censorship should be. Thalberg understood the need to forestall extensive cuts by state censors and had even strategized ways to do so in the Don'ts and Be Carefuls; but he rejected the moral astigmatism, as it were, of Lord's mandates and privileged instead the creative agency of a given studio. Effectively, Thalberg demonstrated an ambivalence towards the very guidelines he helped to draft.

Across the early implementation of the Code, he also showed an impatience with the bureaucratic audits of the Studio Relations Committee. For instance, in a letter to an SRC censor regarding proposed cuts to *Paid* (dir. Wood, 1930), Thalberg points out that Colonel Jason S. Joy, the head of the SRC, had already approved the indicated content ahead of time.[21] And in the draft of a memo regarding *War Nurse* (dir, Selwyn, 1930), another censor complained to Hays that Thalberg's "attitude has been a little bit queer [. . .] Not the usual Thalberg reaction. [The] attitude at the moment is, why should any small group of people decide what the rest of the world should see?"[22] The timing of the memo is interesting: dated September 30, only a few months after the formal adoption of the Code, this account of Thalberg's "attitude" seems to bear out the very frustrations that he alluded to in the February meeting. "The problem of the producer [. . .] primarily is to produce as many pictures as necessary and to give the public the sort of entertainment that they crave,"[23] Thalberg stated—and his alleged response to the cuts to *War Nurse* suggests that he resented the intrusion of the SRC into this ethos.

In the General Principles, Thalberg discusses at length the need for more latitude for producers—particularly in the adaptation of controversial source material. Pointing to the clarity of expression introduced by the talkies, Thalberg argues that novels or plays that would have been too sensational in silent cinema can now

> treat the subject with the exact delicacy and decency required by any proper moral standard. [. . .] [T]he story will naturally be so treated and cleaned up so as to be appropriate for exhibition. [. . .] It is fair to conclude that any book, play or title which has gained wide attention is legitimate material for motion picture use. An unfavorable notoriety gained by the work when circulated in its original field is not a genuine barrier to its presentation as a motion picture providing the motion picutre is itself produced with taste and decency. It is unjust to prejudge the motion picture on account of the doubtful reputation of its source.[24]

This lauding of the opportunities presented by sound cinema recalls Thalberg's appreciation of the broadened field of the talkies, while also acknowledging the studio's responsibility to cover that terrain in a tasteful manner. Interestingly, he proposes a negotiation between "delicacy" in the treatment of controversial subject matter and boldness in the process of adaptation itself. Arguing for a forensic ("exact") handling of the "cleaning up" process, while asserting the more general right of the studio to choose "any" source material, Thalberg calls for a balance of artistic and executive authority. As he would clarify at the February meeting, "[M]any books have been written [. . .] which contained salacious matter [. . .] which is not at all necessary to [their] popularity"[25]—thus suggesting that the process of studio-level adaptation and the accompanying "cleaning up" could offer a welcome revision to a given work in its "original field."

The implications and effectiveness of "cleaning up" were, however, debated between Thalberg and Hays. The former perceives it as part of a broader aesthetic cycle by which the modified filmic adaptations would inspire other novelists to regulate their own "objectionable element[s]"[26] in order to ensure easier adaptation to the screen; Hays, however, points to the obstacles inherent in such a process. "[T]here is a certain group that feels that we shouldn't be allowed to take anything and 'clean it up,'" Hays states, "Whereas, there are still a few that I might designate as rather extreme people [. . .] who think we should take any book and film it just as it is. Of course, that's entirely out."[27]

One such adaptation that tested these principles was *The Divorcée*. Though the introductory anecdote suggested that Thalberg did not think that Shearer was "glamorous enough" to play the title role, the discussions surrounding the film at the AMPP meeting hint at another reason why he would not have wanted his wife to star. Casting Shearer in a scandalous project at the center of fraught debates was, simply, a risk to her image. As Lambert argues, Thalberg had "a feeling that it was not the kind of role great stars of the theater played" (1990: 159)—which is to say, the film would undoubtedly be popular, but not necessarily a prestige picture suited to his wife's elegant image. In considering the transcript of the meeting, however, *The Divorcée* emerges as a significant film in the Thalberg canon: not just as a Shearer vehicle, but in its own right as a case study of his principles-in-action. With fluency and insight, Thalberg's discussion of the film (then titled *Ex-Wife*) provides a context for him to explain in more detail the process by which a creative executive could translate a controversial source to the screen.

A comedic drama that explores double standards of fidelity between man and wife, *The Divorcée* begins with Ted's (Chester Morris) proposal to Jerry (Norma Shearer). She charms him with her assertion of what he calls "a man's point of view": forgiving Ted his romantic past, Jerry remarks, "You're just human, and so am I." But on her third wedding anniversary, she learns that her beloved husband has had an affair; and in an effort "to hold," as Jerry explains, "onto the marvelous latitude of a man's point of view," she herself has a dalliance—for which Ted divorces her. Jerry proceeds to carry on a number of high-society romances, until she realizes her enduring love for Ted and pursues a reconciliation. These diegetic questions of latitude and perspective intersect with those emerging from Thalberg's statements regarding the censorship of source material. As he states in the debate with Lord, "[T]he difficulty confronting us, as an industry, is that we must understand and appreciate that there always seems to be so many different minds [writers, directors, performers]" influencing the development of a film. Thalberg goes on to call for Lord to offer some "definite and concrete thing [in terms of the Code], yet realizing the difficulty under which we have to work." [28]

As Maltby points out, Thalberg's statement relates to a broader concern with "standardization and enforcement [given that] any Code would be susceptible to disagreements of interpretation" (1995: 20). Thalberg also addresses here the tension between being subject *to* the Code and, at the same time, an agent of film production. This theme would feature in the General Principles themselves. Implicit in the latter's sections on adaptation is a desire to have it all—to maximize, that is, the *entertainment* value in a property while nominally acknowledging the pressures of value *judgments*. As Thalberg put it, he sought to preserve the appeal of a work "which has attained wide notice or attracted general interest" while showing a willingness to "clean[. . .] up" the more objectionable elements.[29] As a case in point, Thalberg's extemporaneous defense of *Ex-Wife* as source material illuminates his fluency in negotiating these terms: the film "presents divorce in the light of the growing evil it is looked upon to be, but looking at the subject of divorce with less suspicion than it was looked upon before."[30] Which is to say, the film retains the sensational subject matter of the novel but with a view to maintaining a moral tone; but even that moral tone takes into account changes in social mores.

In stylistic terms, *The Divorcée* translates this ambiguity into montages that materialize the fragmentation of convention, as well as convey the exhilaration of a liberated woman. Veronica Pravadelli has termed this style of montage the "urban dissolve," noting its recurrence in pre-1934 films (2015: 27). Characterized by images of streets, traffic, and city dwellers that create "pure movement [and] energy" (27), these urban dissolves evoke the kinetic sexuality of their heroines by countering contemplative shots of the female body or sly ellipses with bursts of motion. Until the climactic scenes in which Jerry and Ted's marriage collapses, the film proceeds at a near-theatrical pace with long takes in (for the most part) stage-like interior sets. The sequence following their divorce, however, introduces the frenetic energy of the urban dissolve.

Though admittedly the montage does not take place on a city street, it nonetheless captures the nightclub environs so intrinsic to what Jerry wryly calls "the sweet, pure air of 42nd Street and Broadway." The scene features Jerry-as-divorcée at a New Year's Eve party and opens with a long establishing shot of the dancing masses before cutting to a closer shot of the crowds. Overlaying the latter image are shots of the various musicians and instruments that produce the raucous jazz music of the soundtrack. After a brief exchange between Jerry and Ted, she is swept away by the revelers—her image replaced by a literally kaleidoscopic dissolve that rotates shots of dancers, balloons, and streamers. Pravadelli has noted that the urban dissolve as a technique captures "the modern woman's narrative of transformation" (27); on a more specific level, this montage channels the fragmenting momentum of events that have redefined Jerry's identity as wife and woman.

When explaining his approach to the adaptation of *Ex-Wife*, Thalberg notes,

> The result of divorce—as we know in many instances—viewed from the standpoint of its effects on the part of the wife, is a very unhappy one, and where we present it in the light of showing that the husband is desirous of going back to his former situation, it seems to me when we are presenting such a subject that we are positing a very worthwhile problem.[31]

As suggested by Thalberg, then, the film fulfills a certain moral obligation by treating divorce as a kind of draw for *both* the husband and wife: the couple are not happy together, but nor are they allowed to be happy apart. In so acknowledging the "unhappy" effects of divorce on both parties, the film maintains that the pleasures they find while apart are ephemeral, false. Within this conciliatory context posed by Thalberg, though, those very pleasures can nonetheless be shown. Indeed, where the montage of the New Year's party explores the fracturing of Jerry's former life, the subsequent sequence explores its aftermath: "viewed from the standpoint of its effects on the part of the wife," to recall Thalberg's words.

In a series of four vignettes, Jerry fends off the advances of various men. Her rejoinders are witty and, by the end of the sequence, slightly bitter; but more compelling is the graphic continuity over which they play: the medium shots only show Jerry's arms and hands entwined with her suitors'; they are all faceless (see Figures 5.1 and 5.2). It is as if the kinetic anonymity of the New Year's party has slowed down, now allowing Jerry to consider more languidly her opportunities for sexual conquests—and at the same time suggesting her own immersion into the depersonalized archetype of "divorcée." For however ably Jerry defends her virtue in theory, there is little sense that she does so in practice—if only because of the decadence of the imagery. The jewelry and cocktail glasses, her sleeves with sequins and fur trim, all conspire to evoke a world of sensual pleasures that are materially gratifying if morally ambiguous. In the General Principles, Thalberg writes that "the decent presentation of an interesting but originally questionable story theme would do much to counteract its former unfavorable influence"[32]; this sequence, accordingly, presents the questionable theme of sexual liberation from the perspective of a decent woman trying to negotiate the thrills and challenges of her new identity.

It is Jerry's reluctant divorce-court determination to "take all of the hurdles, see all the scenery, and listen to the band play" that introduces the sequences of the New Year's party and the subsequent sexual fencing. In so expressly allying itself with Jerry's pleasure-seeking point of view, the film transforms what she had called "the marvelous latitude" of the male outlook into the quasi-vertiginous, sometimes disjointed experience of a woman realizing her sexual freedom. Equally fractured here is, importantly, any sense of absolute judgment. Even if, as Thalberg contended, the effects of divorce are ultimately shown to be "unhappy," they are not without their carnivalesque thrills—which, through the film, the public itself can share. In this way, *The Divorcée* demonstrates that the process by which the studio would, to return to the General Principles, "treat [a given] subject with the exact delicacy and decency required by any proper moral standard"[33] was relative. The film would be "cleaned-up," as Thalberg termed it—not purified.

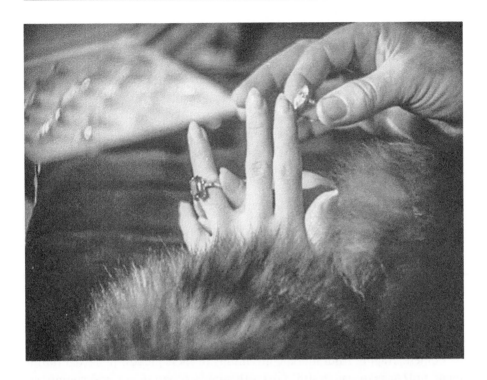

Figures 5.1 and 5.2 Jerry and her suitors.

SPECULATION IN *RED-HEADED WOMAN*

In his debate with Lord, Thalberg suggests a more moderate process by which studios could produce "*better* pictures" that would appeal to a higher-minded public while still releasing films "which may be a little 'off-color.'" When Lord compares this to a banker who admits that "5% of [his] deals are off-color," Thalberg politely but firmly demurs: "A banker might say, 'I am going to invest 95% of my funds very carefully, choosing possibly a 5% of those funds and engaging with them in speculation, which on the whole seem good but may not be *quite* so good.' "[34]

Thalberg himself would go on to "speculate" with certain of MGM's productions between 1930 and 1932. In a particularly extreme instance of risk-taking, Thalberg would even venture into the horror genre with Tod Browning's *Freaks* (1932). Thomas Doherty identifies this tale of a macabre circus as a definitive example of early Code grotesqueries that failed with audiences; but one that nonetheless endures today in "forc[ing] a recognition of sentience and humanity in the deformed" (1999: 317–318). More moderately speculative productions would fall within what Jacobs has termed "the fallen woman" genre (1997: 3), featuring the dramatic, sometimes darkly comic tales of women straying from moral conventions in their pursuit of sexual fulfillment and/or material wealth. Given this intersection of sex and commerce, there is something particularly apt about the metaphor of careful investment opposed to risk-taking.[35] For example, *A Free Soul* (dir. Brown, 1931), also starring Shearer, explores one society woman's destructive sexual attraction to a gangster; *Possessed* (dir. Brown, 1931) follows a young woman's life as a mistress to a wealthy man. Another such film was *Red-Headed Woman*. A box-office success in 1932 (though banned in parts of Canada and cut by state censors), *Red-Headed Woman* managed, as Maltby remarks, to make "comedy out of what had previously been [. . .] the material for melodrama"—that is, the story of the fallen woman (1986: 37, 31).

As Thalberg set out in the General Principles, "Spoken lines permit of much less misunderstanding. Therefore it is both permissible and legitimate to tread on more delicate ground and with perfect propriety to deal with human elements the silent picture was forced to shun."[36] Lil (Jean Harlow), the titular red-headed woman, continually treads on delicate ground: she aggressively and successfully pursues an affair and marriage with her already-married boss, Bill Legendre (Chester Morris); she seduces and blackmails a sanctimonious captain of industry; and when Bill reveals her affair with the latter's chauffeur (played by Charles Boyer), she tries to kill him. Lil's violence not only goes unpunished, but is effectively rewarded, as the closing sequence shows her living in Paris with a wealthy French man—and still in the company of her beloved chauffeur. Loos points out that the film

> outraged ladies' clubs throughout the land [. . .] because our heroine, the bad girl of whom all good husbands dream, ended her career as many such scalawags do, rich, happy, and respected, without ever having paid for her sins. (43)

By Loos's reckoning, then, the film offered a realistic resolution rather than a moralistic one.

Certainly Loos's dry appraisal of the public response is reflected in a censor's 1932 description of Lil as "a common little creature from over the tracks who steals other women's husbands and who uses her sex attractiveness to do it" (qtd. in Jacobs 1997: 18). Perhaps unsurprisingly, one SRC representative described the original script as "the most awful [. . .] I have ever read [. . .] [Thalberg] insisted that he disagreed 100 percent with our opinion [but] suggested many vital changes" (qtd. in Vieira 2010: 179). Thalberg's willingness to compromise over particular details suggests that he wanted to distract from the real danger of the film: Lil herself, who was not merely a "common little creature" but a fully developed character with motivations and desires of her own, however venal. To repeat the Loos quotation cited earlier, "At a time when most Hollywood movies dealt in contrived situations, Irving insisted that plots grow out of character" (38).

This emphasis on psychological substance relates well to Thalberg's concern with great scenes and oblique casting—speaking to a dual awareness of the character's ability to trigger a narrative turning point and the importance of the performer in defining that character. Certainly the notion that "plots grow out of character" recalls more dramatic questions of motivation in films like *The Big Parade* and *Wild Orchids*, as well as Thalberg's insistence on Mimi and Rodolphe's love scenes in *La Bohème*. Yet comedies were equally significant for Thalberg, as revealed by Marx and Loos's respective recollections of developing *Red-Headed Woman*. The former recounts how Thalberg had assigned Bern to the film, given that he "preferred women writers and sexy stories" (1987: 21) and that his "erudition qualified him to bring out the rampant sex" (64) that characterized Brush's original novel. Thalberg and Bern had originally assigned F. Scott Fitzgerald to write the screenplay, but they took him off the project after reading his first draft: "He didn't grasp the point about laughing *with* her," according to Thalberg (qtd. in Marx 1987: 66).

Once Loos began working on the script, she found herself in a story conference in which she and Thalberg talked over the characterization of gold-digger Lil, inasmuch as she presented an obstacle to the maxim "every film had to be a love story" (36). Loos remembered how

> Irving went on pacing and tossing his silver dollar. Finally he stopped. "I think I know what the love story can be. Our heroine must be deeply in love with herself [. . .] The poor girl has the flashy type of looks that frighten off any man with the qualities of a hero. Who *is* there for her to love, when she only attracts fools?" (qtd. in Loos 39)

Accordingly, Lil's narcissism is not only a striking feature of her character but a central factor in the plot itself. Preoccupied with her appearance and physical impact, and perceiving others as expendable in her drive to fulfill sexual and/or material desires, Lil forces the men in her life to submit to her will. As Thalberg's very tone in the anecdote above suggests, however, there is also a kind of humorous fatalism to Lil; she accepts her "flashy" beauty as such and, in turn, capitalizes on the power it brings her.

Indeed, implicit in Thalberg's statement is a sense that the film is not only making fun of the "fools" that Lil attracts, but also of the conception of femininity itself as a threat. Jane M. Greene has discussed the dual impact of comedy: she notes that though "the satiric treatment of the sexually aggressive female was seen as a way to render her ridiculous" (2011: 244), humor itself could be used to "question the very moral standards the Code [was] trying to uphold" (245). Certainly, as conceived by Thalberg and Loos, Lil makes those values ridiculous in themselves: when Bill places the blame for the affair on Lil, telling her "You've only got one filthy idea in your whole rotten make-up," Lil points to his underlying hypocrisy. "Well, if I have," she retorts, "Then don't try to fool yourself that you don't share it." At a time when the proponents of the Code were looking for a way to reconcile conventions of morality with the liberation of expression wrought by the talkies, Thalberg used the latter to show the weaknesses in the former. Like the 5 percent of films with which Thalberg wanted to speculate, the regulations themselves "on the whole seem[ed] good but may not [have been] quite so good."[37]

Thalberg and Loos's glib treatment of the fallen woman genre imbued the production with a self-awareness that complements other films of the era. Michael Curtiz's *Female* (1933), for example, plays upon the deliberate reversal of patriarchal conventions (with Ruth Chatterton portraying an industry magnate and rapacious pursuer of young lovers) to contemplate representations of the ideal feminine; while, as Thomas Doherty notes, Mae West's *I'm No Angel* (dir. Ruggles, 1933) places its star in a carnival context that references her own extra-diegetic sensationalism (184–185). Harlow herself would go on to play a star in *Bombshell* (1933), Victor Fleming's screwball comedy about the machinery of the film industry.

Though, as noted earlier, Thalberg had chided Bern for that "romantic astigmatism" (qtd. in Vieira 2010: 201) afflicting producers, the latter's insistence on casting Harlow as Lil was key to ensuring the success of the film. As Susan Ohmer points out, this early starring role established Harlow as a performer whose comic presence complemented her sensual physicality (2011: 182). Crawford reportedly wanted to play the part (Vieira 2010: 185); but where she often imbued her roles with an undercurrent of intensity or frustration, Harlow approached Lil with a light touch appropriate to Loos's witty screenplay. The star also brought a knowing humor to the role; as Loos relates of Harlow's meeting with Thalberg: "Do you think you can make an audience laugh?" asked Irving. Harlow replied: "Why not? People have been laughing at me all my life" (qtd. in Loos 40).

As Loos recalled, though, the first cut of the film did not foreground the humor. At a sneak preview, audiences "did not know whether to laugh at our sex pirate or not" (43); Thalberg then asked Loos "to contrive a prologue which will tip the audience off that the movie's a comedy" (qtd. in Loos 43). Accordingly, the opening sequence offers a brief montage of Lil's *toilette* as she prepares herself for seducing her boss. She chooses her clothes according to whether one "can [. . .] see through" her backlit skirt, and places Bill's picture in her garter—and begins the film with an utterly self-reflexive line of dialogue. As Lil/Harlow reclines in medium close-up, burnished hair flowing, she grins, "So gentlemen prefer blondes, do they?" All but winking at the camera, Harlow-as-Lil references not only screenwriter Loos's 1925 bestselling novel *Gentlemen Prefer Blondes*, but also the audience's association with her own "blonde bombshell" persona.

Here, the line establishes the coquettish tone of a film that goes on to engage with its own extra-diegetic context and performative nature: Lil/Harlow describes her tryst with Bill/Morris as "like an uncensored movie"; the eponymous theme song is showcased in a later scene, opening with a shot of the sheet music with title emblazoned; and the red-headed woman herself conveys her attraction to her boss in terms of a fan-star dynamic. "You're all I've been able to think about for years," Lil relates. "I've been crazy about you from a distance, ever since I was a kid."

As one censor pointed out, "a certain glamour surrounds" Lil (qtd. in Jacobs 1997: 18)—a kind of aesthetic satisfaction in her production of herself as an object of desire. Not only does Loos and Thalberg's prologue indicate that the film is a comedy, but it also foregrounds Lil's to-be-looked-at-ness, following Laura Mulvey's term (2009: 19). This overt focus on Lil's "flashy good looks," as Thalberg described them, recalls a particular hypothetical narrative posed by Father Lord. At the February 1930 meeting at which he and Thalberg debated the Code, Lord illustrates an "immoral story" by describing a scenario of "a beautiful and bad girl having a hilarious time. She 'plays' around with other people's husbands [. . .] she does about everything in the world." He notes that if at the end of the film this woman goes unpunished, the film is immoral: "Because the audience has been made to feel that the conduct of that girl, which was in itself *evil*, was, in fact, good [. . .] and that all of the time she was having a darned good time."[38] Though such hypothetical situations play out in many films of the era, at least in part—consider *Baby Face*—there is an uncanny link to Lil's own fate in *Red-Headed Woman*. Very simply, the film itself seems to be "having a darned good time" along with her—making the audience complicit in her exploits.

Highlighting this sensibility is the turning-point sequence—the Thalbergian great scene in the film—in which Bill becomes definitively entangled with Lil. After he comes to her apartment to break off the dalliance and pay her to leave town, Lil locks herself into her bedroom with him and refuses to surrender the key. After a furious Bill smacks her—only to have Lil enthuse that she "likes it"—there is a cut to Lil's equally stimulated roommate, Sally (Una Merkel), listening to the sounds of a charged scuffle emerging from the bedroom. A cut back to the disheveled couple reveals Lil lying on the floor, feigning distress. Penitent, Bill carries her to the bed and asks her again to give him the key; and the scene ends as the sniffling Lil recovers enough to slide the key down her blouse. The following sequence presents, logically enough, the dissolution of Bill's marriage in the divorce court.

This sequence is no straightforward depiction of a battle between Bill's (alleged) virtue and Lil's vice. Just as Lil demands Bill's acknowledgment of his lust for her, the film itself insists upon the audience's awareness of the performance in play: Lil virtually narrates Bill's conflict—"Now you're afraid; you're afraid of yourself because you know you love me. You're afraid you're going to take me in your arms. You're afraid you're going to kiss me"; while following the ostensibly discreet cut, Sally acts as a titillated audience. With quasi-orgasmic sighs, she eagerly comments, "She's locked him in!" The camera also takes part in this overt seduction of the spectator: panning forward to frame Lil and Bill in intimate two-shot as she describes her effect on him, then pulling back slightly and reframing to capture the violent jolt of Bill smacking her. After Bill throws Lil away from him and out of the frame, the teasing cut to the closed-door renders this sado-masochistic exchange an off-screen spectacle performed within the consciousness of the viewer and Sally, his/her on-screen proxy.

Even if the interplay between Bill and Lil alternately entices and eludes the gaze of the spectator, the conclusion of the sequence offers still another sensational *ménage*. As Lil lies prone in medium close-up and slides the key down her blouse, the radiance of the lighting—imbuing her hair, skin, and clothing with a near-pearlescent quality—gradually cedes to dusky gray as Bill's shadow heralds his approach. Finally the dark mass of Bill's back is visible to the right of the frame, its darkness moving to the left and ultimately concealing

Lil as he literally blacks-out the shot to access her body. Thomas Doherty has characterized such pre-Code effects as techniques of "figurative literalness," or "timely detour[s] [that] could infuse the onscreen narrative with otherwise censorable material [. . .] for the imagination" (119). The sensory charge to these images, however, introduces a wholly material sensuality: the merging of Bill's body with the film's, an act that simultaneously signals and conceals his merging with Lil's. With both Lil's coquettish self-awareness and Bill's fleshly desire literally incorporated into the filmic body, the material of the movie renders explicit the *implicit* carnality of the scene.

Courting the gaze as surely as the diegetic fallen woman pursues her conquests, the film lures its audience with promises of visual consumption—only to evade consummation and ultimately call attention to this teasing process itself. In so investing MGM's resources in the "off-color" risk of *Red-Headed Woman*, Thalberg underscored his own view of the Code: a set of rules that were made to be negotiated rather than accepted, challenged rather than surrendered to, in the pursuit of entertainment value in filmmaking. His approach to the "delicate ground" of censorship in this film recalls one description of Lil herself in the film: "Strictly on the level, like a flight of stairs."

THE PURPOSE OF A PRODUCER

When discussing the process of adapting *Ex-Wife*, Hays and Thalberg found themselves analyzing the greater issues at stake. Returning to the implications of "cleaning up" source material, Hays asks Thalberg, "Well, would it be your idea to give them [the audience] what is in 'X's Wife' [*sic*]?" To which Thalberg replies,

> Your purpose as producers in this industry is to comply with the wishes
> of the great public and give the people that which your public is demand-
> ing, up to a certain point, with a modicum of discretion, of course; that,
> it seems to me, is our purpose today.[39]

Once again, as in the USC lecture, Thalberg articulates the imperative to provide entertainment value to the audience, bringing to the screen topical and provocative material—"with a modicum of discretion, of course." It was this factor of the producer's discretion that was the most difficult to define throughout the February meeting and, indeed, in the years to come. Resisting the didactic tendencies of the Code, Thalberg sought to protect the intertwined variables of executive oversight and aesthetic vision. In juxtaposing the mandates of the Code with the singularity of the processes of production and spectatorship, Thalberg argued not for moral laxity but for conceptual freedom.

The late 1920s to early 1930s introduced a period of technical innovation and theoretical sophistication for Thalberg's MGM. Running parallel to industrial developments like the rise of sound and the formalization of the Production Code, Thalberg's conceptualization of the medium evolved in rhetorical force and confidence. His approach to story-crafting and star-making helped to inform the broader theory of entertainment value set out in 1929; and that overarching understanding of entertainment value inflected Thalberg's response to the more rigorous imposition of regulations in the early 1930s. Fundamental to each of these individual theories was Thalberg's understanding of the dual nature of filmmaking: it was an aesthetic pursuit for its producers that, in turn, ensured an immersive experience for mass audiences. Loos would laud Thalberg's approach to those aesthetic pursuits, describing them, fittingly, in terms of the love-story model that he himself privileged: "Irving worked for the pure love of creating [. . .] [C]ollaborations with him were, to me, almost like love affairs. They had many of the thrills, none of the drawbacks, and were certainly due to last longer" (174). Where this may have captured the experience of many working with Thalberg in a creative capacity, the next chapter will explore the ways in which, by 1932, the relationship between Thalberg, Mayer, and Schenck was ending.

NOTES

1. Abbreviated hereafter in text as General Principles. Richard Maltby identifies the document as "largely the work of Irving Thalberg" (1995: 15); and in discussing the drafting of the work, Hays himself notes that "Mr. Thalberg did that." (Association of Motion Picture Producers [AMPP], "Discussion of the Production Code in Its Draft Form." MPPDA Digital Archive, Flinders University Library Special Collections. MPPDA Record 671, Record of Meeting. 8-1985 to 8-2132. Available at <https://mppda.flinders.edu.au/records/671> (last accessed 24 October, 2019), p. 2.
2. Though these films are often understood to be "pre-Code" films—consider their marketing in the *Forbidden Hollywood* DVD collections released by Turner Classic Movies—they were in fact produced under the Code. As Maltby notes, "the Code was enforced from its adoption in 1930" (2003: 62).
3. Thalberg's engagement with writers was not always so positive. Screenwriter Lenore Coffee, for instance, remarked that he had a "love–hate" relationship with writers: "[H]e was himself a frustrated writer. He knew he needed writers, but that very need irritated him. He once said to me with ill-concealed contempt, 'What's all this business of being a writer? Just putting one word after another.' My reply was, 'Pardon me, Mr. Thalberg—putting one *right* word after another'" (Coffee 1973: 99).
4. AMPP, "Discussion of the Production Code in Its Draft Form," 136–137; emphasis in original.
5. Ibid., 77.
6. Ibid., 137–138.
7. Margaret Herrick Library, Academy of Motion Picture Arts and Sciences, Metro-Goldwyn-Mayer Legal Department collection. File 28-f.336.

8. MPPDA (Committee on Public Relations, Sub-Committee on Eliminations). "Original Formulation of the Don'ts and Be Careful." MPPDA Digital Archive, Flinders University Library Special Collections. MPPDA Record 341, Report of Meeting. 3-1232 to 3-1234. Available at <https://mppda.flinders.edu.au/records/341> (last accessed 24 October, 2019).

9. Ibid.

10. Ibid.

11. Memo to Will H. Hays. MPPDA Digital Archive, Flinders University Library Special Collections. MPPDA Record 426, Memo. 4-2395 to 4-2396. Available at <https://mppda. flinders.edu.au/records/426> (last accessed 24 October, 2019). MGM is listed second only to First National.

12. AMPP, "Discussion of the Production Code in Its Draft Form," 2.

13. Ibid., 138.

14. Ibid., 136.

15. Ibid., 138; emphasis in original.

16. Ibid., 137.

17. Ibid., 28.

18. Ibid., 14; emphasis in original.

19. Ibid., 137.

20. Ibid., 138.

21. Margaret Herrick Library, Academy of Motion Picture Arts and Sciences, Motion Picture Association of America, Production Code Administration records. Digital Collection. Available at <http://digitalcollections.oscars.org/cdm/compoundobject/collection/p15759coll30/id/11527/rec/3> (last accessed December 4, 2019).

22. Memo on *War Nurse*. MPPDA Digital Archive, Flinders University Library Special Collections. MPPDA Record 1240, Correspondence. 8-1726 to 8-1745. Available at <https://mppda.flinders.edu.au/records/1240> (last accessed 25 October, 2019). Strikingly (as noted in the Digital Archive editorial notes), this passage is scored out in the draft—suggesting the censor's reluctance to highlight resistance at the executive level.

23. AMPP, "Discussion of the Production Code in Its Draft Form," 78.

24. Ibid., 139–140.

25. Ibid., 83.

26. Ibid., 84.

27. Ibid., 86.

28. Ibid., 82–83.

29. Ibid., 139.

30. Ibid., 89.

31. Ibid., 90.

32. Ibid., 139.

33. Ibid., 139.

34. Ibid., 78–80.

35. In related terms, Lea Jacobs has discussed the "emphasis on the idea of exchange" in fallen-woman films like Warner Bros.' *Baby Face* (dir. Green, 1933), noting how camera movements, musical cues, and *mise en scène* stand in place of explicit representation and thus parallel the narrative's own focus on the exchange of sex for status and or/security (1997: 70).

36. AMPP, "Discussion of the Production Code in Its Draft Form," 139.

37. Ibid., 80.

38. Ibid., 64–65.

39. Ibid., 89.

CHAPTER 6

The Intelligent Producer and the Restructuring of MGM

In December 1932, *Fortune* magazine published what would become one of the most famous articles about Thalberg-era MGM. Appraising the studio's financial and artistic success in the midst of the Depression, the anonymous piece identifies Thalberg as "what Hollywood means by MGM" ("Metro-Goldwyn-Mayer" 1976: 257). Mayer receives fairly lengthy commentary in his role as "a commercial diplomat" in charge of "contacts and contracts" (267); the importance of a more corporate figure like Schenck is considered as relatively circumstantial. Thalberg, however, dominates the article and the studio itself:

> His brain is the camera which photographs dozens of scripts in a week and decides which of them, if any, shall be turned over to MGM's twenty-seven departments to be made into a moving picture. It is also the recording apparatus which converts the squealing friction of 2,200 erratic underlings into the more than normally coherent chatter of an MGM talkie. (258)

It is not only Thalberg and the studio that are connected so symbiotically; as *Fortune* tells its readers, the producer relates just as wholly to his audience. Thalberg can

> divid[e] his brain into two parts. One part, reading a script, turns it into a moving picture; the other part watches this imaginary picture and [. . .] is so much like the conglomerate brain of 50,000,000 other U.S. cinemaddicts [that it] tells Mr. Thalberg [. . .] whether or not the picture is good. (262)

As Jerome Christensen would observe of this article decades later, it suggests that Thalberg "*made* the movie in half of his brain (the studio one) and *distributed* it to the other half (the exhibitor one)" (2012: 26; emphasis added).[1] At once sharing the subjectivities of the studio, cinematic apparatus, and spectator, Thalberg is, as *Fortune* states in another context, "changeable as the chameleon industry in which he labors" (259).[2]

As Vieira has noted, *Fortune* was not the only publication to so laud Thalberg in 1932 (2010: 199). Only a few months earlier, *Screenland*'s Alma Whittaker had identified Thalberg as Hollywood's "Hit-Maker": "His is the guiding mind, the driving force which pervades the production activity of that great organization [. . .] [H]is influence appears in every production" (1932: 19). Instead of an interview with Thalberg, this one-page piece offers a "vivid impression" of his presence and accomplishments—and how, through his filmmaking, these coalesce into an identity almost beyond his control. "He doesn't like to be called 'The Boy Wonder,'" Whittaker admits. "[B]ut we can't help it, that's what he is. That's Irving Thalberg!" (19) Positioned in the magazine amid profiles of performers like Garbo and Ruth Chatterton, this article presents Thalberg as not simply a producer but a star in his own right.

Both the *Fortune* and *Screenland* articles reveal much about the Thalberg image as such and how it had solidified by 1932, a year of artistic and commercial prestige encapsulated by the extraordinary success of *Grand Hotel* (dir. Goulding). An ensemble melodrama based on the 1929 novel by Vicki Baum, the film starred Garbo, John and Lionel Barrymore, Joan Crawford, and Wallace Beery. It was the most profitable movie of the year for the studio and would go on to win the Academy Award for Best Picture (Schatz 1996: 119), as well as cement Thalberg's legend as a producer. The film's significance in Thalberg's canon has only strengthened over time: historian Thomas Schatz, for example, acknowledges *Grand Hotel* as "the archetypal MGM picture during Thalberg's regime [. . .] What [it] is about, finally, is the triumph of style" (1996: 119). In response to Schatz, Robert Spadoni finds that the transcripts of the story conferences between Thalberg and director Edmund Goulding illuminate much about the complexities of studio-era authorship (1995: 363). Commentary of the day also recognized the film's importance for MGM's legacy: *Fortune* cites the work as a quintessential example of the "superlatively well-packaged [MGM production]—both the scenes and personalities which enclose the drama have a high sheen" (269). For Whittaker in *Screenland*, *Grand Hotel* is nothing less than Thalberg's "greatest achievement [. . .] [his] conception from start to finish" (16).

1932 was a landmark year for MGM, a critical and commercial zenith for Thalberg and the studio he had helped found. Yet underlying this phenomenal success were a number of professional tensions and personal challenges, all of which set the scene for a radical change the following year. In 1933, Mayer and Schenck would introduce a restructuring that effectively demoted Thalberg from head of production to unit producer. With this decision, MGM would enter a period of instability and, in Thalberg's view, artistic compromise. But how did these massive shifts come to take place so definitively in the simple passage from one year to the next?

One long-term cause was the troubled relationship between Mayer, Schenck, and Thalberg. Though *Fortune* had commented on the "corporate smoothness, that amity among executives" (268) that ostensibly characterized MGM, the camaraderie between these three figures had in fact deteriorated beyond repair. While it was the associate producers—men like Bern, Rapf, and Lewin—that *Fortune* had identified as "just so many extensions of Irving Thalberg's personality" (262), Mayer and Schenck rejected any suggestion that they, too, were defined in relation to the already legendary head of production. Film historians have noted that Thalberg's fame engendered professional jealousy between him and Mayer; the latter and Schenck also resented Thalberg's increasing financial stake in the corporation, which he negotiated to reflect his defining contributions to the studio (Schatz 1996: 120, 122; Crowther 1957: 194–195; Vieira 2010: 216–217). As Crowther would write in his 1960 biography of Mayer, "The nibbling away at [Mayer's] own prestige that Thalberg cultists did was matched in irritation only by the assaults that Thalberg continued to make on the Mayer pocketbook" (1960: 160).

These financial negotiations emerged, in part, from Thalberg's questioning of his professional life, even in a year as triumphant as 1932. His close friend and colleague Bern died under mysterious and violent circumstances in September, after marrying *Red-Headed Woman* star Jean Harlow earlier that year.[3] Thalberg mourned Bern, whose death introduced a period of depression and "reminded [him] of the time limit that had been placed on his own life," according to Bob Thomas (236). As Thalberg would point out, "What's it all for? Why the hell am I killing myself so Mayer and Schenck can get rich and fat?" (qtd. in Thomas 236). Citing fears surrounding his health and the stress of his role at the studio, Thalberg asked Mayer and Schenck for a year's leave; the former saw this as a negotiating tactic. "I believe the boy is getting spoiled," Mayer suggested. "People are telling him how good he is. I believe it is turning his head a little" (qtd. in Crowther 1957: 193). Regardless of Thalberg's intent, Schenck and Mayer ensured his increasingly reluctant presence at the studio by offering him up to 100,000 shares in Loew's itself (Schatz 1996: 122).

The most critical turning point, however, occurred at the end of the year. A few days after the studio Christmas party in 1932, Thalberg suffered a heart attack from which he took over a month to recover. The severity of this event provided Mayer and Schenck with a pretext for neutralizing the authority that Thalberg held over the studio. Early in 1933, Mayer invited son-in-law David O. Selznick to join MGM as a producer—free from Thalberg's supervision and with "first option" on MGM's formidable resources

(Vieira 2010: 225; Schatz 1996: 163). By the spring, while Thalberg and Shearer were taking a recuperative trip to Europe, Mayer and Schenck carried out a full restructuring of the studio (Vieira 2010: 220–225, 236). Jettisoning the role of head of production, they invited Thalberg to return to the studio in a new—diminished—capacity: unit producer of six prestige pictures a year (Vieira 2010: 239; Crowther 1960: 181). As Crowther relates, Schenck advised Thalberg that beyond those six movies, "he was not to bother himself at all with the rest of the films being made" (181).

Since the merger in 1924, Thalberg's executive oversight and theories of production had helped establish MGM's artistic identity. He had guided the studio through the rise of the talkies and the formalization of the Production Code; he had developed the careers of a host of stars and refined the principles of epic filmmaking. For Thalberg, then, to be told "not to bother himself" with any more than six pictures a year would have seemed both a personal affront and professional insult. Mayer attempted to couch the decisions in solicitous terms; for example, he explained that he hired Selznick "to spare Irving, who is so dear to me" (qtd. in Vieira 2010: 226). And in the telegram informing Thalberg of his demotion, Mayer again adopted a beneficent tone: "Am doing this for you" (qtd. in Vieira 2010: 236). In August 1933, still another telegram would tell another story—this time, signed by the New York and New Jersey exhibitors of MGM's films. They described themselves as "incensed because Louis Mayer [is] taking full credit for product and placing you same status as Selznick." The telegram concluded, "Entire industry for you."[4]

The drama of the restructuring remains a vexed chapter in MGM's history, with personal betrayals and affirmations of professional solidarity alike. But the following will argue that Thalberg found a sense of creative purpose by exploring new concepts of filmmaking to accommodate the post-restructuring conditions in which he found himself. This took place in both private and public contexts: letters to Schenck and a November 1933 article with Hugh Weir for the *Saturday Evening Post* entitled "Why Motion Pictures Cost So Much." The foundations of his established theories remain evident in these pieces—the importance of providing entertainment value for the public, the necessity of producing on a great scale, and the need for oblique, creative casting. What emerges in these 1933 works, though, is a reimagining of these familiar themes with conceptual boldness. Thalberg calls for experimentation and risk-taking in financial and artistic terms; he analyses the movie-going experience as an oneiric escape, a way of transcending everyday life; and perhaps most controversially, he argues both *for* an industry that makes fewer—and better—films each year and *against* the rushed manufacturing of mediocre pictures. Undoubtedly, this theoretical turn provided a means through which Thalberg could critique the production practices of a reshaped MGM; but it also represented a new phase in his professional identity. No longer the head of production, Thalberg could—with varying degrees of objective analysis and personal commentary—adopt a reflective view of the studio and the theoretical perspectives he had established.

The process was a fraught one, however, as seen most intimately in the letters to Schenck. In Vieira's discussion of the first of these, dated February 1933, he points out that Schenck and Mayer had put Thalberg in the absurd position of "defend[ing] himself" and his "record" of achievements (2010: 229). Thalberg's tone is, indeed, defensive at points; but the very rationalization of his approach to filmmaking allowed, in turn, for a reaffirmation of the concepts that had made it—and MGM—so successful. For instance, Thalberg declaims his ethos of making "great, not indifferent pictures" (qtd. in Vieira 2010: 228): "The picture business can only exist on the basis of real entertainment, glamour, good taste, and stars" (228). These are statements which Thalberg would reprise later that year, following his July return to the studio (Schatz 1996: 164). His approach, however, had shifted from diplomatic bewilderment to outright frustration. As he wrote to Schenck in December, "Our standards have slipped [. . .] tremendously. The pictures that I see [. . .] are juvenile, immature, uninspired, and lacking that finish that characterized our product for so many years" (qtd. in Crowther 1960: 183). Also troubling to Thalberg was the decline of his relationship with Mayer and Schenck. As he wrote in December,

> I am not talking now as a heavily interested partner in the enterprise because my voice, as such, has been too frequently overruled [. . .] nor am I offering it as the seasoned opinion of an experienced showman whose policies have brought millions of profit [. . .] and whose advice is eagerly sought after by every company but the one with which he is connected. I am offering it as the opinion of a producer employed by the company—a producer of some merit who is sincerely trying to make some good pictures. (Qtd. in Crowther 184)

Thalberg did not conceal his reservations from the wider public. A month earlier, he had posed these same questions around MGM's place in the industry and shifting production standards, as well as his own process as a producer, in "Why Motion Pictures Cost So Much." On one level, this article—co-written with Hugh Weir, "who had polished [Thalberg's] prose" (Vieira 2010: 242)—assesses the financial state of the film industry and the public's response to rising ticket prices. Yet these concerns provided a pretext for Thalberg's process of theoretical affirmation at a time of professional reinvention; the article is a public declaration of the filmmaking ethos that he was privately defending. Consider, for example, how in the following passage Thalberg translates the exasperation of his letters to Schenck into more objective observations:

> A bad picture, or even a fairly good picture which is not so good as it should be, may do the company which puts it out many times as much harm as the cost of the picture itself. So, knowing all this, usually from bitter experience, the intelligent producer will go on experimenting—which, in pictures, means going on spending—until he believes in his own mind that he has made the best possible product. (1933: 10)

Here, the "juvenile, immature, uninspired" pictures produced by MGM read as a collective "bad picture, or even a fairly good picture which is not so good as it should be"—Thalberg thus damning with faint praise the mediocrity of recent releases. Most strikingly, though, the "seasoned [and] experienced showman," "heavily interested partner," and "producer employed by the company" of Thalberg's letter coalesces, transforms, into the portrait of "an intelligent producer."

Though Thalberg only uses the term once, the figure of the "intelligent producer" as such effectively personifies his set of propositions for an aesthetically minded industry responsive to the demands of the public. In this way, the concept signals a departure from the Boy Wonder double that had shadowed Thalberg since his earliest days in Hollywood. The Boy Wonder represented a public idea(l) of Thalberg in a pre-1933 MGM—an ideal constructed by publicity material and industry rhetoric. By contrast, the intelligent producer is a wholly adult and very personal figure: an embodiment of creative values and a third-person projection of Thalberg's interiorized professional identity. He emerges here as not simply the hit-maker of popular culture, but a scholar of his profession; an intelligent producer, that is, whose conceptual understanding of filmmaking merges with the ability to execute those abstract ideas.

This chapter will, accordingly, trace Thalberg's response as an intelligent producer to the conditions of MGM's restructuring, bringing together the public discourse of his "Why Motion Pictures Cost So Much" and the more personal statements of principle expressed in his letters to Schenck. To paraphrase the *Fortune* article, Mayer and Schenck were trying to change "what Hollywood means by MGM" (257); Thalberg, accordingly, sought to define himself by reflecting on the past and exploring the future of theories that had, and would, help shape his professional identity. This conceptual arc was not only chronicled in the written materials, but also took form in three emblematic films of the period: *Strange Interlude* (dir. Leonard, 1932) offered an abstract counterpoint to the melodrama of *Grand Hotel*, in this way affirming Thalberg's belief that "the intelligent producer will go on experimenting"; *The Barretts of Wimpole Street* (dir. Franklin, 1934) provided a context within which to consider Thalberg's discussion of the "dream world" of cinema (Thalberg 1933: 85); and *The Merry Widow* (dir. Lubitsch, 1934) allegorically explored what Thalberg called the "background of glamour and interest that [must be] built up in the star" (qtd. in Vieira 2010: 227) in order to protect their career and, moreover, the studio's reputation.

In "Why Motion Pictures Cost So Much," Thalberg notes that the intelligent producer "must not only make the customers like the picture they see but he must make them want to see more pictures produced under the same name and the same trade-mark" (10). His conceptual signature, as it were, had always been apparent in MGM's films. Monikers such as Hit-Maker and Boy Wonder indicate that his style—or rather the box-office appeal of that style— was nearly over-determined. But that had been the signature of Thalberg as head of production. What would this new role as unit producer, indeed intelligent producer, reveal? He was no longer responsible for the output of the studio; he did not need "to bother himself at all" with anything except for his own six films. What remained of Thalberg's time as head of production, however, were his theoretical convictions—and ambitions. Each ensured that his aesthetic would endure.

"THE INTELLIGENT PRODUCER WILL GO ON EXPERIMENTING"

In his 1933 article, Thalberg explicitly brings together issues of experimentation and expenditure. As quoted earlier, he defined the intelligent producer as one who "will go on experimenting—which, in pictures, means going on spending [on production costs] until he believes in his own mind that he has made the best possible product" (10). Such phrasing recalls Thalberg's statements at the 1930 meeting with the AMPP, in which he conceived of making controversial films as "engaging [. . .] in speculation";[5] even terms like entertainment value and audience values have a fiscal connotation. For Thalberg, financial risk had always been a way of thinking through—or indeed executing—his aesthetic principles and conceptual ambition; and it was the latter that took precedence in his experimentation with *Strange Interlude* in 1932.

Thalberg reflected on what Fitzgerald would later call the "whole equation" of filmmaking:

[N]obody has ever been able to say definitely whether picture making is really a business or an art. Personally, I think it is both.

It is a business in the sense that it must bring in money at the box office, but it is an art in that it involves, on its devotees, the inexorable demands of creative expression. In short, it is a creative business, dependent, as almost no other business is, on the emotional reaction of its customers. (1933: 11)

Since the founding of MGM in 1924, Thalberg had gauged these emotional reactions to technological advancements, a variety of genres and provocative subjects, and a range of performers. He had developed a theoretical approach to production that allowed for the versatility of "creative expression" while maintaining an elemental focus on crafting the most impactful and, ultimately, entertaining motion pictures. In another context, Samuel Marx recalled that Thalberg succinctly defined "box office" as "a combination of a star and a title that the public wants to see" (qtd. in Marx 1975: 217). What Thalberg under-played here, however, were the investments both conceptual and financial that went into producing that success.

In Thalberg's pursuit of critical and commercial excellence, he under-stood that spending money on a film would ultimately help it make money: "Look [. . .] a successful picture may take in ten million dollars at the box office. An unsuccessful one may take a million. If the difference is fifty or a hundred thousand dollars in production" ("Metro-Goldwyn-Mayer" 1976: 262). Financial expansiveness, however, represented only one facet of that "creative business" to which Thalberg referred above; it was not an end in itself, but rather the means through which abstract notions of story and char-acter could find their fullest material expression. As Thalberg notes in the article, he established this approach as early as 1925 with the costly making of *Ben-Hur*—referring to it as "so old now that I can discuss it without fear of seeming to be seeking publicity for it" (83). This invocation of *Ben-Hur* as a defining success explicitly harkens back to the origin story of Thalberg's MGM. It was the point at which he began to define himself as an "intelligent producer," in his terms, or what popular culture would perceive as "That Perfect Boss" (Leslie 1926) and, in 1932, "The Hitmaker." He recalled,

A poor picturization of Ben Hur [*sic*] would have cost us in prestige far more than the half million dollars' worth of junked film. The good picturization, which we did finally make, not only earned back the huge sum of money it cost but it built up a goodwill the value of which it is almost impossible to estimate. (83)

Very simply, the money put into the film for retakes and set design paid off at the box office and, more importantly, in industry recognition ("prestige"). As Thal-berg relates, fiscal timidity—releasing a mediocre film out of fear of "junk[ing]" an existing investment—would have translated into poor entertainment value, which in turn would have damaged the studio's reputation. Ultimately, MGM needed to experiment with the possibilities of rescuing that troubled film.

Years later, the transcripts of the *Grand Hotel* story conferences would reveal that for Thalberg, money continued to be no object in the creation of the artistic product. He observed in one instance, "It's just as important to see that [money is] spent as to see that it isn't" (qtd. in Schatz 1996: 116). This sense of largesse as an aesthetic, rather than economic, principle came into play through the sheer number of stars in *Grand Hotel*. The cast endures as the *ne plus ultra* example of what *Fortune* called Thalberg's "galactic arrangement[s] whereby two or more 'stars' appear in one film" (269). Its unquestionable success validated this strategy—but as Thalberg reminds his readers in "Why Motion Pictures Cost So Much," "If picture making were as easy as that, we'd be making Grand Hotels [*sic*] every week in the year" (85).

But it was not Thalberg's intention to make *Grand Hotels* repeatedly. He wanted, in a manner that anticipates his 1933 article, to "go on experimenting" (10): not only with the development of a given film, but with his entire *oeuvre*. Certainly *Strange Interlude*, released in the summer of 1932, was not another *Grand Hotel*. An adaptation of Eugene O'Neill's 1928 play, *Strange Interlude* followed a core cast of characters from youth to old age in what Gavin Lambert has termed "the first attempt in Hollywood to come to terms with Freudian material" (1990: 166). The film explores the love triangle between troubled Nina Leeds (Shearer), her psychiatrist and lover Ned Darrell (Clark Gable), and her husband Sam Evans (Alexander Kirkland). Also infatuated with Nina is her long-time family friend, Charlie Marsden (Ralph Morgan). The "galactic arrangement" of performers was fairly modest: Shearer and Gable, co-starring again after *A Free Soul*, effectively dominate the film's cast of supporting players, though future stars Robert Young and Maureen O'Sullivan feature in small roles.

By Marx's account, *Strange Interlude* "had failed" (1975: 197). Marginally less expensive than *Grand Hotel*—a budget of $654,000 compared to $700,000—the film received no Oscars and made a profit of only $90,000 (260–261). It is, however, a definitive Thalberg production of the time, uniting what *Fortune* called his characteristic "fine eye for contour and polish" (270) with radical challenges to conventions of sound and spectatorship. As the article noted, the "sophisticated stuff" of the film suggested an appeal to Loew's audiences in "urban centers," while also "[giving] the hinterlands the idea that sex didn't need to be represented in terms of Marlene Dietrich's garters" (270).

However patronizing, this comment speaks to the film's experiments with how to represent sexual desire on the screen. Where the Production Code attempted to regulate the moral terms of a given film, and the Studio Relations Committee monitored explicit imagery and dialogue, the psychological portraiture of *Strange Interlude* revealed characters' *implicit* motivations. Throughout O'Neill's original play, the characters declaim their thoughts about a given situation through soliloquies delivered to the audience; in the film, voice-over monologues from each character's perspective accompany the scenes and signal the juxtaposition between superficial interaction and authentic feeling. This continually shifting hierarchy between the visual and aural registers—with the latter itself split across interpersonal dialogue and the voice-overs—demands a spectatorship attentive to the nuances of each verbal and facial expression. Such a relay creates still another love story in the film: one between the characters and the viewer who becomes both interpreter and confidant.

Photoplay lauded *Strange Interlude* for this innovation, declaring, "From a technical standpoint—the most daring picture ever produced [. . .] The utterance of unspoken thoughts makes the film both novel and interesting" ("Brief Reviews" 1932: 129). In the September issue of the magazine, MGM marketed the film as "A New and Amazing Development in Talking Pictures! *For the first time, you hear the hidden, unspoken thoughts of people.*"[6] Where *Grand Hotel* constructs a spectacle of exteriority—each of the characters playing out their respective and interrelated dramas; the hotel functioning as a liminal space at a remove from the personal and domestic; even the title credits introducing the stars themselves with an accompanying close-up—*Strange Interlude* explores an interior, psychological territory. As Lambert has noted, "no one except Thalberg would have considered producing" such complex source material on the screen (1990: 166).

Throughout the film, there are clear traces of the theoretical questions that had guided Thalberg's work at MGM up to this juncture. Casting Gable as a psychiatrist represents an instance of oblique casting, given his early association with a more rugged or aggressive masculinity; the sensational nature of the story, dealing with adultery and madness, challenged the dictates of the Production Code; and the innovative use of voice-overs endures as a broadening of that already "broadened field" (qtd. in Manners 1929: 94) that Thalberg identified in the rise of the talkies. There is, of course, one great sequence—a narrative turning point that functions as a marker by which to gauge the dramatic scale of the film as a whole.

Following her marriage to Sam, Nina has an affair with Ned both out of physical attraction and a darker motivation: Sam's mother has warned Nina that madness runs in his family; and though a child would ensure his happiness, there would nonetheless be a risk of perpetuating the tragic tendency. With her husband remaining totally ignorant, Nina bears Ned's child and raises him as hers and Sam's. After the baby's birth, Ned visits the couple—only to find Charlie, ever jealous of and devoted to Nina, in the house as well. The sequence captures the film's overarching fluidity between conventions of high romance—recalling Loos's contention that "to Irving Thalberg every film had to be a love story" (36)—and more experimental modes of representation.

It begins with an extended exchange between Ned and Nina, in which the former lovers stand on a balcony and debate the future of their affair. Filmed with just three cuts and entirely in two-shot with an emphasis on the performers' profiles, the intimacy of the compositions recalls the Garbo–Barrymore love scenes in *Grand Hotel*. Shadows envelop the frame, broken by the intermittent flashing from a nearby lighthouse and the lighted room in the background. There are no voice-overs or extra-diegetic music; only the sound of waves and the charged dialogue. A quintessentially "high sheen" ("Metro-Goldwyn-Mayer" 1976: 269), recalling the terms set out in *Fortune*, envelops the scene and effectively suspends the more challenging dramatic discourse of the film. As much about the beauty of the stars as the troubles of the characters, this is a romantic interlude within *Strange Interlude*.

The sound of Sam returning to the house shatters this idyll, and Ned rushes inside to tell him about the affair. Once within the domestic space, the interior monologues begin again: Ned thinks through his unwillingness to hurt Sam, and so speaks only pleasantries to his old friend; Nina, standing behind and above the two men in a classic triangle composition, expresses her relief: "There, that's settled for all time." The closing shots of the sequence, in which Nina gathers her husband and admirers around her, underscore its import for the remainder of the film. As she stands alone in medium shot, Nina appraises her control over the situation in voice-over: "My three men. Their life is my life [. . .] That makes it perfect." The next shot captures a low-angle ensemble portrait of Nina standing tall in the center of the frame, with Sam, Charlie, and Ned seated around her deferentially and (except for Sam) resignedly. Far from the sensuality and conflicted romance of the scene between Ned and Nina, in which the two shared the frame at all times, the expressionist qualities of the shot illustrate the narcissistic satisfaction of Nina's voice-over (see Figure 6.1). To return to *Fortune*'s comments on the film, the scene demonstrates that "sex didn't need to be represented in terms of Marlene Dietrich's garters" (270)—it could, instead, be considered in terms of a far more troubling *ménage* constructed out of one character's drive for validation.

This is the last sequence in which the characters are young, so to speak; in the next scene, the ensemble has moved well into middle age. By the end of the film, following Sam's passing, an elderly Nina and Ned finally part ways. She turns to the ubiquitous Charlie, and he speaks the last lines aloud as he embraces her: "God bless 'dear old Charlie,' who passed beyond desire [and] has all the luck at last." With this assertion of platonic neutrality, the film concludes with a "passing beyond desire" into a time–space that is neither past nor present, and certainly not wholly material. Dressed in a white wig and with gentle lines to signify old age, Shearer-as-Nina muses, "I feel as if I were a girl again, as if you were my father and the Charlie of those days made into one." Just as in the earlier love scene between Nina and Ned,

Figure 6.1 Nina's three men.

this exchange takes place outside and without voice-over monologues. Displaced from that subjective commentary, the emotional valence of the scene is conveyed through tropes like falling autumn leaves, withering flower petals, and a string score. Uncannily, these conventional markers of pathos come together to function as a final destabilizing element—now it is the absence of the inner voices, rather than their presence, that unsettles the viewer. For this absence signals not just the end of the film, but also the imminent death of the characters.

In contrast to the scope of *Grand Hotel*, which explores a highly exteriorized experience within a condensed time frame, *Strange Interlude* traces the development of the characters' subjectivities across entire lifetimes. Certainly both films share a preoccupation with mortality: in *Grand Hotel*, John Barrymore's Baron dies violently and Lionel Barrymore as Kringelein suffers from a terminal illness; and in *Strange Interlude*, Nina's obsession with controlling the men in her life derives from the death of her first love. The former, however, ends with an exaltation of the ever-renewing course of desire—Kringelein's remaining days will be spent with the lovely young stenographer Flaemmchen (Joan Crawford); the Baron's death will provide another reason for the narcissistic Grusinskaya (Garbo) to revel in her melancholy; and after they depart, a car arrives at the hotel with a new cast of characters and hints of unfolding dramas. *Grand Hotel* concludes, that is, with the hope of a future; by contrast, *Strange Interlude*'s world "beyond desire" folds in upon itself.

Given the complexity of Thalberg's *oeuvre*, it is not necessary to argue for one ending—or indeed one film—to stand as more or less quintessential to his aesthetic. For all of *Grand Hotel*'s now legendary status in MGM's history, it coexists with the more obscure *Strange Interlude* as a Janus-faced feature of Thalberg's final year as head of production. Each "hold[s] the mirror up to life" (Thalberg 1933: 85), to borrow one of Thalberg's statements about cinema, but their reflections effectively look in different directions. One affirms the persistence of the human drama, with a parade of characters cycling into the hotel-as-microcosm through a literally revolving door; the other compels intimacy between viewer and character even as it highlights the ambiguity of that closeness, excluding the audience with a final zoom-out. One film is kinetic and public, the other contemplative and private—but the traces of both *Grand Hotel* and *Strange Interlude* would be seen in Thalberg's 1934 productions.

THE DREAM WORLD OF WIMPOLE STREET

Time functions in a unique way in Thalberg's "Why Motion Pictures Cost So Much." Unlike his lecture at the University of Southern California, which focused on "currency" in filmmaking and technology, or his statements regarding the development of the Production Code, which were by necessity concerned with the future of regulation in the industry, the *Saturday Evening Post* piece positions Thalberg as simultaneously a commentator on Hollywood's past, an oracle of its future, and an expert in present conditions of filmmaking; the article both reflects (on) the past and offers projections of the future.

This sense of oversight—and foresight—would be complemented by Thalberg's more abstract imagery in the piece; namely, his discussion of a cinematic dream world. In context, this passage refers to the specific impact of the performer, but its broader implications relate to the transformative capacities of the medium itself:

> [The actor], more than the author, more even than the director, must hold the mirror up to life. By his ability to convey the author's and the director's ideas to the screen and to the people out front, he must transport his audience into a dream world. (1933: 85)

In earlier concepts like entertainment and audience values, Thalberg had explored the various ways through which the filmmaker could maximize a picture's potential for success. Such value added, as it were, would reap benefits both critically and commercially. What is fascinating in the above passage, however, is Thalberg's more holistic view of the cinematic experience. Where in the General Principles he had described film as "one vast reflection of every image in the stream of contemporary life [. . .] as contemporary as a newspaper or a comic strip,"[7] here he conceives of a poetic realm for the movie-going public. The themes and characters might be connected to "contemporary life," but the experience of spectatorship itself was suspended from such circumstances. For Thalberg in 1933, cinema undoes prosaic limitations in an immersive and intimate fashion: "hold[ing] the mirror up to life" only to dissolve the distinction between the reality of the seats "out front" and the ideality of the screen up there.

Vieira relates this passage and its focus on the oneiric to Thalberg's extensive "time in darkened projection rooms and [. . .] recent [. . .] anesthetizat[ion]" following his health problems (2010: 242–243), thus crafting a compelling link between his personal life and professional perspective. Along these biographical lines, it is also clear that the notion of a liberating cinematic experience, a dream world in itself, would have been particularly meaningful to Thalberg in his new, relatively restricted working conditions. Just as *Strange Interlude* highlighted Thalberg's experimental aesthetic at the height of his success, so too does *The Barretts of Wimpole Street* reveal much about his concern with triumph over circumstance following the restructuring.

By the time he wrote the *Saturday Evening Post* article, Thalberg's daily life at the studio had changed considerably. As Marx recalled, "[S]uddenly, [Mayer] had absolute power over a vast organization" (1975: 204). This shift in hierarchy was further manifested through the introduction of new creative producers. In January 1933, Walter Wanger moved from Columbia Pictures to MGM following negotiations with Mayer (of which Thalberg was admittedly aware) (Schatz 1996: 162). According to Wanger, Mayer had drawn him to MGM with the request to "build up the biggest collection of talent so that this studio can't fail" (qtd. in Bernstein 1994: 82). It was, however, the presence of Selznick and his access to stars, stories, and directors that entirely unsettled Thalberg. As Marx described it, Selznick and Thalberg's personal and professional amity endured—but this did not prevent the latter from "running into obstacles he had never known before. He had to contend with Selznick's extensive use of the MGM stars. The other producers on the lot were also his competitors" (216, 220). By December, Thalberg found the situation nearly intolerable. In his letter to Schenck that month, Thalberg wrote,

> The difficulties I encounter, as a producer, are specifically an inability to acquire talent and an inability to make that talent give its best efforts. The first is due to the fact that unless I wish to exercise the rights under my contract I cannot get a first-class person employed on our lot. (Qtd. in Crowther 1960: 184)

He goes on to cite his challenges in keeping quality writers on his projects, noting that he is "forced to work with and give opportunities to the continuously-availables and out-of-work writers that I can pick up" (185). The "first-class" colleagues were, by contrast, working with Selznick and Wanger (184).

Vieira notes that Thalberg had resisted the studio's new "dual goals of *more* production and *less* supervision" (2010: 228; emphasis added) as early as February 1933; as he wrote to Schenck, "Someone must do the job I have done in the past [. . .] [T]he successful lots are those dominated by a single idea" (qtd. in Vieira 229). Which is to say, a single aesthetic vision—Thalberg's own. The hiring of Selznick and Wanger had diluted this single idea, not only introducing a shift in the studio's leadership but effectively splitting the resources on the lot between creative producers. Equally problematic was the elevation of associates who had formerly reported to Thalberg. The Thalberg Men, who had once considered him a mentor and figure of authority, had shifted their allegiance. Crowther explained the change in terms of a royal court, through which Mayer functioned as "a rajah" overseeing "a peerage of producers, a classification of dukes on a level above directors" (1960: 182). Where in the "old regime" (182) Mayer and Thalberg had co-ruled MGM, the latter now found himself effectively deposed. Symbolic of this new era was the practice of claiming producing credits on the screen. This began with Selznick and *Night Flight* (dir. Brown, 1933); as Marx notes, MGM producers began to announce their status thereafter, with the exception of Thalberg (1975: 209).

For all of these challenges, they nonetheless provided Thalberg with the opportunity to put his theory of entertainment value over "indifferent pictures" (qtd. in Vieira 2010: 228) into action. In "Why Motion Pictures Cost So Much," Thalberg recast his difficulties as part of a broader view on producing fewer and better films, thus making a virtue out of what was supposed to be a restriction: that is, the small number of pictures under his purview. Thalberg would explain this process of meaningful film production to the moviegoing public, transposing personal frustrations regarding mediocre personnel and limited resources to a comprehensive vision of what filmmaking could be. Early in the article, Thalberg acknowledges both the crisis of the Depression and the perception of Hollywood as "extravagant" (10, 11), thus setting the scene for his proposed intervention. In evoking an ideal industry that crafted only quality productions for which viewers would be glad to buy tickets, Thalberg predicted,

> By eliminating the making of many pictures, we will increase the attendance of the pictures that are produced; and by decreasing the poor pictures that are made, we will capture a vast new audience of potentially regular picture goers who have been disappointed too frequently to make picture going a habit [. . .]
>
> By decreasing the number of pictures, we will eliminate at once the incapable player, the incapable writer and the incapable director, and concentrate in a single picture the best talent necessary to the proper development of each story.

By not restricting the time, we will permit each flaw to be cor-
rected until the result is genuinely fine, and frequently inspirational,
entertainment. (84)

"Genuinely fine," "frequently inspirational"—such phrases could describe
equally well the most effective cinematic dream worlds. What the above
indicates, however, was that Thalberg had lost confidence in his colleagues'
production methods and, therefore, their ability to craft that transporting
experience for the viewer. Feeling disenfranchised from MGM itself, Thalberg
here sought a more sympathetic perspective in the *Saturday Evening Post* read-
ership—that is, in his very audiences. He appeals to the logic of the spectator
with whom he has consistently shared such a sensitive rapport; and in so doing,
Thalberg expands upon the dialogical engagement that had characterized his
approach to the talkies in the USC lecture and to the Production Code in the
General Principles. In direct address to the public, Thalberg effectively confers
with them at still another point of redefinition.

In his early works as a unit producer, Thalberg pursued "genuinely fine"
(1933: 84) talent and projects (his troubles with finding writers notwithstanding). He personally produced five films, to varying degrees of success. *Outcast
Lady* (dir. Leonard, 1934) starred Constance Bennett and was an adaptation
of Michael Arlen's 1924 novel *The Green Hat*—first adapted by Thalberg for
Garbo in *A Woman of Affairs* (dir. Brown, 1928). Broadway star Helen Hayes
played the lead in the adaptation of the J. M. Barrie play *What Every Woman
Knows* (dir. La Cava, 1934), and Lubitsch would direct Jeannette MacDonald
and Maurice Chevalier in *The Merry Widow*. Shearer also starred in films for
her husband—the only two, in fact, that made money at the box office. *Riptide*
(dir. Goulding, 1934) was a sophisticated comedy and a modest success, offering its own take on the dialogue between public reputation and personal affairs.
(It also featured Thalberg's name in print advertisements [Vieira 2010: 248].)
The Barretts of Wimpole Street, however, represented a more significant project. Based on a Rudolph Besier play, the film follows the courtship of Elizabeth
Barrett (Shearer) and Robert Browning (Fredric March). An invalid confined
to her suite of rooms in the family home, which is itself dominated by tyrannical patriarch Edward Barrett (Charles Laughton), Elizabeth publishes poetry
and carries on an epistolary relationship with Robert. The latter's admiration
for Elizabeth's poetry leads him to declare his love in person—which ultimately triggers the revelation of her father's incestuous attachment.[8]

Where it would be understandable to view the film exclusively in terms of
its perverse love triangle, *The Barretts of Wimpole Street* and its poet protagonists also enabled a diegetic meditation on the construction of dream worlds in
the terms established by Thalberg. The film "holds the mirror up to" historical
lives: Browning and Barrett are the main characters, though they exist on the

screen as "Elizabeth" and "Robert"—leads in a romantic drama. Indeed, it is Elizabeth and Robert who fall in love with each other through their respective works of art; that is, the dream worlds of their poems. Thinking of the role of the performer him/herself in Thalberg's concept, Elizabeth-as-poet and Shearer-as-actor share the role of artist and mediator between reality and imagination. Appropriately enough, much of the film revolves around Elizabeth/ Shearer—not simply in the arc of the story, but in its very landscape. For as this film illuminates, the evocation of the cinematic dream world is both spatially and emotionally charged: requiring the synthesis of diegetic world on the screen and the "people out front" to be "transport[ing]" in its affect.

Rather than iterate commonplace binaries of public/exterior and private/ interior, the film sets up a world that integrates these registers to sometimes uncanny effect. Anticipating William Wyler's *The Heiress* (1949), director Sidney Franklin uses deep space to craft a domestic labyrinth. Public rooms on the ground floor feature sweeping archways and doorframes hinting at more chambers beyond; massive windows and floor-to-ceiling drapes offer glimpses of the outside world. Though it makes sense to associate this interior space with the incestuous patriarch, the outside world bears its own sense of insulation. The residential square is as ordered as the mansion, and even in the scenes where Elizabeth and Robert carry out their courtship outside of the home, they meet in manicured parks and adjoining greenhouses.

Certainly the dramatic terrain owes much to the demands of filming on a studio backlot; but it also reveals how this family drama, like the cinematic dream world itself, plays out on a continuum between personal and shared experience. Elizabeth's sitting room in the family home serves as a particularly intense focal point for this exchange. The *mise en scène* crafts an exaggerated verticality within the room, introducing a Carrollian effect to this historical drama: there is a vast door through which family members and doctors come and go, and beyond which stairs head both up and down; there are bookcases, a wardrobe, and ornate molding on the walls; candlesticks, book spines, and lamps; floor-to-ceiling windows through which the seasons change; and even the visitors themselves, who often stand tall. Each of these elements serves to highlight the horizontality of Elizabeth's form as she lies prone on the sofa. Confined to her chaise longue for roughly the first half of the film, Elizabeth exists as an axis around which the family affairs revolve. Where Edward dominates the house proper, Elizabeth occupies what is effectively the heart of the home; her brothers and sisters congregate here, engaging with Elizabeth as a maternal presence.

Robert's first visit to this room, however, introduces a frisson of romantic attraction to a space long defined in terms of Elizabeth's confinement. He is, as Edward later calls him, "an outsider" to the home, but he ingratiates himself into its premises with ease. Tall and handsome, he aligns with the longitudinal dimensions of the room; yet as the scene progresses, he joins Elizabeth on the chaise and inclines towards her—their occupation of the same plane thus capturing their growing intimacy. Robert immediately recognizes the space as one belonging to his *own* "imagination," or dream (world) of her: "You may think, Miss Barrett, that this is the first time I've been here, but you're quite wrong [. . .] I've seen this room more times than I can remember."

Connected to this recognition of Elizabeth's personal space is a commensurate recognition of her very identity, made external through her published writing. Elizabeth's poems have, as he describes it, revealed her "hopelessly, utterly, entirely"; so much so that Elizabeth acknowledges, "I'm afraid it will be quite useless, my ever trying to play-act with you [. . .] I shall always have to be just myself." The incorporation of long takes, especially at the points where Robert and Elizabeth share the sofa in medium-long shot, emphasises the intensity of their attraction. Yet even as they inhabit the foreground of these shots, the window in the background—placed between the couple—continually draws the eye. At first, the sight of snow falling upon the tree branches offers a reminder of the reality outside of that dream world. The fact that the window is out of focus, however, only sharpens the sensations between the two in their shared inner life: in sitting so close and holding her hands, Robert brings Elizabeth what she calls "a series of electric shocks." It is, then, the dream world that is real.

Equally seductive, though, is Robert's ease in negotiating personal and public space, moving fluidly from Elizabeth's sitting room to the crowded square below. This awakens Elizabeth's own desire to bridge those dimensions; the desire, that is, to expand the parameters of her physical and emotional experience. When Robert leaves, she draws herself onto her feet for the first time in the film to watch him through the window. The next sequence begins in the spring, with a reprise of this image. Elizabeth has learned to walk with relative ease, and she goes downstairs on her own to meet with a delighted Robert—only to encounter her father's disapproval and insistence that she return to her sitting room. What follows is a highly expressionist, near-gothic image: standing at the foot of the stairs, Elizabeth appears miniscule as she looks up to her room (see Figure 6.2). Her form is framed deep in the background and in the middle of the shot through the bannister of the staircase, which itself is steeped in shadows in the foreground. Indeed, the darkness of the angles between balusters and stairs—the former vertical, the latter horizontal—present an ominous extension of the geometry of the sitting room. Taking the film's overarching emphasis on deep space to an extreme, the shot captures, and lingers on, more than Elizabeth's worry over not making it up the stairs on her own. It frames her fear that she will be trapped in the room to which those stairs lead.

Figure 6.2 Elizabeth and the stairs.

Lambert has described this scene as one of the work's "moments of vir-
tuoso movie acting, almost silent, relying on purely visual effects" (1990: 210).
Certainly it conveys the uncanny liminality of Elizabeth's situation. Hesitat-
ing on the steps, with (as seen in the previous shots) both Robert and Edward
watching her, Elizabeth is neither totally insulated as the latter would wish
nor free to come and go as the former. Both men exist within parameters that
they themselves have drawn clearly—the father who literally closes the curtain over Elizabeth's picture window, for example, or the lover who has total
liberty. Read within the Victorian context, this shot presents Elizabeth as an
everywoman caught within a patriarchal bind; torn, that is, between the role
of daughter and sweetheart. But Elizabeth is also a poet, an artist who longs to
expand the horizons of her dream world of inner subjectivity and outer artistry
to include travel, love. The crisis here is not simply that Elizabeth must divide
her allegiance between Robert and Edward Barrett; it is that she may endure
an existential paralysis as crippling as her physical illness. Most unsettling of
all is the denouement of the scene, in which Edward sweeps Elizabeth up and
carries her to her room.

Underscoring the film's—and Thalberg's—thematic concern with the possibility of overcoming limitations, Elizabeth's story does end happily. The final
scenes highlight Elizabeth's fluency of motion as she slips out of the house to
elope with Robert, moving swiftly up and down the stairs that had challenged
her. Elizabeth ultimately transports herself into this proverbial happy ending,
standing as the diegetic counterpart to Shearer-the-actor, who, returning to
Thalberg's theory, "must transport [the] audience" (85) into the dream world
of the film. In a style different from Garbo, for example, whose very passivity

drew audiences *to* her, Shearer suggested both the agency and the commitment to bring the spectator *with* her—whether she was "transport[ing] [her] audience" into the experimentalism of *Strange Interlude* or the historical melodrama of *Barretts*. In this post-restructuring period, Shearer emerged as an intelligent star for Thalberg's intelligent producer.

Beginning with *Ben Hur*—or even as far back as Universal's *Hunchback of Notre Dame*—Thalberg had explored questions of audience immersion and visual and dramatic impact. But at this point of effective displacement from the MGM he had known, Thalberg reflected upon the emotional and psychological stakes of the cinematic experiences he was producing. The success of a film was measured not simply through its entertainment or audience values, but through the cohesion of those elements into a "genuinely fine," "frequently inspirational" dream world. As his own circumstances changed, Thalberg reaffirmed his commitment to the creation of such worlds.

SEDUCTION VALUE: *THE MERRY WIDOW*

Though *The Merry Widow* did not do nearly as well as *Barretts* at the box office, it was the film about which Thalberg felt the most enthusiastic (Vieira 2010: 256). It represented a return to stylistic elements that had been successful for him in the past: the film was a musical remake of von Stroheim's 1925 film starring John Gilbert, which Thalberg had produced; it highlighted the advancements MGM had made in the musical genre since *The Broadway Melody of 1929*; and it featured the kind of multi-faceted love story that Thalberg had refined in the early days of sound and the Production Code. Adapted from the Franz Lehar operetta, *The Merry Widow* follows the courtship of dashing Count Danilo (Maurice Chevalier) and Sonia (Jeannette MacDonald), the titular widow. When Sonia, the wealthiest woman in Marshovia, leaves the small country for Paris, the king calls upon Danilo to bring her back and so restore the fortunes of the nation. Though Sonia has a number of beaux who pursue her, it is Danilo who awakens her interest. She explores these desires by adopting the persona of "Fifi," a high-class prostitute at legendary café Maxim's who seduces Danilo—nearly—and falls in love in the process.[9] Even in the guise of Fifi, however, Sonia knows not to rush things. Pointing to a portrait of Napoleon, she cautions an overzealous Danilo: "His only mistake was [that] he attacked too early. That's how he lost Waterloo."

In his February 1933 letter, Thalberg had expressed—more passionately— a similar sentiment. He advises Schenck about the vulnerability of star personas under the assault of mass production, offering a near-clinical comparison of MGM's current stars with those from competing studios. It is unlikely that Thalberg would have made these comparisons (in) public: "Certainly there is not that much difference between Joan Crawford and Claudette Colbert [. . .] or between Jean Harlow and Miriam Hopkins" (qtd. in Vieira 2010: 227). What differentiated these leading ladies was MGM's commitment to quality productions, defined by "real entertainment, glamour, good taste" (qtd. in 228). Noting that "[s]tars are not that much more beautiful or that much more talented than the ordinary player" (qtd. in 227), Thalberg points out that exposure in mediocre productions can compromise their allure.

> The destruction of stars is a very subtle process. You scarcely notice that it is happening [. . .] Sometimes what seems to be quite a good picture somehow tends to destroy the background of glamour and interest that has been built up in the star. (Qtd. in 227)

Which is to say, the post-restructuring ethos of MGM—"more production and less supervision" (228), recalling Vieira's words—endangered both the studio's reputation and the strength of its performers. By Thalberg's reckoning, the star him/herself was a complex entity composed not simply of photogenic impact or performance style, but of the foundational support of their studio. Particularly notable is the reference to the building-up of a star's "background," or the idea that a star could infuse each film with the memory of past roles or the trace of a public persona. Though he does not mention it directly here, Thalberg's concept of oblique casting was paramount in developing the depth of that "background" context.

In the *Saturday Evening Post*, Thalberg makes equally conceptual statements about the dangers of such rushed production practices. Discussing not only the destruction of stars but all creative personnel in the studio, Thalberg allows himself a more forceful tone than the one that characterizes the piece as a whole. Though up to this point he had effectively translated passages of personal communications into more palatable terms for the general public, he does not conceal his frustration in this concluding section.

> If it were not for the unreasonable pressure of time that is put on [performers, writers, directors] and ridiculous attempts made to have them work on silly stories and play silly parts and direct half-finished continuities, they would soon prove their worth [. . .] [T]hey cannot be forced to make hundreds of pictures to be rushed through on schedules [. . .] because the human mind is incapable of doing creative work regularly under conditions that call for time-table delivery of their creative efforts. (1933: 85)

Though the letter to Schenck only alludes to the "destruction of stars" as a "subtle process," the above outlines that process in grim detail. Recalling the

1929 discussion of early sound films recording running water just for the sake of it, Thalberg identifies the abortive and absurd processes that have emerged from industrial complacency. The mechanization of artistic enterprise, the "silly" products emerging from that assembly-line mentality, and the demoralization of creative talent—these are the stages of "destruction" not just for studio personnel, but for the creative business of filmmaking itself. Though Thalberg does not cite MGM directly, both its post-restructuring production methods and his personal warnings *against* those methods are recognizable here. The intelligent producer had made his case definitively: in "attacking" film production so aggressively, to paraphrase Sonia/Fifi's comment to Danilo, the studio was inviting its own Waterloo.

Just as *Strange Interlude* put into practice Thalberg's theory of the virtue of experimentation, and *The Barretts of Wimpole Street* mapped out his conception of a cinematic dream world, *The Merry Widow* represents a romantic parable about the triumph of authentic "glamour and interest" (qtd. in Vieira 2010: 227) over the artifice of "silly" and "rushed" affairs (in both senses of the word). The film allegorically reframes Thalberg's emphasis on entertainment value—the very value he implicitly defends in the above passage—as *seduction* value. Where the former calls for quality of artistry over quantity of films, the latter demands a balance between promising thrills and holding out for love. In both value systems, it is imperative that neither the studio nor the figure of desire give too much away; that they hold out for the real thing, as it were.

Nicholas Smedley argues for Sonia's significance as just such a figure of desire in Lubitsch's canon of heroines, noting that she represents "the complementarity of sex and respectability in women" at a time in Hollywood when such "values [were] embodied in two different characters" (2011: chapter 4). Such "complementarity" in a single female lead was not, however, unique to Lubitsch. Sonia represents a quintessential Thalberg heroine in the tradition of Shearer as Jerry in *The Divorcée* and Nina in *Strange Interlude*, or Garbo as Lillie in *Wild Orchids* and Grusinskaya in *Grand Hotel*. Sonia's elegance belies a profound sensuality that she explores in playing the part of Fifi, allowing her to vacillate between the projection of her inner desires and the public identity of merry but virtuous widow.

Indeed, throughout the film there is a *de facto* love triangle between Danilo and Sonia's dual identities of merry widow and loose woman. Where Sonia is a respectable, if coquettish, widow, and Fifi is a prostitute both romantic and sensuous, Danilo is a serial womanizer living by excesses. He is a celebrity within the world of the film, a veritable Valentino of Marshovia, with women literally chasing him as frequently as he chases them. Sonia, by contrast, can only express her intensity of feeling in poignant arias and the pages of her journal. The mask of mourning that Sonia wears upon first meeting Danilo captures this sense of the elusive—or, as Thalberg might term it, the "glamour and interest" (qtd. in Vieira 2010: 227) that Sonia/Fifi cultivates throughout the film. When Danilo initially courts Sonia with the *noblesse oblige* of a legendary seducer, he pleads with her to remove the mask and show him her entire face. The mask thus stands as a clue of beauty withheld and made more intriguing; but it also provides a means by which Sonia may later play the part of Fifi without Danilo recognizing her. Because Sonia does not rush to reveal herself, she may both act out her alter ego and defer Danilo's pleasure in recognizing her as the merry widow he has been sent to woo.

As the following suite of scenes makes clear, the mask is only one of a number of accoutrements meant to build up (in Thalberg's terms) Sonia's allure. Indeed, her bedroom itself functions as a physical "background of glamour and interest." It is a vast space featuring luxurious textures and accents almost entirely in white: crystal candelabras with flickering flames; net curtains; satin headboard on the bed; and gauze draped over the dressing table with silver accessories. Dressed in the black lace of mourning with ruffles and a train, Sonia occupies the room as a kind of inversion of that platinum opulence—no less elegant, but at another chromatic extreme. A series of shots show Sonia's maids helping her undress by returning her hat, shoes, dress, and corset into separate wardrobes, each filled with numerous versions of the respective items.

As the film goes on, it becomes clear that the bedroom stands as a behind-the-scenes space. The sheer volume of these items suggests the production of Sonia's beauty, the idea that there are any number of costumes literally at her disposal to craft an image of respectable widowhood. Heightening this sensibility are the proscenium arches and curtains of the wardrobes themselves. For all of their performative connotations, however, these elements are charged with the intimacy of Sonia's personal desires. It is in this bedchamber, surrounded by these *objets*, that Sonia sings "Vilia," an aria of longing and loneliness ("The night is romantic and I am alone"). This environment also provides the context for Sonia to write in her journal about the intensity of her attraction to Danilo. With every page upon which she writes about how very much she is forgetting him, her preoccupation only grows. Finally, Sonia declares that "there's a limit to every widow" and decides to go to Paris. A series of dissolves show the pieces of black clothing turning to white and other lighter shades, with the maids opening the doors of the wardrobe as if drawing back the curtains of a stage. Here, the audience witnesses Sonia's evolution from somber widow into the Merry Widow herself; the scene ends, in fact, with her exalting the charms of Paris in the spring.

Leo Braudy has described the "Lubitsch touch" as one through which the director "reveal[s] previously hidden motivations, the sexual story, by [. . .] a focus on a significant object" (1983: 1078). This style aligns the spectator with "the director's [. . .] knowingness" rather than with the characters themselves, cultivating "irony and distance" towards the diegetic world (1078). Through this lens, the emphasis on the *mise en scène* of Sonia's bedchamber suggests the gentle absurdity of a woman who has everything pining over a man whom everyone (including her maids) has had. But looking at the sequence with an eye to the Thalberg touch, as it were, highlights Sonia's own "creative efforts" (1933: 85) in bridging subjective desire and objective appearance to create the persona of the Merry Widow as such. Sonia does not just perform the alter ego of Fifi in this film; she also effectively makes a star out of herself.

Her contemplative process is at odds with the anonymous processional of women whom Danilo sings about in "Maxim's," and to which Sonia later pretends to belong. They promise the "time-table delivery" (Thalberg 1933: 85) of sexual satisfaction, taking place in the suites above the café itself. Where the charge of the personal characterized Sonia's bedchamber, the suite at Maxim's offers a contrived intimacy: the door is always open, literally and figuratively, to other women. This charade of seduction contrasts the great romance for which Sonia/Fifi longs; and finally, disenchanted by Danilo's cavalier ways, Sonia/Fifi calls the young women into the suite at Maxim's. Crowded into the doorway in medium long shot, all but indistinguishable with their blonde hair and classic profiles, these women represent the mass-produced and virtually disposable "entertainments" of an evening. Yet Danilo has recognized the authentic seduction value in Fifi and realises the weakness of the fakes. To draw from Thalberg's terms, Danilo has learned that "[s]ometimes what seems to be quite a good picture" (qtd. in Vieira 227)—or, in this case, entertainment—is in fact just an imitation of the real thing.

When Danilo recognizes Sonia as Fifi at a state ball in the following sequences, they begin to reconcile. It is, in fact, their dancing to the "Merry Widow Waltz" that cements their relationship (in spite of the screwball antics that delay their marriage until the very last scene). In a series of extreme long shots linked by dissolves, Danilo and Sonia waltz alone across a number of vast rooms in the palace, only to be joined by dozens of other couples. In Busby Berkeleyesque formations, these dancers grow increasingly more kaleidoscopic in their shifting choreography and attributes: in some shots, they wear black in contrast to Danilo and Sonia's lighter costumes; in others, the women are entirely blonde compared to Sonia's darker hair (see Figure 6.3). By the climax of the sequence, Danilo and Sonia have disappeared, and a seemingly endless stream of dancers revolve through the corridors and ballroom only to be further reflected in a mirror. Given that this famous tune would have been long awaited by the audience, the sequence presents a spectacle of sensory fulfillment: soaring music, bird's-eye shots of opulent settings, impossibly complicated choreography.

Figure 6.3 "The Merry Widow Waltz."

What anchors the excesses, though, are the recurring shots of Danilo and Sonia, who both open and close the sequence with their private waltz in more intimate medium-long shots. Far from the "rushing through" of "time-tabled" satisfaction, this musical number presents the rewards of building up "glamour and interest"; it is the fulfillment of that seduction value promised throughout the film. For all of the orgiastic splendour of the "Merry Widow" spectacle, that dream world of sensation derives from the emotional authenticity of the central relationship. And as Thalberg might have argued, the latter resonates off-screen in the spectator's own immersion in the "*real* entertainment, glamour, good taste" (qtd. in Vieira 228; emphasis added) presented by MGM at its best.

WHAT PICTURES COST

For all that Thalberg translated his personal frustration into a more objective public consideration about the state of filmmaking, the final paragraph of "Why Movies Cost So Much" is as passionate as anything that he wrote to Schenck.

> To continue the present destructive policy of rushing out pictures poorly made, of destroying stars by robbing them of their glamour and their ability to give distinguished performances, of bewildering the best

creative efforts of the best writers through forcing them to work on silly material and rushing them on good material, of loading down good pictures with the production costs and selling expenses of pictures which nobody wants to see—to continue any such suicidal policy is to continue giving the one inescapable answer to the question of why pictures cost so much, and to invite a condition of public apathy in which there won't be any pictures at all. (85)

Just less than a year before, *Fortune* had exalted Thalberg's existential affinity with the cinematic form. And even more than being this sensitive producer of given films, he embodied the studio itself: "what Hollywood means by MGM" (257). Following the restructuring, however, Thalberg had to question what MGM could mean to Hollywood. Where *Fortune* had lauded MGM's "superlatively well-packaged [productions]" and "scenes and personalities [with] a high sheen" (269), it was Thalberg who illuminated how those very virtues were under threat. "Destructive polic[ies]," "destroying stars," "bewildering the best creative efforts" of key personnel—each danger falls under the overarching "suicidal" ethos that MGM had adopted at the beginning of 1933. What Thalberg chronicles here is not simply why movies cost so much for the audience, but what poor movies could cost the industry.

Vieira points out that Thalberg found the studio's "resources even harder to tap" (2010: 243) after the publication of this article. Between 1934 and 1935, though, the shifts in the MGM power structure would stabilize—relatively speaking. The stratified system instituted by Mayer, through which he represented the highest point of authority over a phalanx of producers, gradually evolved into what Schatz describes as "a *modified* central-producer/unit-producer system" (1996: 165; emphasis added): Thalberg, Selznick, Wanger, and former Thalberg associate Hunt Stromberg represented the height of the producing talent and worked "independently," while "second-string producers" such as Bernie Hyman, Laurence Weingarten, and original MGM producer Harry Rapf consulted with Thalberg over "more routine productions" (165).

If the death knell—the Waterloo—that Thalberg sounded in "Why Movies Cost So Much" did not signal MGM's actual demise, it did capture the end of the studio as Thalberg had conceived of it. Through the external challenges posed by the rise of sound and the establishment of the Production Code, Thalberg's MGM had remained a constant; the locus of ever-evolving, but consistently high, entertainment value. What the 1933–1934 series of private correspondence and public statements reveals, however, was that that stability derived from Thalberg's conception of its importance. Mayer and Schenck's restructuring of the studio displaced, rescaled, the "single idea" (qtd. in Vieira 2010: 229) that Thalberg had developed for MGM. But the *Saturday Evening Post* article suggests that in destabilizing the central producer model, and therefore undoing the intimate identification between Thalberg and MGM, the new system allowed for his public renaissance. The intelligent producer, as defined by Thalberg, may directly address his public and is not beholden to a specific studio; though professional pride means that he seeks to "make [audiences] want to see more pictures produced under the same name and the same trade-mark" (11), he himself is defined by creative ambition and singular vision. In no longer embodying MGM, Thalberg found that he could speak for himself.

NOTES

1. Elaborating on this point, Christensen explores the vertiginous logic of the article: it "celebrates the genius of a man who concocts personalities that people will admire and animates them in stories that people will believe—and who can do so not only because he knows what they want but, more importantly, because he sells to no one what he has not already sold to himself as the self-created customer of his wares" (2012: 30).
2. Scholars have commented on the anti-Semitic undercurrents of the article as a whole. Vieira finds that "it characterize[s] Thalberg as brilliant and effective, even if he did happen to be a Jew" (2010: 218); and Kathleen A. Feeley notes that the piece "recycle[s] anti-Jewish stereotypes [in discussions of] his potentially awesome *and* fearsome power" (2016: 50).
3. In *Deadly Illusions: Jean Harlow and the Murder of Paul Bern* (1990), Samuel Marx and Joyce Vanderveen offer a detailed account of Bern's death. Though Hollywood lore has long set out that Bern died from a self-inflicted gunshot wound, Marx and Vanderveen argue that MGM perpetuated this story to cover up his murder.
4. Margaret Herrick Library, Academy of Motion Picture Arts and Sciences, Irving G. Thalberg and Norma Shearer Papers. File 1-f.2.
5. Association of Motion Picture Producers [AMPP], "Discussion of the Production Code in Its Draft Form." MPPDA Digital Archive, Flinders University Library Special Collections. MPPDA Record 671, Record of Meeting. 8-1985 to 8-2132. Available at <https://mppda.flinders.edu.au/records/671> (last accessed 24 October, 2019), p. 80.
6. Advertisement for *Strange Interlude*: *Photoplay*, September 1932: 11.
7. AMPP, "Discussion of the Production Code in Its Draft Form," 137.
8. As Vieira notes, Thalberg needed to ensure that the issue of incest would be conveyed "without alarming censors" (2010: 252). Laughton maintained, "They can't censor the gleam in my eye" (qtd. in Vieira 252).
9. With its insouciant take on provocative subject matter, *The Merry Widow* raised concerns in the Production Code Administration. In consultation with Will Hays and Martin Quigley, Joseph Breen ordered thirteen cuts which, as Thalberg protested, made the film "jumpy and choppy" in certain scenes (Vieira 2010: 260).

CHAPTER 7

"What can we do to make the picture better?"

In "Why Motion Pictures Cost So Much," Thalberg discusses the initial reception of melodrama *The Sin of Madelon Claudet* (dir. Selwyn, 1931). Noting that it had "brought tears to the eyes of every man and woman in the studio" (1933: 10) during production, Thalberg wryly recounts the audience's contrasting response at a preview:

> [W]hen we took a sample print out to a little theater just outside Los Angeles [. . .] there wasn't a wet eye in the house.
> All the company had cried, but the audience didn't. The pathos of the mother who sacrificed all [. . .] for some reason did not get over on the screen.
> In other words, what we had thought was pathos was only bathos. (10)

Thalberg goes on to explain that in order to redeem the film, as well as the nascent screen career of theatrical star Helen Hayes, "we simply had to spend whatever might be needed to make that picture right" (11). Though Thalberg does not explicitly say that retakes were the solution to *Madelon Claudet*'s problems, his signature strategy of reshooting key scenes, introducing new material, or revising the screenplay following unsuccessful previews—no matter the cost—suggests that they were the greatest protective measure he could grant the film. Framed within the article's broader context (or as argued in the previous chapter, pretext) of discussing industry costs for studios and spectators, this anecdote functions as a case study of how investing time and money in films could reap aesthetic and commercial benefits. The film made $145,000 at the box office, and Hayes won the Academy Award for Best Actress (Marx 1975: 172, 259).

However emblematic, the experience above was only one of a number of times that Thalberg used previews and subsequent retakes in order to "make

[a] picture right" (1933: 11). Samuel Marx would note that Thalberg's focus on previewing films emerged from an understanding that "a paying audience provided clues to strong points and weaknesses" where the "studio showings"—as noted in Thalberg's account above—could generate a misleading and complacent response (1975: 136). By the same token, Thalberg understood the preview to be what he called "a testing ground" rather than a final judgment; in his words,

> it is no proof that a picture is a failure or a success. Rightly used, a preview tells you what parts of the picture are good and should be retained; which characters do not appeal to an audience and should be cut. (Qtd. in Marx 1942: section 2)

The journey to this testing ground was routine: on the night of a preview, associated studio personnel would join Thalberg on a trolley, playing bridge and dining on food from the studio commissary as they traveled to smaller theaters outside of Los Angeles proper (Marx 1975: 136–137).[1] Once at the movie theater, Thalberg left his colleagues to their designated rows and "moved further front, to find a single seat for himself, a silent observer, like a troubled doctor searching for hidden ailments" (137). As Bob Thomas notes, the success or failure of the preview shaded the mood back to the studio (1969: 139)—though Thalberg would respond to poor screenings with equanimity. His abiding question was, "What can we do to make the picture better?" (qtd. in Thomas 140)

Across chronicles of Thalberg's years at MGM, the retake emerges as a point of continual discussion and (mostly) admiration—but why, particularly? Certainly the process captured Thalberg's aesthetic standards and perfectionist drive; and like the "creative business" (11) Thalberg describes in the *Saturday Evening Post*, it has an elemental duality. The retake is a practical process emerging from an intuitive awareness of what the film could be, with results both abstract (audience appreciation) and quantifiable (box-office success). But the most compelling quality of the retake relates to Thalberg's understanding that a film, like any living form, had the capacity for renewal and rehabilitation. The first cut of a film was only one stage of its development; the work would reach its full potential through an intimate understanding of its strengths and vulnerabilities. Producer David Lewis, who worked with Thalberg late in his tenure at MGM, described this as a "creative sense of doctoring" through which Thalberg "felt that he could find the weak spots [in the previews] and redo them later. He was like a surgeon, exploring, examining, and ultimately healing" (1993: 81). This approach contrasted the standard practice of the early industry; as actor Conrad Nagel points out, "[u]p until Thalberg, you had a schedule, you finished the picture, and that was the end of it. Good, bad, or indifferent, it was released" (qtd. in Rosenberg and Silverstein

1970: 188). Far from this fatalistic acceptance of a given work's condition, Thalberg's retake affirmed the cinematic body's propensity for evolution.

For all of this retrospective analysis from his colleagues, Thalberg's discussion of *Madelon Claudet* expresses with an air of immediacy his commitment to the retake as both a practical process and concept of filmmaking. The historical circumstances of the article, however, introduce still other implications for this iteration of the theory. As discussed in the previous chapter, Thalberg published the piece in response to the restructuring of MGM; in this way, his emphasis on retakes implicitly critiques the new studio leadership that resisted such expense.[2] More abstractly, Thalberg's meditation on the retake here is part of a broader reflection on his production style and role at the studio at this time of change. To frame the issue in terms of his public persona: where the "Boy Wonder" established the retake as such, it was the intelligent producer who claimed it as part of an industrial ethos. But given the fact that Thalberg would die less than three years after the publication of "Why Motion Pictures Cost So Much," the retake and its associations with the living form of cinema assume all the more significance.

Thalberg's death in September 1936 brought a famously untimely conclusion to his work as a producer and theorist of filmmaking. His artistic aspirations and professional ambitions were high: with several films in development and a series of successful productions between 1935 and 1936, Thalberg had overcome the conflicts of the 1933 restructuring to cement his professional identity as MGM's intelligent producer. Director and friend Jack Conway recalled Thalberg telling him, "I'm in a running battle with L.B. [Mayer] but I'm going to beat him" (qtd. in Marx 1975: 246). In terms of political activities, Kathleen A. Feeley points out that Thalberg also devoted time to anti-Nazi initiatives, including the Hollywood Anti-Nazi League; he also helped to found the Community Relations Council of the Los Angeles Jewish Community Committee (2016: 54). Most strikingly in this period—and to be discussed in more detail—Thalberg had arranged to form his own production studio following the expiration of his contract with MGM in 1938 (Crowther 1957: 236).

Like the films that Thalberg healed, as it were, through retakes, his career was itself a work-in-progress—one with a still-evolving future. In order to explore the significance of the retake at this juncture in Thalberg's life and career, this chapter will argue for its range of meanings across a series of films from 1935 to 1937. The first section will establish the terms of the original process itself, which effectively diagnosed a film to "make it better." The next two sections will consider Thalberg's broader retake, or revision, of his cinematic style in historical epics *Mutiny on the Bounty* (dir. Lloyd, 1935) and *Romeo and Juliet* (dir. Cukor, 1936). In these works, Thalberg celebrates the crafting of epic narratives, spectacles in scale and concept. Equally epic, however, are the films' integration of and expansion upon Thalberg's classic tenets of filmmaking. Across these works, oblique casting would find a counterpart in Thalberg's oblique *interpretation* of classic tales and character relationships; his concern with love stories, as seen across his *oeuvre* and particularly in the negotiations over the Production Code, plays out in unexpected dialogues between the ethereal and sensual; the focus on one great scene evolves to include a series of interlinked "decisive moments" (Thalberg 1936: 1); and the dream world of cinema itself, which Thalberg discussed in the *Saturday Evening Post*, re-emerges in expressly oneiric representations of diegetic landscapes.

The final section will address the crisis faced by wife Shearer over how to reprise Thalberg's legacy in his unfinished film *Marie Antoinette* (dir. Van Dyke, 1938). As she would recall, "Irving produced that. He was dead, but it was still *his*" (qtd. in Lambert 1990: 99). What, then, do unfinished projects like *Marie Antoinette* and, indeed, his proposed independent studio illuminate about Thalberg's immediate posthumous legacy? Though it was *The Good Earth* (dir. Franklin, 1937) that the studio dedicated to Thalberg as his last film, this chapter will view *Marie Antoinette* and the plans for his studio as a collective vestige of his vision of filmmaking.

Thalberg died at a threshold point in his professional life. In 1936, he was the intelligent producer of MGM on his way to becoming an independent producer in his own studio; and just as the retake process itself was predicated on Thalberg's understanding of a given film as ever-evolving in its possibilities, so too was his work in cinema unfinished. Biographers have noted Thalberg's awareness of his mortality in this period, as well as his engagement with films about death (*Romeo and Juliet*, *Camille* [dir. Cukor, 1936], *The Good Earth*).[3] The following analyses, however, will consider his works not in terms of what would be, but like Thalberg, what had *been*. For in that final year, he would reflect on his past and ask himself how he could make better pictures—whether at MGM or in his own studio.

RETAKE VALLEY

Though Marx suggests that Thalberg's focus on previewing films began in earnest following the rise of the talkies (1975: 136), a piece of footage from 1926 indicates that he had developed the accompanying process of retakes from the earliest days of the studio. While on a weekend away at San Simeon, Hearst's California castle, Thalberg, Gilbert, and director Anthony Asquith made a short home movie entitled *The Unchaste Chased Woman*.[4] In the words of Gilbert biographer Eve Golden, it is "over-the-top hilarious" (2013: 171) with the actor playing a heroic cowboy, Asquith a predatory male, and Thalberg dressed in apron, shawl, and kerchief as the titular woman. Replete with intertitles, the film is also over-the-top knowing in its depiction of melodramatic conventions and "Irvina's" own production practices. "Now . . . if my little Irvina will only retake me that all may end well!," cries Gilbert's cowboy as he races to the rescue.

According to Nagel, Thalberg's focus on retakes helped make MGM "the Tiffany of Hollywood": "The retake became policy. They would finish the picture. They would take it out and preview it. Then they'd come back and fix it up" (qtd. in Rosenberg and Silverstein 188). In his 1957 history of MGM, Crowther describes Thalberg's process of previewing films as a way of "testing finished films against the actual responses of audiences to try to discover [the films'] flaws [. . .] 'Irving doesn't make pictures, he remakes them'—they used to say" (181). In similar *comme on dit* terms, Thomas notes that "Retake Valley was the name applied to M-G-M [*sic*] by local jesters" (140). Thalberg was sanguine in response to such criticisms and would continue to privilege his perspective in the editing of a film. For example, when director Lewis Milestone protested that he "improve[d] [his] films thirty-three percent in the cutting room," Thalberg replied, "Tell him I improve mine one hundred percent" (qtd. in Marx 1975: 187).

Bringing together intellectual curiosity and practical action, the guiding question of "what can we do to make the picture better?" took shape in numerous interventions: the addition of love scenes in *La Bohème*, for example, and the enhancement of "the war" as such in *The Big Parade*; or using a more dynamic camera to heighten the impact of the musical numbers in *The Broadway Melody of 1929*. Thalberg would also advise associate Hunt Stromberg over the editing of his picture *The Great Ziegfeld* (dir. Leonard, 1936). Noting that "[i]t still needs something," Thalberg found another song to include as a musical number; as Beth Day outlines, "It cost the studio an additional $250,000 to shoot this [. . .] on a revolving stage and cut it into the finished film. But it paid off at the box office. The number was the hit of the show" (1960: 215). This holistic engagement with a given film at every stage of its development also reveals much about Thalberg's frustration with the strictures of the early Production Code; his impatience, that is, with intrusive cuts that would not "make the picture better," but rather less distinctive and complete in itself. Consider, for example, the violence of a "mutilated picture"[5] as cited in Thalberg's draft of the 1927 Don'ts and Be Carefuls—a term that conjures images of films edited to damaging, rather than restorative, effect.

Associate producer Albert Lewin would later explain,

> Irving was [. . .] a great editor. He was a perfectionist. If we had an extremely successful preview [. . .] most people would pat themselves on the back and be awfully satisfied. He would tear the picture apart and improve it. He would push and push to get the very last bit of excellence into a production. [. . .] Sometimes three or four days of retakes will

improve a picture enormously, and Irving never hesitated to spend the extra money. His successors were not like that. (Qtd. in Rosenberg and Silverstein 113)

With a diagnostic perspective and an interventionist approach, the Thalberg of Lewin's description considered a given film at a molecular level—pursuing "the very last bit of excellence" that could, conversely, create a spectacular whole. As Thalberg himself would explain, "The difference between something good and something bad is great, but the difference between something good and something superior is often very small" (qtd. in Crowther 1957: 181). With forensic insight, Thalberg perceived that margin of possibility; with the holistic understanding cited by his colleagues, he maximized it.

As Thalberg would write in the *Saturday Evening Post*, the "creative business [of filmmaking . . .] should be conducted with budgets and cost sheets, but it cannot be conducted with blue prints and graphs" (11). Nor, as these accounts illuminate, could Thalberg conduct it without a personal connection to the film. Particularly illuminating is the "doctor" imagery that various scholars use, a medical discourse employed to help convey the sensitivities of Thalberg's process. Nagel would recall the way that Thalberg "had an uncanny ability to see exactly what was wrong with something and to be able to doctor it up" (qtd. in Rosenberg and Silverstein 188); and Crowther notes that "supervisors and other people at the studio came to depend upon [Thalberg] as an infallible 'doctor' when their pictures were in need of care" (1957: 183). Recalling the fluid subjectivity posited by the *Fortune* article, in which Thalberg assumed the identities of cinematic form, spectator, and the studio itself, the retake process evolved from a multi-faceted understanding of film production. In watching a given film from the seat of a paying customer, Thalberg inhabited the position of an informed viewer rather than an executive; going on to "fix" the films, as it were, he then exceeded the roles of producer, director and editor to act as healer.

Indeed, what made the retake process particularly radical was Thalberg's consideration of the audience itself as collaborator. Though, as Bob Thomas notes, some colleagues criticized Thalberg for taking the opinions of suburban— and therefore "unsophisticated"—audiences so seriously, he found that such viewers represented "the vast numbers who supported" MGM's productions (145). The preview-and-retakes of *The Sin of Madelon Claudet* provides a case study of this approach, as does the production of *Anna Karenina* adaptation *Love* (dir. Goulding, 1927). As Thalberg recounted in his 1929 speech at the University of Southern California, the suburban public's dismay at the tragic ending of the Garbo and Gilbert film necessitated an alternate conclusion. "There was such a demand for the happy ending and there was a great deal invested in the picture," Thalberg explained. "[I]t seems pointless to argue with the public [so] we acceded to the demand [. . .] which proved to be more successful in smaller towns" (1977: 123). To reframe this in the terms set out in that same USC speech, Thalberg ensured, and privileged, the entertainment value of a given work through retakes. Though introducing glaring problems of (in)fidelity to the original text, this incident speaks to Thalberg's greater commitment—fidelity—to the movie-going public who could make the film itself a success. Anita Loos would recall that "Irving paid small attention to professional critics, putting them down as impersonal theorists; but he read those postcards [from the audience] with the greatest respect" (1974: 42). As a highly *personal* theorist himself, Thalberg was attuned to both the intimacy of the individual perspective and the potential of the entire film.

Taken together, these accounts define the retake as a curative process emerging from Thalberg's sense of creative conviction and concrete action. The suburban theater and cutting room coalesce into an operating room, with studio personnel and spectators alike consulting with Thalberg. In a practical sense, he is a surgeon unafraid to "tear the picture apart" (in Lewin's words, qtd. in Rosenberg and Silverstein 113) because he knows he can put it back together even better than it was; to recall Crowther's terms, "'Irving doesn't make pictures, he remakes them'" (1957: 181). For all of this anatomical knowledge, however, there is also a certain shamanism that underscores descriptions of Thalberg's process. Nagel, for example, cites that "uncanny ability" to intuit the vulnerabilities of a film—invoking Thalberg's preternatural power that had first mesmerized Hollywood in the early 1920s. As a fundamental part of his professional identity, the retake brought together the mystique of the Boy Wonder and the analytical precision of the intelligent producer.

Thalberg could not, however, fix MGM on his terms. The rehabilitation that he had called for in 1933 did not take place; instead, 1934–1936 introduced still more changes for the studio. Wanger left MGM in 1934, following conflicts with Mayer over the leftist sensibilities of *Gabriel Over the White House* (dir. La Cava, 1933) and a difficult working relationship with Garbo during the production of *Queen Christina* (dir. Mamoulian, 1933) (Schatz 1996: 165). Of the prestige producers, only Thalberg, Selznick, and Stromberg remained, and each continued to develop their respective styles. Selznick distinguished himself with the critical and commercial success of films such as *Dinner at Eight* (dir. Cukor, 1933), *Manhattan Melodrama* (dir. Van Dyke, 1934), and *David Copperfield* (dir. Cukor, 1935), and Stromberg had hits with *The Thin Man* (dir. Van Dyke, 1934) and *The Great Ziegfeld* (dir. Leonard, 1936) (Schatz 1996: 169). Thomas Schatz points out that where Thalberg and Selznick considered the making of each film as unique in itself—thus resisting the formulaic nature of unit producing per se, with its recurring use of certain directors, stars, and even genres—Stromberg tended to "reformulate" past successes produced by himself or his colleagues (1996: 169).

For all his contributions to MGM, Selznick followed Wanger and, in 1935, resigned from the studio. He would, of course, go on to develop his own production company, Selznick International Pictures. (As David Thomson notes, Thalberg was an early investor [2004: 241].) A piece in *Variety* suggested that Selznick and Wanger had left "due to 'too much interference'" from Mayer; interestingly, the article also posited that "most associate producers on the lot have been seeking full dictatorship and authority over their representative units as was enjoyed by Irving Thalberg" (qtd. in Bernstein 1994: 90). Though Thalberg personally felt the strain of continued conflicts with Mayer (Marx 1975: 245), such commentary suggests that the wider industry viewed the former's influence as unchanging. Indeed, in 1936, *Photoplay* editor Ruth Waterbury would highlight Thalberg's resilience: "A year and a half ago Metro was full of political factions [. . .] His own health wasn't at its best. The will to succeed in the man, however, wasn't in the least downed" (11).

Thalberg's will to execute his vision of the creative business of filmmaking came to the fore in a mid-1930s dispute with the Screen Writers Guild, a union that aimed to support its members' struggles against "lack of security in their jobs, the inequities of awarding screen credit, [and] their insignificant status compared to stars and directors" (Thomas 267). Perceiving such unionisation as not only detrimental to the studio but also personally disloyal (Vieira 2010: 308), Thalberg offered staff the compromise of the Screen Playwrights company union (Thomas 267). When the Guild still threatened to strike, Thalberg summoned the MGM writers to a meeting at which he declared,

> If you proceed with this strike [. . .] I shall close this studio, lock the gates, and there will be an end to Metro-Goldwyn-Mayer productions. And it will be you—all of you writers—who will have done it. (Qtd. in Thomas 268)

The Guild did not strike, and the company union took precedence in MGM. Thalberg's rejection of the Guild notwithstanding, he did not allow members of the Screen Playwrights to bully their counterparts in the SWG. As he said to two members of the latter, "You're entitled to your opinions" (qtd. in Vieira 2010: 313).

Such a balance between personal conviction and diplomacy characterized the best of his working relationships; as Vieira describes it, Thalberg at this stage of his career "was both autocratic and enlightened" (2010: 314). Lewis recalled, "He didn't demand obedience. He always listened. In case of a disagreement he would say, 'We'll try it both ways. Mine first'" (73). Thalberg's negotiations with Clark Gable over the role of Fletcher Christian is a case in point: in this quintessential example of oblique casting, Thalberg had to convince the star that the period role was appropriate for him. "I think this is a good part for you," he told Gable. "[I]f I'm proved wrong when the picture is released, I'll never again ask you to play a part that you don't want to play" (qtd. in Marx 1942: section 2). In related terms, Thalberg also explored new angles on established practices. For instance, when he began to work with the Marx Brothers on *A Night at the Opera*, he suggested they test the material in front of live audiences: "Take the five big comedy scenes in the script. Play them in vaudeville houses with a connecting narrative on the screen. You'll find out in a hurry whether the stuff is funny" (qtd. in Thomas 284). More than underscoring his commitment to the preview as such, this account speaks to Thalberg's understanding of the process as versatile in its relationship to the conceptual thrust of a given film. The Marx Brothers were live performers as well as cinematic comedians; their work demanded the investment of an audience. Where the classic execution of the preview implicitly considered the film as an animate work-in-progress, this live variation foregrounded the preview's inherently dialogical engagement between on- and off-screen subjectivities.

Though Thalberg's 1934 films had largely disappointed at the box office, 1935 represented a year of accelerated productivity and popularity. Of the five films he produced that year, four made a profit: *China Seas* (dir. Garnett) brought Jean Harlow and Clark Gable together with Wallace Beery in a high-seas drama; *A Night at the Opera* restored the movie careers of the Marx Brothers; and *No More Ladies* (dir. Griffith) starred Joan Crawford in an adaptation of a Broadway society comedy. *Mutiny on the Bounty* emerged as the biggest hit of all, winning the Oscar for Best Picture and earning over $4 million (Schatz 1996: 172).[6] As a legacy of the restructuring, Thalberg had first encountered *Mutiny on the Bounty* because of fellow prestige producers Selznick and Wanger. The latter had wanted to adapt the Nordhoff and Hall novel (1932) before leaving MGM, while Thalberg acknowledged Selznick's *David Copperfield* as instrumental in his own desire to produce a celebrated literary work (Schatz 1996: 172). The period tale starred Charles Laughton as the tyrannical Captain Bligh, Gable as Fletcher Christian, the leader of the mutiny, and Franchot Tone as Christian's reluctant ally Roger Byam.

Its popularity was tremendous, with *Motion Picture* describing the work as "destined to live as one of the true epics of all film history" ("Big Last Minute Reviews" 1936: 16). For Thalberg, though, *Mutiny* "lived" alongside another epic: *Romeo and Juliet*, the adaptation of which he called "the fulfilment of a long cherished dream" (1936: 1). Indeed, there is an oneiric quality to the latter film that belies both the violence of the tragedy and the sensuality of the lovers' attraction. More passionate, in fact, in its depiction of relationships is *Mutiny*; as Loos notes, the "rivalry" between Christian and Bligh was "so bitter it could only have been based on the strongest mutual fascination" (36–37). In this way, the two films illuminate the evolution of Thalberg's fascination with not simply epic narratives but the complexities of representing human desire. Just as *Grand Hotel* and *Strange Interlude* explored the dialogue between public and private, so too do *Mutiny on the Bounty* and *Romeo and Juliet* present still other dual facets of longing: the sensual and the ethereal. *Mutiny* is charged with physicality and an unexpected passion, whether for survival or revenge; *Romeo and Juliet*, by contrast, commits to a dream-like envisioning of an age-old romance.

Turning from the retake as a production process, then, the following sections will explore how Thalberg expanded upon—retook—his established themes through films that, with their opulence and emphasis on spectacle, attested to his still-evolving love affair with the screen itself.

"PEOPLE ARE FASCINATED WITH CRUELTY"

Advertisements for and reviews of *Mutiny* heralded the immersive experience of the film. The text of a full-page ad evokes a world that sweeps "[f]rom the blood-drenched decks of a man o' war to the ecstasy of a sun-baked paradise isle . . . from the tyrannical grasp of a brutal captain to the arms of native beauties who brought them love and forgetfulness."[7] The reviews highlighted similarly visceral qualities. For *Motion Picture*, "It brings to your ears the sharp thud of whips on human flesh, the tortured cries of broken creatures in irons. It brings before your eyes the pitiful wasting away of starving, thirsting human beings" ("Big Last Minute Reviews" 16). *Photoplay* found the film to be "a brutal, sweat-and-blood tale of man's inhumanity to man [. . .] It is not a pretty film, but it is grand and real" ("The Shadow Stage" 1936a: 48). The sheer sensory impact on the spectator—from romantic embraces to "sweat-and-blood" struggles—defines, to borrow from Thalberg, the entertainment value of the film. This insistent and at times violent appeal to the senses, moreover, allows for the reanimation of the historical event; as *Motion Picture* would conclude, "It is the dark record of a dead past, brought suddenly to life" ("Big Last Minute Reviews" 16).

For Thalberg, the vivification of that "dead past" required retakes. Douglas Shearer, for example, remembered how Thalberg called for a correction of the set design: "Those sails on the *Bounty* are too gray for a bright sunny day" (qtd. in Rosenberg and Silverstein 383). Thalberg also collaborated with screenwriter Talbot Jennings and associate producer Lewin in refining the script; as Thomas notes, "the three men spent the whole day viewing film and working on scenes that Thalberg thought might be improved" (277). He worked with editor Margaret Booth to cut the film and concluded the process with a final preview at Grauman's Chinese Theater (Thomas 278). These material interventions parallel the broader, conceptual retakes that Thalberg would enact—particularly in his shifting approach to the theme of conflict. In

The Big Parade, one of the most immediate points of comparison to *Mutiny*, the "dark record" of World War I served to illuminate the nobler side of human nature in a sweeping romantic drama; in *Mutiny*, however, the violence on the ship captures a more elemental struggle for survival through a microcosmic commentary on personal experience. The big parade of history, that is, had been reduced to a tormented voyage. Indeed, when Mayer suggested that the lack of female leads in the film could be a problem, Thalberg maintained that the film did not require the conventions of romance in its exploration of still other, darker lures. "It doesn't matter that there are no women in the cast. People are fascinated with cruelty, and that's why *Mutiny* will have appeal" (qtd. in Thomas 274).

The question of cruelty defines the film from its opening sequence, in which Christian leads a press gang that forces men into service on the *Bounty*. The subsequent scene of departure, for all its characterful exchanges and bright exterior shots, bears flourishes of this intrinsic brutality: the wrenching farewell between a young sailor and his wife and baby; the sadism of Bligh ordering the public flogging of a sailor who has already died. Vieira has keenly noted the influence of Eisenstein's theory of montage in this production, citing the eloquent manipulation of shots as evidence of Thalberg "using film *as film*" rather than an extension of the theatrical stage (2010: 326). Certainly this depiction of the departure from port overtly channels Eisenstein's concept of each shot as "a montage cell (or molecule)" (1977: 53) in the construction of an entire concept. As if in homage to Eisenstein's chronicle of another ill-fated voyage in *Battleship Potemkin* (1925), the sequence establishes the violence of a kinetic and fragmented environment. A series of high-angle close-ups of the officers alternate with extreme low-angle long shots of the anonymous sailors, moving in tandem across expressionist coordinates of rope ladders, billowing sails, and jutting masts. Particularly striking is one of the final extreme low-angle shots, in which the camera remains static as the massive sails balloon and cruise on overhead (see Figure 7.1). Amid the pageantry of this "anchors aweigh" sequence, the strain of cruelty reveals itself yet again through the shot of an officer beating the young man who has just been separated from his wife.

This is, however, only one of many times that Thalberg expressed his inherent fluency in the cinematic medium; consider his vision of the most impactful construction of sets and camera angles in works such as *Broadway Melody* and, fundamentally, *Ben-Hur*. The near-abstract quality of the sequence, in fact, suggests a broadening of Thalberg's intentionality in using "film as film": where in the chariot race sequence he had experimented with scale to "prove" to the audience that the set was not fake (Thomas 72), here he called upon overtly stylized editing to convey a more psychological reality.

Figure 7.1 The *Bounty*.

In the early stages of developing the script, Thalberg had worried over its dramatic arc. He found the scenes to be "like a string of sausages, each one good, but not satisfying. I'm left hungry. I want a big steak!" (qtd. in Thomas 275). Where one great scene allowed for a turning point against which to measure the scale of the narrative itself, Thalberg found here a problematically sustained mood—"good, but not satisfying" in impact. Yet in the final production, the kaleidoscopic angles and rapid cuts of this early montage generate a visceral (if uneasy) satisfaction that establishes the primary theme of cruelty on a sensory level as well as an expositional one. The editing recalls both the rocking of the waves and the lashings of the whip used on the dead man, and the ballooning of the sails captures the fraught energy of a journey just beginning—each accustoming the specta-tor, like the sailors, to the rhythm of life on the *Bounty*. So completely does the montage create the effect of an insulated and vertiginous world that it is still another shock to see the ship in its entirety in more conventional long shots.

As if to increase the entertainment value of this early scene, the mutiny itself reprises the montage effect and expands upon the menace suggested in the earlier sequence. In the Eisensteinian sense, the "collision of [the] indepen-dent shots" of the men as they attack each other creates the idea of *mutiny* (49); yet transposed to Thalberg's terms, the mutiny is a retake of the establishing montage, showing the audience how the same men who once worked in tandem now turn against each other. If the mutiny is the "big steak," or great scene, for which the viewer waits, the sensory recall of that earlier montage heightens its affective power.

Even through such material and dramatic fragmentation, the *Bounty* herself abides. As Laughton explained in a *Photoplay* interview, the film

> is not a tale of men, nor of years, nor of purposes, but the moods of a ship as she leaves the port; as she breasts forward before the wind; as she twists and turns in a storm; as she arrives at her destination. (Qtd. in McAllister 1936: 104)

The ship serves, then, as the spatial and emotional center of the film for characters and audience; the vessel, in literal and figurative terms, for the drama itself. This existential affinity comes to the fore in the periodic rolling of the sets in the shipboard scenes, reminding the viewer of the fundamental instability of the seamen's existence. Even in the scenes taking place in Tahiti, where the men find respite from the torments of the voyage, the land represents only a temporary refuge—a dreamscape composed of long shots of sea and hazy sky, often transitioning through ethereal dissolves. By contrast, the dominant symbiosis of "moods" between man, vessel, and the sea itself establishes that primary cruelty of which Thalberg spoke: the volatility and brutality of nature both human and environmental.

The Big Parade, as a counterpoint, underscores the continuum between civilisation and the no-man's-land of trenches and battlefield; consider, for example, the bird's-eye shots of trucks moving to the front. Through such a connection, the landscape of the war allows for the flourishing of nobler virtues: loyalty, love, even mercy. In *Mutiny*, however, the forced communion of man and sea calls upon a more primal drive for survival. Even when united in their rebellion, the conflict between the men does not necessarily abate: quarrels over the aims of the mutineers linger for the rest of the film. In this way, Bligh embodies the diffuse cruelty that tempers the very atmosphere of the voyage—his limitless brutality providing, in turn, a direct object for the discontent of the men. Thalberg would heighten Bligh's presence in a revision to actual events, adding him to the scenes featuring the hunt for the mutineers. Though Bligh himself had not captained the *Pandora* in its pursuit, Thalberg included him in this "third act" of the film (Vieira 2010: 286–287). Vieira rightly points out that this gives a "lift" to the end of the film; but it is intriguing to consider why, exactly, Thalberg found this retaking of the historical incident to be necessary.

In so focusing on Bligh's hunt for Christian, Thalberg underscored the nature of the film as not simply a historical adventure but an epic of darker, even fated passions. Bligh's lust for revenge brings the *Pandora* to destruction in a wreck on what an intertitle—in an echo of silent-era storytelling—describes as "the uncharted and treacherous reefs of the Great South Sea." Though the reefs themselves are uncharted, the *Pandora* and her men seem to follow a predestined course. Finding themselves back on a ship captained by Bligh, the captured mutineers and officers (who had been unwilling accessories to mutiny) experience an uncanny reprise of the circumstances on the *Bounty*. Bligh orders them to be placed in irons in the hold of the ship, subject to torture for not revealing Christian's whereabouts. Where the early montage foreshadowed the volatility of the *Bounty*'s voyage, couching its inherent violence in the thrill of adventure, the comparatively staid shots in the bowels of the *Pandora* signal the resolution of this journey. In a series of medium and medium-long shots punctuated by the periodic rolling motion of the set, the men cluster together in a gray landscape of filth and chains; in contrast to the expressionist compositions of the departure from port, with the sharply contrasting forms of man, ship, and sky, the human figure here merges with the squalor of the background (see Figure 7.2). Distinctions of rank and social class, even of individual purpose, have ceded to a depersonalized but shared suffering.

Breaking this stagnation is the moment in which Bligh finally runs the *Pandora* upon the reefs. With a shudder and creaking noise, the *de facto* prison comes to life for the first time—only to signal the danger of imminent death as water gushes in the portholes and floods the hold. The camera movement remains minimal: observing the men through the oblique angle of a broken ladder as they try to free themselves; framing individuals in medium shot shouting for help. Even the effect of shuddering in the hold takes place through the

Figure 7.2 Prisoners on the *Pandora*.

movement of the set itself and a slight zoom-in. Contrasted with cuts to the action above deck—gusts of wind, rolling waves, and men climbing into life-boats—the stillness of the camera conveys a resignation to, indeed, the cruelty of whatever may happen to the men. Those who survive the shipwreck are condemned to hang; only Byam will ultimately escape death.

What Bligh's historically inaccurate but, as Thalberg perceived, dramatically necessary presence on the *Pandora* conveys, then, is the fated nature of the voyage. More than a villain, Bligh is nemesis; the continual cutting to his role in the action above deck signals his responsibility for the turmoil. And more than Christian's enemy, he is the latter's double. In a grotesque expression of that "mutual fascination" outlined by Loos, Bligh's destruction of the *Pandora* anticipates Christian's own burning of the *Mutiny* at the end of the film, after landing with the remaining mutineers on Pitcairn Island. Mortally repelled and drawn to each other from opposing moral poles, each is willing to destroy his ship to protect his future.

In *Mutiny on the Bounty*, the retake is both internal to the film's construction—an aesthetic volatility—and external in its relationship to context—Thalberg's reconsideration of earlier themes and historical events. In this study of survival, Thalberg frames mutiny in terms of an embodied conflict: between individual and nature, between literal shackles and violent liberation. If, as Laughton set out, the *Bounty* herself functions as the center of the narrative, then the camera and screen are themselves collaborators in projecting the emotional and spatial variability of that environment. Dynamic at the start of the voyage, the cinematic form captures the hysteria of what is to come; resigned at the end, the camera bears witness to the fate of man and ship. This shift in style makes evident the film's own capacity for change, revision, even as the men find themselves trapped in a predetermined cycle. The final scene, in fact, shows Byam happily setting out on another, far more civilized ship; but this sense of the uncanny returns a last time with the reprise of an extreme low-angle shot from the *Bounty*'s departure, in which the camera remains static as the massive sails balloon overhead. With "Rule Britannia" surging on the soundtrack and the flag of the Royal Navy flying, the return of the image codes as triumphant and redemptive; but the more sensory cues of looming sails and vertiginous camera angle hint at the memory of recent turmoil. And a cruelty which could, like the shot itself, re-emerge.

IMAGINATION, POETRY, VITALITY

Unlike *Mutiny on the Bounty*, *Romeo and Juliet* invites the viewer to appreciate, rather than surrender to, its representation of a bygone age. Though *Photoplay* finds that Leslie Howard makes Romeo "intensely ardent, human, and appealing" ("The Shadow Stage" 1936b: 53), it is the "sheer physical beauty" (53) of the *mise en scène* that first gains praise in the review. "[W]ith accuracy and lavishness, with fidelity and touching loveliness all the glory of the Renaissance" (53) appears on the screen. An advertisement for the film strikingly invokes Thalberg himself in the creation of this classical world: "To the famed producer Irving Thalberg go the honors for bringing to the screen, with tenderness and reverence, William Shakespeare's imperishable love story."[8] Given his rejection of screen credits, Thalberg's inclusion in the publicity introduces two simple questions—why so overtly claim *Romeo and Juliet*, and why at this point in his career?

In one regard, Thalberg's presence in the publicity lends credence to Lambert's observation that "the picture is [. . .] more concerned to *be* a classic than find the essence of a classic" (1973: 104). Where *Mutiny* is publicized as a film that viscerally engages with the public, *Romeo* emerges as a film *for* a public as reverential to the source material as Thalberg himself was. Vieira notes that "Shakespeare was in the air" in mid-1930s Hollywood, with Max Reinhardt's Hollywood Bowl production of *A Midsummer Night's Dream* in 1934 and his subsequent 1935 film (2010: 336). For Thalberg, however, *Romeo and Juliet* represented far more than an acquiescence to the cultural vogue.[9] As he would explain to Marx,

> Every picture is under obligation to its customers. In making [this] we are obligated to customers not yet born. This picture may play to more present-day audiences if we adapt the Shakespeare dialogue to modern tastes, but we must maintain our integrity to all the public. They'll reach upward to the highest levels we can set for them, but they'll never stoop over an inch. (Qtd. in Marx 1942: section 2)

In a reprise of his statements at the 1930 meeting with the AMPP, Thalberg here sets out a statement of purpose: to provide meaningful pictures that entertain and, in this case, elevate the public. Where films like *The Divorcée* and *Red-Headed Woman* were, paradoxically, conventional in their very risks—bringing up routine questions of sexuality and morality—*Romeo and Juliet* introduced a more unexpected and defining challenge. In effect, the intelligent producer needed to balance fidelity to one of the most famous texts in literature with his desire to make formidable material both inviting and rewarding for audiences. As Marx explains, Thalberg "saw [the film] as a monument to his career" (1975: 249) and, it could be added, to his sensitive engagement with the public.

Once Thalberg had supervised the scoring and editing of the film (Vieira 2010: 349), he began the process of previews. From fan magazine interviews of the day to Marx's retrospective study, the preview features as a key element in accounts of *Romeo and Juliet*—though in a variety of iterations. Cukor recalled "the current of uneasiness shifting through the theater" (qtd. in Small 1936: 47) as the crowd realized the unannounced film was a Shakespeare adaptation, only for that unease to defuse in their enjoyment: "They realised we weren't trying to declaim [. . .] They were so delighted they nearly crowed" (47). Shearer, however, spoke of a preview in which the spectators "sat transfixed, but that's not a sure sign of anything [. . .] When they just sit, you can't be sure—anyway, not when you're as nervous as we were" (qtd. in Zeitlin 1936: 61). It was only when the preview cards came in that Thalberg, Shearer, Cukor, and Howard knew the audience liked the film (61). Decades later, Marx would recount Thalberg's concern over a screening for a crowd of underwhelmed university students; "attuned to their reactions, he sensed the disappointment" (1975: 250) in the theater.

This emphasis on the preview experience as opposed to the retake process captures, if only by omission, the relative limitations of the latter for this particular film.[10] As Marx goes on to explain,

> [R]etakes could only be made to a certain degree. There was no way to alter the motivations, cut out characters and replace them with others, or change the climactic situation, as [Thalberg] had done in so many films in the past. He was trapped by the classic construction of the play, for changes in Shakespeare would be called sacrilege. (250)

Vieira expands on Marx's statement to point out that Thalberg did emphasise some conventional draws, including comic moments with Edna May Oliver as the Nurse and the final swordfight between Romeo and Paris (2010: 350). Yet in place of the more dramatic interventions that could occur in almost any other production—even his adaptation of *Anna Karenina*—Thalberg encountered an elemental stasis in the conception and execution of the narrative. "He was trapped," to use Marx's words, by overdetermined material and audience foreknowledge.

But as Thalberg would explain to his colleagues in another context, "Movies aren't made; they're remade" (qtd. in Thomas 139). With this abiding theory in mind, Thalberg found creative latitude in *Romeo and Juliet* not through altering the diegetic world, but in recasting his modern-day principles of production in the context of a centuries-old artwork. To expand on Lambert's statement above: the film speaks to Thalberg's concern with what *makes* a classic, as well as with it *"be[ing]* a classic" (1973: 104) in its own right. William Strunk Jr., the academic Thalberg hired as a consultant to the production, had explained that "Shakespeare would have made the best movie producer in history" (qtd. in Vieira 2010: 341) with his appreciation of gripping narratives and, at times, collaborations with other storytellers. For Thalberg, then, the process of adapting the play explicitly aligned its classical status with his own vision of contemporary

filmmaking, and in turn cemented his identity as the inheritor of a Shakespearean legacy. The intelligent producer *remade Romeo and Juliet* by retaking his
own long-established catalogue of techniques and aesthetic concerns—great
scenes, the evocation of a dream world, and love stories—to claim the cultural
value of Hollywood's entertainment value.

In the preface to the souvenir program, Thalberg foregrounds this discourse by defining a classic as such: "A classic is a work of beauty which has
emerged victor over time. It is the winner in the most intense competition of
all, an aesthetic popular vote over a period of years" (1936: 1). Continuing
in these terms, Thalberg clearly identifies Shakespeare as the master of producing entertainment value: "[M]an of the theatre that he was, [he] employed
every device to entertain his audience. He wrote not for the few, but for the
many" (1). Framed within this context of mass appeal, Thalberg's Shakespeare
anticipates the theories of narrative and sensory impact that the film producer
himself would transpose to the screen:

> It is especially appropriate to present Shakespeare on the screen because
> his dramatic form is practically that of the scenario. His was a stage of
> action. His theatre had no curtain. His method, like that of the scenarist,
> was to write not in acts but in scenes—dramatic scenes dealing with a
> decisive moment in the lives of his characters. [. . .] But Shakespeare did
> more than write a perfect scenario. He wrote magnificent poetry. (1)

In so arguing for Shakespeare as a cinematic storyteller, Thalberg here aims to
undo any daunting associations with classical literature that would risk intimi-
dating the everyday spectator. At the same time, he also identifies Hollywood
filmmaking itself with the Shakespearean tradition—thus ensuring both the
approachability of the latter and the symbolic gravity of the former. Eliding
the distinction between stage and screen, past and present, Thalberg presents
Romeo and Juliet as a classic—a "work of beauty"—that belongs to its audience as well as its producer(s). And by concluding with the praise of Shakespeare's "magnificent poetry," Thalberg implicitly invites a consideration of,
a curiosity about, how that poetry could be seen on the screen. As Thalberg
notes earlier in the piece, Shakespeare's "play is addressed to the eye as well
as the ear" (1).

Certainly the opulence of the *mise en scène* emerged as a central feature in
the film. A *Photoplay* article of the day listed what Cukor called the "staggering
statistics" (qtd. in Small 99) of various materials and personnel[11]; later, in conversation with Lambert, Cukor would recall the conflicts over costumes and set
design. Established MGM figures Cedric Gibbons and Gilbert Adrian found
themselves reluctantly sharing the responsibility with Oliver Messel, Cukor's
personal choice of set designer. This division of artistic sensibilities—a "tug of

war [about which] Thalberg sat like Solomon and never committed himself," in Cukor's words—led to an allegedly vague aesthetic. Cukor explained, "The result is what you see, neither one thing nor the other. It's original at moments [. . .] and conventional at others" (qtd. in Lambert 1973: 104).

What Cukor perceived as a relative weakness, however, contributes an inherently oneiric quality to the production. Recalling Thalberg's statement in the *Saturday Evening Post*, the actor, writer, and director must collaborate to "transport [the] audience into a dream world" (85). Accordingly, *Romeo and Juliet* needed to reflect both the intensity of feeling and classical elegance of Shakespeare's "magnificent poetry" (1936: 1). The adaptation introduced still another concern: namely, how would Thalberg offer a definitive representation of a romance that had been shared by audiences for literally centuries, across many different formats? What Cukor remembers as Solomonic detachment can, in the context of Thalberg's abiding emphasis on versatility (oblique casting, the experimentation of the intelligent producer), be considered as the latter's implicit acknowledgment that there were many ways to depict a dream world so entrenched in the cultural imagination.

The prologue establishes this sense of plurality, with a framed tapestry coming to life to feature the chorus—who, even as flesh-and-blood actors, sit and stand almost motionless before a painted backdrop. Effectively awakening the classic play while heralding its status as a work of art, the prologue claims a constellation of styles from the immediate and animate to the detached and illustrative. Indeed, where the driving synthesis of man, sea, and ship in *Mutiny* captures an elemental struggle for survival, the shifting look of *Romeo and Juliet* follows a more emotional logic determined by the characters' "decisive moments" (Thalberg 1936: 1). The euphoria of love-at-first-sight plays out within the kaleidoscopic patterns of the masquerade ball, choreographed by Agnes De Mille; the despair of Juliet contemplating her half-death in the potion scene corresponds with the Deco minimalism of her bedchamber. Similarly, crowd scenes taking place in the town square share a naturalistic quality of light and shot composition, while the confidences and sweet partings in the gardens of the Capulet mansion feature a more theatrical insularity. Such perpetual visual fluidity helps bring dynamism to a legendary tale—one that, as Marx pointed out, could not itself be modified. In order to win that "aesthetic popular vote" of which Thalberg wrote, he had to demonstrate to audiences that *Romeo and Juliet* was still very much alive.

In proving that, as he maintained in the program, "The notion that a classic is dry as dust is in most cases mistaken" (1936: 1), Thalberg returned to still another, more recent classic: the conventions of silent cinema. As he explained in the 1929 USC lecture, "Certain subjects are best interpreted through the silent form, and the silence itself is often a great virtue" (1977: 126). This notion found new expression in the masquerade ball sequence in which Romeo and Juliet first see each other and fall in love, identified by Thalberg as one of Shakespeare's defining scenes (1936: 1). In order to convey this sense of profound attraction, particularly in a film with dialogue to which any member of the audience could have known the words, Thalberg foregrounds the eloquence of silence. At roughly three minutes long, the moment of love-at-first-sight generates, in fact, from the more sustained rhythm of Romeo's admiring glances that only ends when Juliet finally returns his gaze.

Like the animated tapestry of the prologue, the sequence overtly evokes a dream world of aesthetic counterpoints: the fixed pattern of the gleaming floor juxtaposed with the shimmering reflections of the dancers that play upon it; the decorative trees held by the page boys paralleling the willowy grace of the women; and perhaps most strikingly, the white-satin-covered heads of the dancers calling all the more attention to Juliet's brunette curls (see Figure 7.3). In a series of point-of-view shots from Romeo's perspective, Juliet appears as the focal point in the spectacular ballet. She dances in long shot and close-ups, drawing the extra- and intra- diegetic eye with her precision of movement and lustrous costume. Romeo, by contrast, stands still and apart from the crowd, alternately wearing and taking off his mask. Unlike Garbo's first appearance in *Anna Christie* or *Grand Hotel*, the appearance of Shearer as Juliet does not

Figure 7.3 The masquerade ball.

appeal to a sense of delayed gratification; the audience has seen her before, even if Romeo has not. But so reframed within this lyrical number, featuring only the voices of a children's choir, Juliet appears anew to both spectator and Romeo. In a construction of alluring innocence that explicitly recalls the love scenes upon which Thalberg insisted for *La Bohème*, the viewer has a second chance to process their impression of Juliet as a romantic heroine.

Running parallel to this stylistic dynamism were Thalberg's oblique interpretations of still other decisive moments in the film. The funeral of friend and colleague John Gilbert, who had died in January 1936, inspired this approach. Struck by the histrionics of a mourning Marlene Dietrich, who had been Gilbert's lover, Thalberg resisted more conventional angles on Romeo and Juliet's tragedy: "No, it's overdone," he commented on viewing the rushes of a farewell scene. "It's beautiful, but the parting would have much more poignancy if it were done with a smile [. . .] It's better to underplay a scene than to act as they did at Jack's funeral" (qtd. in Thomas 299–301).[12] Lambert found this approach generated the "low emotional temperature" (1990: 229) in the film; and indeed, Romeo and Juliet's love appears somewhat subdued compared to the unlikely passion of the attraction–repulsion between Bligh and Christian. Production Code restrictions meant that even the sequence of Romeo and Juliet's wedding night could only suggest the consummation of their love. Following their embrace, there is an elliptical montage that links together illustrative backdrops of the Capulet balcony and a starry sky with naturalistic shots of the coming dawn (replete with trees, birds, and rising sun). But in so underplaying tragic and sensual circumstance and committing to Shakespeare's "magnificent poetry" (Thalberg 1936: 1) through more allusive imagery, Thalberg's *Romeo and Juliet* offers a dream world in which desire is both a thing of beauty and an utterly natural condition.

The potion scene, however, interjects an intensity that reveals the nightmarish quality of that world. Thalberg had particularly admired this monologue: "What Shakespeare did with that potion scene! By his own imagination, poetry and vitality, he had Juliet describe what the potion was going to do for her. It's brilliant" (qtd. in Thomas 299). Cukor filmed the soliloquy in a single shot, with the camera steadily reframing to follow Juliet/Shearer's movements in the relatively spare environs of her bedchamber. Without the dramatic pull of cuts, musical score, or bold *mise en scène*—Juliet/Shearer declaims the speech before a bedcurtain and a blank wall—the sequence relies on, indeed, the "imagination, poetry and vitality" of Shakespeare's words and Shearer's performance.

Where *Strange Interlude* contrasted interior emotions and outward articulation, the potion scene insists upon their intertwining as Juliet narrates her present and future experience: she questions the motivations of the Friar, dreads her tortured awakening in the tomb, and finally sees the projections of

Figure 7.4 The potion scene.

her fears embodied in Tybalt's ghost. If the masquerade ball presents a reprise of silent-era romantic conventions, then the potion scene celebrates the capacities of sound by making both the words and Shearer's voice the spectacle. The entertainment value of the sequence lies not in the lushness of set design or, as in *Mutiny*, the expressivity of the editing; instead, it derives from the imagery that Juliet/Shearer conjures on an imaginative screen within the cinematic dream world (see Figure 7.4).

The scene closes on a more overtly expressionist image, with the camera zooming in for a final extreme close-up while the extra-diegetic score begins at last. At this point, Juliet holds the bottle of potion high and declares, "Romeo, I come! This do I drink to thee." It is the *this* that Shearer emphasizes in her line reading and, in so doing, expands its referential scope—defining it as not just a potion, but an entire experience of horror and uncertainty that she is willing to endure for Romeo. *This* is what underlies the dream world of Romeo and Juliet's love story; *this* is the unexpected source of visceral intensity, raising the "emotional temperature" of which Lambert wrote. Though the scene itself was filmed, ironically, on one of the few days that Thalberg was away from the set (Crowther 1957: 233–234), its impact captures what he had already seen in Shakespeare's words.

On August 26, *Romeo and Juliet* premiered in New York (Lambert 1990: 230). Thalberg contracted pneumonia on September 12, following a severe cold that he had caught on Labor Day weekend (Vieira 2010: 364). He died at home two days later at the age of 37, surrounded by family and his closest MGM colleagues. Considered within the context of the production itself, his passing introduced a poignant coda to the Shakespearean tragedy; to borrow Thalberg's words, it was the final decisive moment in the romantic epic that he had created with such passion and care. But just as Thalberg had spent his last year at MGM exploring how he could make better films, he spent his last days still attentive to their success. The night before he died, Thalberg woke from his sickbed to ask, "*Romeo and Juliet.* What were the weekend grosses?" (qtd. in Vieira 2010: 367).

"AS LONG AS IRVING LIVES . . ."

Up until his death, Irving Thalberg was making plans for the future. Primary among these was his development of the I. G. Thalberg Corporation, an independent film studio, and productions of *The Good Earth*, *Camille*, and (in a more incipient phase) *Marie Antoinette*. While completing two of the greatest works of his career, Thalberg found himself on the threshold of a new professional era. Filled with potential and creative enterprise, this transitional period would attract commentary both nostalgic and, at times, hagiographic in the years following Thalberg's passing. As the following will discuss, such impulses recall the broader conceptual implications of the retake—this time, for understanding the studio and films that *could* have been.

The I. G. Thalberg Corporation was to be established following the December 31, 1938 expiration of his contract with MGM (Vieira 2010: 298). The overarching structure of the studio was clearly split between the creative and the logistical, with Thalberg producing the films and Loew's distributing them (Crowther 1957: 236). A draft of the 1935 contract agreement with Thalberg and Loew's elucidates, and indeed legalizes, a professional sovereignty which the former had long sought. The document acknowledges Thalberg as the central creative force with total control of the filmmaking process; interestingly, the agreement also notes that Thalberg would seek to end his contract with MGM earlier than 1938.[13]

Wide support for the venture had existed at least as far back as the restructuring in 1933, as made evident by the telegram from New York and New Jersey exhibitors cited in Chapter 6. They declared: "Hope you organize your own company and make great pictures you are capable of making and preserve your freedom."[14] Many years later, David Lewis would recall the plans for the company in equally idealistic terms:

> [Thalberg] was to have total autonomy—it was to be the first real production company financed by a major studio, yet totally independent [. . .] He told me at the time that he was even allotting shares of this new company to his associates [. . .] If he had lived, I would have been rich beyond my wildest dreams. (93)

These accounts, set out sixty years apart, capture the romance of the intelligent producer becoming an *independent* producer. For the exhibitors, Thalberg emerges as a hero "preserv[ing]" artistic integrity in the industry; and Lewis's admiration is intertwined with a wistful vision of his own role in that epic narrative of liberation. Indeed, Thalberg planned to share his success, viewing the studio as an opportunity to continue creating great work with his most valued colleagues. He intended to bring with him producing associates, including Bernard Hyman;[15] stars like Shearer, Laughton, and the Marx Brothers;[16] and even directors (Lewis 93). The terms of Thalberg's contract also allowed him, as Crowther notes, to cultivate "any new stars or other talents" (1960: 203) with whom he worked at MGM up to the point of his contract ending. As Hyman had once declared, "As long as Irving lives, we're all great men" (qtd. in Marx 1975: 252); and certainly, the very idea of Thalberg's independent studio seemed to assure a "great" new epoch of filmmaking.

For all of the enthusiasm and idealism that surrounded the venture at the time—and would again in later nostalgic discussions—Thalberg encountered disheartening challenges. In a legalistic statement dated February 1936, Stromberg recorded an account of his aborted negotiations with Thalberg, who had invited him to join the studio. Though a dramatically aggrieved Stromberg protests that he felt used by Thalberg as a pawn in his conflicts with MGM, it is clear that the former also leveraged his discussions with Thalberg to gain a better contract with Mayer and Schenck. In a particularly striking section of the document, Stromberg effectively congratulates himself for stalling a venture that could have been a key competitor for MGM.[17] The twists and turns of Stromberg's narrative—detailing who met whom where and when, and outlining the great deal he finally cut with Mayer and Schenck—read like an affidavit; yet what they also implicitly reveal is a collective anxiety over Thalberg as a threat to the studio he had helped found. If Stromberg resented being Thalberg's alleged pawn, then he was certainly rewarded for being Mayer and Schenck's informant.

In the same month, Thalberg would briefly acknowledge this situation and still other worries in a letter to potential partners Mary Pickford and Sam Goldwyn. For instance, Thalberg expresses frustration over his unsuccessful attempts to cancel his contract with MGM before 1938. Such a sentiment distils the day-to-day aggravations of working with Mayer to their essence: Thalberg wanted out of MGM as much as Mayer wanted him gone. (On the latter's own terms, that is; Vieira comments on Mayer's anger upon learning of Thalberg's arrangement with Loew's [2010: 298].) At the same time, Thalberg had reservations over the financial risks that Pickford and Goldwyn would be taking by investing in the studio. Noting that the company was not due to begin operations for three years, Thalberg points to the vagaries of economic and personal circumstances—including his own health.[18] Which is to say: Thalberg had plans for the future, but he also had concerns.

Lewis's recollection of the corporation captures the best of its possibilities, both artistically and commercially; to paraphrase Hyman, there is no question of the great works and careers that the I. G. Thalberg Corporation would have produced, had Thalberg lived. But the picture looks somewhat different with a shift in perspective. Moving from the conditional future recorded by friends and colleagues to the present-tense of Thalberg's own experience, captured in part through those historical documents, reveals that his studio was another work-in-progress. Just as he could see the value in and vulnerabilities of a film in production, Thalberg also understood the complex potential of his own company. He knew, that is, that "the difference between something good and something superior is often very small" (qtd. in Crowther 1957: 181); what these documents suggest is that Thalberg was still pushing that margin of excellence for his own company. Just as he was, in fact, for *Marie Antoinette*.

In four years of preproduction, Thalberg hired eleven writers to craft the perfect screenplay and invested nearly half-a-million dollars in the picture (Vieira 2010: 384); as T. L. Larkin notes, he also engaged in extensive negotiations with Joseph Breen about the more sensational elements of the biography (2019: 151). Thalberg would not, however, be present for the actual filming of *Marie Antoinette*. Before his death, he had overseen the development of *Camille* per his standard process of story conferences and viewing rushes; Garbo had even balked at one of his visits to the set because "she was preoccupied" (Lambert 1973: 106, 111–112).[19] And as early as 1934, Thalberg had sent crews to China to begin compiling footage for *The Good Earth*. He had also guided the development of the screenplay and had chosen leading actors and the director (Thomas 304–306). The production included one of Thalberg's more demanding great scenes: a locust plague. As Vieira notes, this scene cemented Thalberg's use of montage (as seen in *Mutiny*) as a dramatic device (2010: 326). When the production manager expressed his concerns over filming the sequence, Thalberg gestured to the capacities of the retake. "If it doesn't work," he said, "we'll fix it later" (qtd. in Vieira 326).

Though Thalberg died before these films reached completion, his direct engagement in their productions from conception to execution render them liminal works; cinematic passages, as it were, between one MGM era and the next. By contrast, 1938's *Marie Antoinette* remained a film at that much more of a remove from Thalberg: in theory "still *his*" (qtd. in Lambert 1990: 99), as Shearer would declare, yet in certain respects very much her own. But from the perspective of the retake, what makes the work especially fascinating is the way in which it attests to a broader imperative to carry on Thalberg's legacy. If, as Marx notes, "[Shearer] was [Thalberg's] greatest production" (1975: 69), then her role in the making of *Marie Antoinette* captures her desire to establish her own identity as the heir to Thalberg's dynasty. As a 1937 gossip item in *Photoplay* would put it: "Despite the aching loss of her husband [. . .] the work [Shearer] inherited from [him] must go on" (York 88).

As Larkin points out, there are diverging accounts of how Stefan Zweig's 1932 biography of the queen came to the screen, with scholars alternately giving credit to Shearer and Thalberg for recognizing its cinematic potential (127). Such ambiguity, though academic, suggests that from its inception the project was a kind of hybrid, belonging to both producer and star. However Thalberg committed to the production, he believed that it would be one of the *chef d'oeuvres* of both his and Shearer's careers. The film would have presented a conclusion to their triptych of period works exploring female subjectivities, following on from Elizabeth Barrett Browning and Juliet. In May 1935, before the making of *Romeo and Juliet*, Thalberg had even announced, "Juliet and Marie Antoinette will mark the end of Norma's acting career" (qtd. in Lambert 1990: 220).

For all of Thalberg's preparation, it is impossible to know what *Marie Antoinette* would have been with his direct guidance. Would the film have featured an oblique interpretation of the events, underplaying Marie Antoinette's tragedy just as Thalberg underplayed *Romeo and Juliet*'s? Would it have emphasized the brutality of the French Revolution, recalling that lust for vengeance that helped shape *Mutiny on the Bounty*? Or would the production have crafted a dream world that made historical fact as much of a storybook romance as *La Bohème*? Even aside from its significance for Shearer's career, *Marie Antoinette* would have provided Thalberg the opportunity to further refine the theories that had guided his productions at MGM: the dramatic tableaux of great scenes of history; the intersection between private woman and public queen; and a love story that encompassed familial bonds, extra-marital affairs, and even chauvinism. In the end, however, what emerged was a film as much about Hollywood history as the French Revolution. The concern over Thalberg's legacy helped to direct the course of the production, and knowledge of this extra-diegetic context informed/s both historical and contemporary audiences' appreciation of *Marie Antoinette*. Ultimately, it is a film about loss—of youthful illusions, love, and finally, life itself.

As Lambert remarks, Shearer's desire to carry on with the project and play the historical queen derived from her perception of the "parallels" between them, thus leading to a process in which Shearer "gave two performances, as Marie Antoinette and Queen of the Lot" (1990: 261, 260). Shearer worked indefatigably in these roles—"as if she wanted to make up for someone who couldn't be there," according to *Photoplay* journalist Kirtley Baskette (1938: 85). As he would explain,

> Right now as never before, Metro-Goldwyn Mayer misses Irving Thalberg and his peerless tradition. Norma Shearer still exemplifies that as does no one else in Hollywood. They were the royal couple and she is still queen. As queenly as Toinette herself. (86)

Maintaining her identity as Queen of the Lot presented Shearer with more challenges than such popular commentary reveals, however. Though her marriage to Thalberg had exalted her during his lifetime, it inspired enmity after his passing. Through Thalberg's estate, Shearer became a key stockholder in MGM, as well as the beneficiary of a percentage deal that entitled her to his share of the studio's profits (Lambert 1990: 254). Mayer first attempted to cut Shearer out of the percentage agreement and convince her to sell her shares; and even after the resolution of the legal conflict, during which Shearer terminated her original contract with the studio, he proceeded to launch an unofficial campaign to unsettle the star. Conferring with producer Stromberg, Mayer replaced Shearer's preferred director, Sidney Franklin, with a less sympathetic W. S. Van Dyke. Renowned for his "one-take" efficiency, Van Dyke represented not just a point of potential conflict but a jarring contrast to Thalberg's own meditative filmmaking process (Lambert 1990: 243–245, 254).

Even Baskette, in the same article that heralded Shearer's return to the screen, admitted that the production was troubled: "[T]here was a tense, strained air for a long time about the set [. . .] Norma was nervous. The cast walked around on tiptoes. The atmosphere was electric—charged with something about to happen" (85). For all of the strain of reprising her husband's conflicted relationship with Mayer, Shearer also perceived an opportunity to cement a new public identity. As Lies Lanckman points out, Thalberg's death introduced the gravity of widowhood into Shearer's persona, offsetting her previous "balance between upper-class respectability and [. . .] modern freedom" (2016: 78). Director William Wellman would, in fact, cite Shearer's "magnificent behavior" following Thalberg's death as an inspiration for the conclusion of his classic *A Star is Born* (1937) (Lambert 1990: 244).

Subsequent articles would further emphasize Shearer's power in the industry and, tellingly, over her own career. In the 1936 *Motion Picture* interview cited earlier, Shearer had declared, "Most of my decisions are made for me. Which is pleasant, because I trust the *decider* so completely. But he *is* the decider" (qtd. in Zeitlin 33). Two years later, Baskette would revise this history: "The popular conception of the professional relationship between Norma Shearer and Irving Thalberg is that he guided her completely in everything. The truth is she often disagreed with him; she always had a mind of her own" (22). Indeed, Lewis recalled a discussion with Shearer in which she stated that she would not follow her husband's interpretation of the Queen—that is, a heroine in the tradition of those

> classic traged[ies] [. . .] illuminated by characters who, through their own folly, brought themselves to ruin, but who, in the face of their enemies rose to great dignity and honor and paid for their sins with true nobility of spirit. (111)

By contrast, Shearer stated that she had "no intention of playing Marie Antoinette as a foolish woman or an unsympathetic character. She said no audience would accept a star in that kind of role" (111). Ever mindful of her on-screen image,[20] Shearer emerged in the production process as a business-minded and creatively aware performer.

If Thalberg perceived *Romeo and Juliet* as a monument to his career, then Shearer—with this new sense of agency—perceived *Marie Antoinette* as a monument to her husband. It is fitting, then, that the two films would share a similar stylistic duality. Where *Romeo and Juliet* adopted an internal alterity to heighten the dynamism of the classic text, *Marie Antoinette* parallels its heroine's transformation through shifts between romantic and realist perspectives. The first half of the film "[caught] the spirit" of Versailles (qtd. in Lambert 1990: 261), as Gibbons put it, through an opulent *mise en scène* that matches the court's pleasure-seeking excesses. In lavish gowns and headdresses, adored by the courtiers, Shearer-as-Marie Antoinette is, in effect, a star. The second half of the film, however, highlights Thalberg's notion of the Queen's (eventual) "nobility of spirit," with her emergence as a virtuous wife, mother, and socially conscious ruler. Here, the work assumes the gravitas of a bio-pic with flourishes of the melodramatic. A documentary-style sequence of toiling workers highlights the historical crisis of poverty and unrest—narrated, however, by the modulated tones of the treacherous Duke d'Orleans (Joseph Schildkraut); and in tracing the rulers' attempted escape after the Revolution, the scene moves between exterior shots of a forest to the intimacy of a studio-constructed village street.

The final sequence, in which a tumbrel carries Marie Antoinette to the guillotine, presents the climax of this duality. In a relatively fast-paced series of cuts contrasting the earlier, more languid editing rhythm, the sequence follows Marie's journey in both bird's-eye views of the mobbed city streets and medium close-ups of her face. Quasi-naturalistic images are intercut with stylized elements: an exterior dolly shot shows the Queen trundling along in the back of the tumbrel, as a breeze moves the rim of the bonnet covering her shorn hair; while in the subsequent image, a medium shot frames her and three guards before a process screen of the city street. The camera then zooms in to a close-up that captures Marie Antoinette/Shearer's beatific face—only to cut to an exterior medium-long shot of the sunlit crowd as they alternately weep for and disparage the monarch. Finally, in the shot before Marie Antoinette faces her execution, the painted buildings and skyline evoke a fairy-tale quality that serves to highlight the grim immediacy of the guillotine itself.

Rather than indicate an imbalance, however, the climactic intertwining of these realist and romantic elements offers a quickening of experience before the end of the film and the passing of its heroine. The close-ups reference the idealizing projections that transformed Marie Antoinette into a *de facto* star of Versailles, and the naturalism of the exterior shots reveals the body that had remained hidden beneath the highly-constructed, lavish gowns. Certainly the concluding image of the Queen herself captures this essential cohesion of past and present. As Marie Antoinette waits upon the scaffold in medium close-up, she tearfully looks off into the distance while a vision of her as a young girl is superimposed over the image of the tragic present. Clapping her hands with joy, the Marie Antoinette that was exclaims, "Think of it—I shall be Queen! I shall be Queen of France!" (see Figure 7.5).

This special-effect process of superimposition was, in fact, Shearer's idea (Vieira 2010: 392); it is not certain whether the overt sentimentality of the image, however affecting, would have appealed to Thalberg's emphasis on oblique interpretations of key scenes. The conception of the shot did, however, definitively cohere Shearer's two roles as Queen of the Lot and Marie Antoinette. For the rest of her life, the past remained present for Shearer through her devotion to Thalberg's memory and his filmmaking legacy. *Marie Antoinette* itself performed respectably at the box office and received favorable reviews,[21] and Shearer was

Figure 7.5 Marie Antoinette, past and present.

nominated for an Academy Award. Baskette virtually predicted the defining role that *Marie Antoinette* itself would play in the Thalberg–Shearer dynasty, describing it as

> much more than a comeback picture for Norma Shearer [. . .] It's more than the most carefully prepared movie re-creation [*sic*] of a historical era ever attempted [. . .] It is more than any material thing. It is a testimonial to one of the greatest real life loves Hollywood has ever known. (20)

Shearer's post-*Marie Antoinette* career did not, however, regain its Thalberg-era momentum. Despite the critical and popular success of *The Women* (dir. Cukor, 1939), her roles in the relatively unpopular *Idiot's Delight* (dir. Brown, 1939) and *Escape* (dir. Mervyn LeRoy, 1940) led to her retirement from the screen in 1942. As Hedda Hopper would later comment, "*Marie Antoinette* capped anything [Shearer] ever did" (1952: 135).

In the late 1930s, Shearer did make a bid to play Scarlett O'Hara in *Gone With the Wind* (Haskell 2009: 61)—an overture that, appropriately, recalled Thalberg's own passing engagement with the project. Albert Lewin would remember pitching the Margaret Mitchell novel to Thalberg in the summer of 1936, only to find that the latter was not interested: "It's sensational. The role is great for Gable and it will make a terrific picture. Now get out of here with it" (qtd. in Thomas 315). When Lewin balked, Thalberg explained,

> Look, I have just made *Mutiny on the Bounty* and *The Good Earth*. And now you're asking me to burn Atlanta? No! Absolutely not! No more epics for me now. Just give me a little drawing-room drama. I'm tired. I'm just too tired. (Qtd. in Thomas 315–316)

The *Gone With the Wind* anecdote has emerged over the years in various accounts, to various effect. For sympathetic biographers like Thomas and Vieira (2010: 320), it underscores Thalberg's exhaustion in that final year, as well as his equanimity in the midst of squabbling over material; for more sardonic chroniclers of Hollywood, the story provides proof of Thalberg's fallibility (Friedrich 2014: 25). As much as anything, though, Thalberg's brief encounter with the project introduces still more questions about the films he did not, and could not, make.

Over time, such questions have become part of Thalberg's cultural memory, heightening the poignancy of his early passing with the temporality of what-could-have-been. As Vieira suggests, even stars like Garbo and Jeanette MacDonald—not to mention Shearer—would have had more longevity in their careers "[i]f Thalberg had lived" (2010: 397). An independent studio, longer careers for MGM's stars of the 1930s, another *Gone With the Wind*—all of these populate the landscape of Thalberg's conditional Hollywood. But all the more intriguing is to trace his legacy in the actual films that succeeded him. For instance, would Selznick's phenomenal success with *Gone With the Wind* have been the same without the precedent of Thalberg's theory of maximizing entertainment value in each film? Would the burning of Atlanta—which Thalberg himself implicitly identified as the great scene of the picture—have had the same impact without the influence of, for example, the *Ben-Hur* chariot race? And would Gable have seemed so perfect a Rhett Butler without his oblique casting as the violent but virtuous Fletcher Christian? Roland Flamini has pointed out that "Thalberg deserves a full biography for what he did, not what he might have done" (1994: 7); to paraphrase this, the following chapter will argue that Thalberg's presence in cinema post-1936 is not simply connected to what could have been, but to what he had already produced.

NOTES

1. Marx explains that the trolley "cost $400 a night. It was ordered so often that Pacific Electric laid a spur directly onto the lot" (1975: 136).
2. As Albert Lewin would recall, "Irving never hesitated to spend the extra money [on retakes]. His successors were not like that" (qtd. in Rosenberg and Silverstein 113).
3. See Thomas 1969: 297; Lambert 1990: 220–221; Vieira 2010: 357.
4. Available at <https://www.youtube.com/watch?v=HxNeuvf2yxk> (last accessed October 24, 2019).
5. MPPDA (Committee on Public Relations, Sub-Committee on Eliminations). "Original Formulation of the Don'ts and Be Careful." MPPDA Digital Archive, Flinders University Library Special Collections. MPPDA Record 341, Report of Meeting. 3-1232 to 3-1234. Available at <https://mppda.flinders.edu.au/records/341> (last accessed 24 October, 2019).
6. Only *Biography of a Bachelor Girl* (dir. Griffith) failed to make a profit. See Appendix to Vieira 2010.
7. Advertisement for *Mutinty on the Bounty*. *Photoplay* December 1935: 2.
8. Advertisement for *Romeo and Juliet*. *Photoplay* May 1936: 2.
9. Vieira also points out that the late-1935 production of *Midsummer* was "too late to influence [the] decision to film *Romeo and Juliet*" (2010: 336).
10. A gossip item in *Modern Screen* would, however, wryly recount that just as Leslie Howard was getting ready to leave Hollywood ("bags were all packed"), Thalberg called him back to the studio for retakes (Townsend 1936: 98).
11. This list includes "Ninety thousand flagstones, two hundred tons of cement, [. . .] eighty books of gold leaf, five hundred yards of carpets, [. . .] twelve bootmakers, two hundred and fifty seamstresses, thirty embroiderers, [and] five hundred painters" (Small 1936: 99).
12. This approach recalls Thalberg's oblique interpretation of a romantic scene in *Camille*. Thinking through angles on the sequence in which Marguerite (Garbo) and Armand (Robert Taylor) discuss their elopement, Thalberg decided that "[t]hey should play this scene as though they were plotting a murder!" (qtd. in Lambert 1973: 111). As Cukor explained in an interview with Lambert, "This was a very interesting idea, and if you remember the scene, it has a kind of tension and no sentimentality at all" (qtd. in Lambert 111).

13. Margaret Herrick Library, Academy of Motion Picture Arts and Sciences, Irving G. Thalberg and Norma Shearer Papers, File 1-f.11.
14. Ibid., File 1-f.2.
15. Ibid., File 1-f.11.
16. Ibid., File 1-f.19.
17. Margaret Herrick Library, Academic of Motion Picture Arts and Sciences, Hunt Stromberg papers. File 16-f.221.
18. Margaret Herrick Library, Academy of Motion Picture Arts and Sciences, Irving G. Thalberg and Norma Shearer Papers. File 1-f.19. Thalberg also mentions in this letter that Stromberg would have likely signed with him if he had been offered more money.
19. Cukor recalled that Thalberg was "always quite shy with [Garbo] [. . .] He said, 'Well, I've been turned off better sets than this,' and left with the greatest grace. He looked and behaved like a prince" (qtd. in Lambert 1973: 106).
20. While directing Shearer in *Romeo and Juliet*, Cukor described her as a "highly self-critical woman who has schooled herself to give an impression of self-confidence," noting that "she looks at her work with the mind of a producer" (qtd. in Vieira 2010: 344, 349). Shearer's brother, sound engineer Douglas, offered a similar insight into the star's *modus operandi*: "Norma had a bent right knee. She learned to always turn it out. By studying hundreds of photographs of herself, she learned how to present this idealized image" (qtd. in Vieira 2010: 349).
21. The film made almost $3 million, before losses of over half-a-million; and *Variety* called the film "a pride to the entire industry" (qtd. in Vieira 2010: 394).

Conclusion: Once a Star, Always a Star

This book began with the image of Thalberg flipping a coin in the air. The introduction argued that the number of interpretations of this single act represented the desire to understand a figure so integral to film history and popular culture. Now, after exploring Thalberg's significance as a theorist of film production, the continual back-and-forth of the coin offers all the more allegorical resonance. In so tracing the evolution of his vision for popular film-making across industrial and technical shifts, as well as across a number of stars and films, these analyses have followed Thalberg's trajectory from the historical to the theoretical; the "dream factory" of MGM to the dream worlds of his motion pictures. But here, at the conclusion of this work, the motion of the coin runs parallel to a final journey for Thalberg: that one between the past and present of cinema. Why, and how, does Thalberg still matter today?

Martine Beugnet has noted that "the question of the multiple origins and genealogies of the medium of the moving image" (2015: 200) is one that preoccupies scholars, particularly in the digital age. Equally fascinating is discerning a figure such as Thalberg's role in those intertwined histories—not only in terms of the medium itself, but also in the industrialization of filmmaking. He helped to found one of the greatest studios in film history, and as its head of production refined—and in certain cases pioneered—processes of star-making and storytelling, editing and sound technology. Thalberg collaborated on the drafting of the Production Code that defined an entire era; he established a relationship with his audience through previews and retakes. In 1932, *Fortune* posited that "[Thalberg] is what Hollywood means by MGM" ("Metro-Goldwyn-Mayer" 1976: 257); now, in the 2000s, a question to consider is what Thalberg still means to Hollywood.

Complicating this is the strength of the Thalberg mythology, which emerged almost immediately after his death and has at times threatened to overshadow the gravitas of his work as a producer. The Boy Wonder grew into the intelligent producer; he, in turn, became a figure of romance evoked in fiction and historical accounts alike. Over time, Thalberg became a kind of screen on which to project fascinations with nostalgia, classic cinema hagiography, and artistic integrity in the corporate sector of Hollywood. Or as F. Scott Fitzgerald—so elemental to the producer's posthumous exaltation—put it: "Thalberg has always fascinated me. His peculiar charm, his extraordinary good looks, his bountiful success, the tragic end of his great adventure" (1993: xxxi). Just as producer studies seeks, as Spicer et al. have described it, to establish the value of a role that has been "easy to caricature but [. . .] difficult to define" (2014: 1), this book has illuminated new elements in the critical importance of a figure who has long been easy to idealize.

In order to map Thalberg's path from the past to the present, the following will trace the development of his afterlife—distinguishing between, while acknowledging the interconnectedness of, the allure of his myth and the importance of his cinematic and theoretical contributions. Fittingly, a concept established by Thalberg himself provides the framework: "Once a star, always a star. Actors aren't athletes. When you're a champion in this business, you're always a champion" (qtd. in Marx 1975: 149). This "once a star, always a star" ethos speaks to more than just the longevity of a career; it is a kind of prophecy articulating the continual re-emergence of Hollywood's, and Thalberg's, history in the contemporary moment. For all of its enduring "fascination," to paraphrase Fitzgerald, the myth of Thalberg has always been sustained by the significance of his productions—motion pictures and theories alike.

"WHEN YOU'RE A CHAMPION IN THIS BUSINESS, YOU'RE ALWAYS A CHAMPION"

Thalberg's "once a star, always a star" concept emerged in the 1920s, and its meaning would shift across the decades. Initially, it stood as another facet of his star-making principles, alongside oblique casting and considerations of audience and entertainment values. Over time, though, the theory would gain new meaning in relation to Thalberg's own celebrity, even in the midst of studio politics and posthumous struggles over his contributions to MGM.

Crowther cites an exchange between screenwriter Frances Marion and Thalberg as fundamental to his view of enduring stardom. In the late 1920s, Marion asked Thalberg to give her old friend Marie Dressler a leading role in the comedy *The Callahans and the Murphys* (dir. Hill, 1927).

Thalberg obliged, even though Dressler had not performed in some time. He noted,

> My theory is that anybody who hits the bull's-eye—it doesn't matter in what profession—has the brains and the stamina to do it again. So I figure a woman who scored as often as Miss Dressler did should be able to repeat. She's probably been the victim of bad writing—and bad advice. (Qtd. in Crowther 1957: 174).

Though the film itself was not a success, Dressler would go on to become one of the most popular box-office stars of the early 1930s in films like *Anna Christie* and *Dinner at Eight*, and would win the Best Actress Oscar for *Min and Bill* (dir. Hill, 1931).

Dressler was only one of the performers whose careers Thalberg helped to revitalize. Her frequent co-star Wallace Beery also found new opportunities at MGM (Crowther 1957: 175), as did Maurice Chevalier, Spencer Tracy, Ruth Chatterton, and the Marx Brothers (Lewis 1993: 72). Thalberg approached the comedians after they had parted ways with Paramount; as Chico Marx put it to a skeptical Groucho: "[Thalberg] had to fight with Mayer, who thinks we're all washed up in pictures, but Irving is firm; he wants us to work with him" (qtd. in Thomas 1969: 281). With Thalberg's support—and insistence on a love story between the comic set pieces (Thomas 281)—*A Night at the Opera* re-established the Marx Brothers as viable stars. David Lewis would explain at length,

> If people had real talent, [Thalberg] knew that talent could always be redeemed through careful nurturing, even though it had failed elsewhere. He knew many failures were to be blamed on bad material and bad handling, and he delighted in giving talent a chance to reclaim itself; it was never just to prove what he could do. (73)

As Lewis suggests above, Thalberg's attention to cultivating entertainment value in all facets of filmmaking—from story development and casting (oblique or otherwise) to shooting and editing the final picture—included an understanding of how a single production could, in turn, introduce new possibilities for a performer. Just as the retake allowed for a given film to undergo a process of reinvention, rehabilitation, Thalberg explored opportunities for "reclaim[ing]" established talent. As he would, ultimately, declare to Samuel Marx, "Once a star, always a star" (qtd. in Marx 1975: 149).

   These accounts attribute to Thalberg a kind of alchemical power through which he could heal both problem films and stalled careers. His sensitivity to reinvention, however, signaled his greater sympathy with the performer rather than a strategic *noblesse oblige*. Bob Thomas writes of how Thalberg "understood [actors]. He recognized their follies, their outpourings of ego, their fickle nature, but he also realised they were unusual human beings" (100). Ruth Waterbury's tribute to Thalberg after his passing highlighted this affinity with performers: "He sympathized and advised, directed and helped. Because of his generosity of spirit, Metro never had trouble with its actors [. . .] He could soothe the most troubled back to peace" (1936: 12). Such a sensitivity allowed for the triumphs cited above, as well as for disappointments; for instance, Marx notes that Thalberg was greatly distressed by John Gilbert's struggles to find success in a variety of roles in the 1930s (1975: 148). Considering the challenges that Thalberg himself faced in the studio restructuring, it is clear that he, too, would come to know the threat of falling from grace. Waterbury, in fact, connects Thalberg's collaboration with the struggling Marx Brothers to the machinations of "political factions [that] ar[ose] around" him (12). As she would conclude: *A Night at the Opera* "brought the Marxes back to fame. It left Thalberg untouched in his primary simplicity" (12). Which is to say—Thalberg's ability to rise to the challenge posed to him only reinforced the singularity of his abilities and sense of purpose.

These redemptive events exceed film history to assume a biographical importance, with their emphasis on vivification and reanimation implicitly underscoring the pathos of Thalberg's early passing. For all his capacity to grant, effectively, cinematic life—"never just to prove what he could do" (Lewis 73)—his own off-screen existence was grievously abbreviated. Waterbury described Thalberg as "a guiding star to heights which [MGM] could not have attained without him" (11); and this felicitous slippage between terms of cinematic celebrity and aesthetic vision highlights the fact that his "once a star, always a star" theory of resilience applied equally well to Thalberg himself. In fact, it resonates all the more profoundly when considering how his influence endured for the remainder of MGM's classical era.

Given the divisiveness that had characterized Thalberg's final years at MGM, raising questions of professional loyalty and competing artistic visions, the studio's response to his loss was fraught. Screenwriter (and close friend) Charles MacArthur described going to work at MGM "like going to the Automat" (qtd. in Crowther 1957: 239); as Crowther elucidates,

> That may have seemed a slightly biased estimation [. . .] But it gave a fair indication of the post-Thalberg regime. The sense of an inspirational influence, a *genius domus*, the studio had while he was there, even under the unit system, existed no longer when he was gone. [. . .] The air that emanated was one of remote authority [from Mayer]. (1957: 239)

After his death, the aesthetic aspirations and sense of shared enterprise that Thalberg cultivated in the studio had finally ceded to Mayer's control. David Lewis found that "[e]veryone wanted to diminish the Thalberg charisma—they wanted to obliterate his distinctive stamp of perfectionism [. . .] The entire [. . .] upper echelon wanted to erase the fact that there had ever been an Irving Thalberg" (96). Vieira, however, rejects the received wisdom that defines MGM's post-Thalberg productions as "saccharine and intellectually lacking" (2010: 396). Personal assessments from either perspective notwithstanding, the one thing that could not be erased was the "stamp" of Thalberg's influence. The genres, themes, and strategies for casting that Thalberg had instituted would thrive for the rest of the decade, becoming all the more embedded in the studio with which he had shared such a by-turns triumphant and troubled relationship.

Granted, Thalberg was not necessarily present in the hugely popular *Andy Hardy* and *Dr. Kildare* series instituted by Mayer in the late 1930s: the first starring Mickey Rooney as a wholesome, All-American youth growing up in an idyllic family and town; the latter featuring Lew Ayres as a benevolent young doctor (Balio 2018: 140–143).[1] Such franchises aside, Thalberg's style would continue to guide MGM's major productions: *The Broadway Melody of 1929* would serve as the model for the 1936, 1938, and 1940 sequels; and Garbo's career, struggling after Thalberg's passing, hit a brief resurgence with an instance of oblique casting in comedy *Ninotchka* (dir. Lubitsch, 1939). Moreover, the "social problem film" (Balio 2018: 127) that Thalberg had helped establish with his emphasis on currency in motion pictures, and through works like *The Crowd* and *The Big House* (dir. Hill, 1930), gained more traction with *Boys Town* (dir. Taurog, 1938) and *They All Come Out* (dir. Tourneur, 1939); and the cycle of Jeannette MacDonald and Nelson Eddy musicals recalled the period romanticism so associated with Thalberg. These MacDonald–Eddy pairings included *Maytime* (dir. Leonard, 1937), which Thalberg had been developing before his death.[2]

World War II introduced a radical new point of focus for the studio and its audiences. It is intriguing to consider what Thalberg's own response to wartime production might have been, given his emphasis on the need for films to engage with shifts in contemporary thought. How would his theories of filmmaking have mapped onto the demands of the Office of Wartime Information, or accommodated the limitations of wartime shortages (Schatz 1997: 142)? Particularly interesting in this era, however, was the realization of Thalberg's 1933 vision of MGM producing fewer films of higher quality. As Thomas Schatz sets out, the constellation of wartime circumstances enabled studios to privilege "top product" and abandon minor films (1997: 170). Finally forced to execute Thalberg's ideal model of production, MGM maintained its strong box-office presence through dramas like *Mrs. Miniver* (dir. Wyler, 1942) and

The White Cliffs of Dover (dir. Brown, 1944), battlefield thrillers *Thirty Seconds Over Tokyo* (dir. LeRoy, 1944) and *Bataan* (dir. Garnett, 1943), and the cementing of its dominance in the musical genre. Arthur Freed, a songwriter who had co-written the musical numbers for *The Broadway Melody of 1929*, was by then head of his own production unit—a move that led to highly popular films including *Meet Me in St. Louis* (dir. Minnelli, 1944) and *The Harvey Girls* (dir. Sidney, 1946), both starring Judy Garland.

By the end of the 1940s, however, Mayer found himself facing a crisis reminiscent of the one that he had introduced into Thalberg's career. Where once Mayer and Schenck had collaborated to minimize Thalberg's authority, Mayer now learned that the studio wanted a new intelligent producer to negotiate the challenges of postwar production. As Schenck very succinctly advised Mayer in 1948, "Find another Thalberg" (Schatz 1997: 337). Dore Schary left RKO to become MGM's vice president in charge of production (337); in 1951, following continual discord with Schary, Mayer demanded that Schenck choose between them (Crowther 1957: 299). Schenck chose the new Thalberg, who ran MGM until 1958. Mayer resigned in the summer of 1951 (300)—almost exactly fifteen years after the death of Irving Thalberg.

Aside from the artistic heritage that Thalberg left to MGM—stars and films; approaches to developing screenplays; insights into cultivating entertainment value and winning audiences—the more bottom-line questions of his stake in the studio continued to be problematic, just as they were in his lifetime. This would come to the fore in the mid-1930s with a struggle between Mayer and Shearer. Upon his death, the terms of Thalberg's contract entitled him to 37.5 percent of the studio's profits; but even though his contract would not expire until 1938, Mayer and Rubin began to share out Thalberg's percentage between themselves (Vieira 2010: 380). Shearer contested this in a long-running legal battle that was eventually resolved with the following conditions: the percentage deal would be restored until 1938, with Thalberg's estate then receiving 4 percent from all MGM productions made between 1924 and 1938 (Vieira 2010: 381; Lambert 1990: 245).

This conflict was the last of many over how to quantify Thalberg's contributions to MGM. Thalberg and his descendants could keep earning money on films that were produced through the late 1930s, though there was no way to account for future films that could not have been made without the work that he did. Yet however unexpectedly, this 1936 decision also illuminates something of the intersection between Thalberg's historical moment and sustained influence across the decades. As Vieira has noted, a key stipulation in the settlement "included profits from television and any medium not yet invented or known" (2010: 381). Though Thalberg would not directly produce any more pictures for MGM, the representatives for his estate anticipated the monetary and cultural value of his films, and indeed his stars. In the years to come, each would be reanimated across a mediascape that itself shifted from the movie palace to the television screen to, today, a multitude of viewing devices—mobile phones, computers, tablets. For a figure who did not receive a screen credit in his lifetime,[3] the name *Thalberg* went on to denote the highest cinematic values; and just as MGM continued to meet the demands of a changing popular culture, so too did its founder—and his productions.

"THE GHOST OF IRVING"

The attention paid to Thalberg from the beginning of his career set the foundation for his posthumous idealization: the *Vanity Fair* article by Jim Tully in 1927, the various accounts of his Boy Wonder-dom in fan magazines, his own publications and many interviews. These works chronicled his theories of filmmaking and have served as valuable primary materials for this study, but they also figure as the collective origins of the Thalberg mythology that would develop after his passing. Recalling his own emphasis on developing a "background of glamour and interest" (qtd. in Vieira 2010: 227, 228) for MGM's stars, Thalberg's presence in the press during his lifetime established the qualities of his perpetual stardom: he would be forever romantic, intellectual, preternaturally gifted.

Various media disseminating Thalberg's image, words, and name cultivated this allure after his death. The Irving G. Thalberg Memorial Award represented the industry's initial integration of the Thalberg charisma (to follow Lewis's terms), honoring "creative producers whose bodies of work reflect a consistently high quality of motion picture production."[4] Darryl Zanuck was the first recipient of the award in 1938, and the Academy would go on to grant it to figures like Ingmar Bergman, Alfred Hitchcock, and Jack Warner. The design of the award itself—featuring a likeness of Thalberg's head—went through several phases: according to the Oscars official website, Shearer was unhappy with the original 1930s version and commissioned two different busts in the 1940s and 1950s.[5]

Though the online material casts this as a "quirky history" in the crafting of "the three faces of Thalberg,"[6] the tale reveals much about Shearer's anxieties over the authenticity of her husband's posthumous image. This would again come to the fore in the casting of Robert Evans as Thalberg in Chaney bio-pic *Man of a Thousand Faces* (dir. Pevney, 1957). As Evans recalls, Shearer discovered him at the Beverly Hills Hotel pool and decided that he would be right to play Thalberg; but she insisted that Evans not wear make-up in the film because, as she said, "Irving would never wear make-up" (2013: 211). Though affronted when the production team rejected her advice, Shearer would go on to suggest Evans for the role of Monroe Stahr in the proposed adaptation of

The Last Tycoon (213). She told Evans, "You *are* Irving. Onscreen as well as in person" (qtd. in 213). Adding to the *mise en abyme* of Hollywood generations was the presence of Selznick, no less, who planned to produce the film and denied Evans the part (213).

Achieving the most appropriate representation of Thalberg, whether in a bust or on the screen, preoccupied Shearer. She sought to preserve the integrity of her husband's image in popular culture, conscious of both the passing of time and his embeddedness in Hollywood's history. Shearer was not alone in this pursuit: Samuel Marx, before publishing his three studies of Thalberg-era MGM, would commemorate his mentor in articles for *The Hollywood Reporter*. In 1942, Marx anticipated his own role as chronicler of Thalberg's MGM when he dedicated one piece to "the biographer of Irving Thalberg who must come along some day" (section 2). Marx would elaborate on this endeavor in another article published ten years after Thalberg's death:

> [T]his is for the boys and girls who have come into the studios during this past decade and who have heard writers say Irving was a great writer even though he never wrote a line [. . .] Or they've heard directors say he had a tremendous feeling for dramatic scenes, although he never directed a foot of film.[7] Or they've heard he was the greatest producer the film business has ever known, even though his name never appeared on a single motion picture during his lifetime. (1946: section 2)

Here, the desire to record the complexities of Thalberg's time at MGM—some inaccuracies born of rhetorical flourish aside—merges with a kindred impulse to explain how Hollywood used to be. Of the producers who briefly configured MGM's post-restructuring pantheon in 1933, each would respond differently to changes in the industry: Mayer would retire (under duress) from MGM in 1951; Selznick would struggle to recapture the extraordinary success of his 1930s–1940s productions; and Stromberg would leave the industry in 1950 (Vieira 2010: 396). Only Wanger prevailed through the 1950s and early 1960s, producing the sci-fi drama *Invasion of the Body Snatchers* (dir. Siegel, 1956) and epic *Cleopatra* (dir. Mankiewicz, 1963) (Bernstein 1994: 302, 343). Thalberg, however, remained untouched by the vagaries of time, and questions of what he would, or would not, have done reverberated beyond his own person in broader attempts to capture the ethos of the *ancien regime*. Indeed, Thalberg's symbolic significance for the industry would, at times, conflict with the very values that it wanted to commemorate—as was the case with the Oscars award itself. Shearer explained in conversation with biographer Roland Flamini, "Irving wouldn't have liked that award. He hated that kind of publicity. I told them so at the time" (qtd. in 1994: 13).

More creative tributes would emerge, particularly in literature. In 1941, novelist Budd Schulberg—the son of producer B. P. Schulberg, Thalberg and Mayer's old neighbor back in the Mission Road days—would feature Thalberg in a kind of cameo role in *What Makes Sammy Run?* Glick's amoral success story presents a sinister parallel to Thalberg's own Boy Wonder narrative; as one character describes it, "There hasn't been anything like it since the rise of Irving Thalberg" (2011: 142). Though brief, this direct reference to Thalberg punctuates Schulberg's more sustained focus on the Screen Writers Guild conflicts of the 1930s with which the former was so concerned. Most famous of all, though, was Fitzgerald's *The Last Tycoon*, left incomplete upon his death in 1940. In an imaginative variation on Marx's own historical imperative, as well as Shearer's more intimate determination to honor Thalberg's memory, Fitzgerald recast the producer as Monroe Stahr—the lead of a Hollywood love story.

The Last Tycoon explores the singularity of Stahr's artistic vision, juxtaposing his authority in the film studio with the poignancy of his personal longings. However fictional its rendering, the novel incorporated biographical elements that helped preserve certain qualities of Thalberg's once and future stardom. Fitzgerald captured the logistical tensions of life at MGM—conflicts with labor unions, for example, and what he called, in his notes, "the deadly dislike [. . .] between Thalberg and Louis B. Mayer" (xxxii). The author also recorded more revealing, and defining, aspects of Thalberg's character. Strikingly, Fitzgerald repeated almost verbatim an exchange that he and Thalberg had about the nature of leadership:[8] "You've got to decide [. . .] You can't test the best way—except by doing it. So you just do it" (20). As Zelda Fitzgerald would explain after her husband's passing, "Those minds which so nearly control the direction of public sentiment engaged Scott deeply. He wanted to render tangible [their] indomitable constancy of purpose and [. . .] driving necessity to achievement" (qtd. in 1993: lxx).

Fitzgerald's chronicling of Thalberg's "indomitable constancy of purpose" would refract further in Elia Kazan's 1976 adaptation of the novel. In 1928, Thalberg had produced the backlot comedy *Show People*, with its merry-go-round of Davies's impersonations and celebrity cameos; almost fifty years later, Thalberg would himself become a character *à clef* in a film that paid homage to *Fitzgerald's* homage. It was a film, as Vincent Canby stated in the *New York Times*, "full of echoes" (1976: 59) of the past through the voice of the present, featuring elements that were anachronistic to the Hollywood that Fitzgerald and Thalberg would have known: the Method intensity of Robert De Niro's performance as Stahr; the abstract quality of Harold Pinter's screenplay. Heightening this uncanny alignment of classic and New Hollywood was the presence of a number of stars—Dana Andrews, Tony Curtis, Ray Milland, Robert Mitchum—who embodied the gravitas of another age, only a generation or two removed from Thalberg. These men had aged but the love story of Thalberg himself, portrayed by one of the finest young actors of the day, had not.

Still other modes of commemoration would attempt to "render tangible" (following Zelda Fitzgerald's terms) the Thalberg charisma—though in relatively more prosaic ways. Two years after he died, MGM established the Thalberg Building. In 1961, publicist and film critic Ezra Goodman would briefly comment on its significance:

> By Hollywood's standards, Thalberg was a sort of Shakespeare of the screen and had intimations of immortality [. . .] Thalberg's successors never enjoyed the esteem he did. It has been said that the imposing M-G-M [*sic*] executive building, named after Thalberg, is air-conditioned and hermetically sealed 'so that the ghost of Irving can't get in to see what they are doing.' (170–171)

Though facetious, Goodman's sketch highlights the studio's vexed response to Thalberg's legacy and the lingering traces of *haute* MGM. The Thalberg Building as such memorialized one of the studio's founders, offering a literal *domus* in tribute to the *genius* of which Crowther wrote (1957: 239); and in this way, it implicitly housed MGM's present actions within the context of its past. Yet by the same token, its "hermetically sealed" conditions—allegedly protecting the contemporary studio from unwelcome intrusions of its own history—contrasted with the external diffusion, indeed transmission, of those early works. The spectre of Thalberg might not have been able to "get in to see what they [were] doing," but he was already haunting screens of the day.

Goodman himself commented in *provocateur* fashion on this media renaissance: "For [. . .] bad moviemaking, it would not have been easy to beat some of the pictures Thalberg turned out in the early Thirties, as television audiences, who can see many of them today, are painfully finding out" (170). Though facile, Goodman's statement hits upon the circulation of Thalberg's films in that televised medium anticipated in the terms of his estate. In 1956, Schenck's successor Arthur Loew began to lease MGM's early films to TV networks (Balio 2018: 194); by 1960, the practice of screening classic films on television was so normalised that Billy Wilder could parody it in *The Apartment*. In an early scene, C. C. Baxter (Jack Lemmon) settles down to eat his TV dinner in front of *Grand Hotel*, drawn in by the sheer number of great stars listed by the announcer—only to be thwarted by the incessant commercials.[9] For romantic Baxter, who fills his titular apartment with phonograph records and prints from art exhibitions, *Grand Hotel* represents still another world of glamour barred to him by the banality of modern life.[10]

By the time *The Apartment* was released, "the ghost of Irving"—to borrow Goodman's phrase—was floating freely between memorial awards and buildings, novels and published reminiscences, bio-pics of his stars and broadcasts of his films. In their variety and diffusion, these modes of preserving Thalberg's memory reflect the complexities of his identity as a producer. He did not take a screen credit for MGM's productions, but oversaw almost all of them; he would die only twelve years after helping to found the studio, but his theories of filmmaking would live on in its subsequent productions. Even the construction of Thalberg's legend itself recalls those very theories and his overarching sense of dramatic impact: he would be cast, if not totally obliquely, in roles such as Fitzgerald's imaginary hero, literal icon on a pedestal, and beloved husband; the great scenes of his life provided both inspiration for future generations and a record of what Hollywood had been; and each version of Thalberg represented a desire to retake his accomplishments, making the best of him even better. Above all, the legend was a love story authored by those who knew Thalberg, for those who wished they had.

Beyond Thalberg's own theoretical framework, the juxtaposition of cultural mythology and cinematic form that characterizes his posthumous identity brings to mind Gilberto Perez's conception of film itself as the "material ghost." Like the dream world theorized by Thalberg, this entity emerges at the intersection of the technical and ineffable:

> The images on the screen carry in them something of the world itself, something material, yet something transposed, transformed into another world: the material ghost. Hence both the peculiar closeness to reality and the no less peculiar suspension from reality, the juncture of world and otherworldliness distinctive of the film image. (1998: 28)

Perez here discusses the capacity of the medium to unite indexicality with ethereality, evoking a liminal register through which the resurrection of a recorded world (enabled by the mechanical processes of camera, projector, and screen) generates a spectral sensation (28). As conceived by Perez, the specific act of film viewing and the uncannily intimate relationship between pro-filmic reality, image, and viewer conjures the material ghost. Mapped onto the present terms, however, this concept helps frame a parallel journey through which the material world of Thalberg's films generates, and sustains, the otherworldliness of his legend.

Perez has perceived an auratic resonance in the photographic image itself, noting that it captures "the uniqueness, the original particularity," of that which was present before the lens (33). To push this further, the "distinctive stamp of [Thalberg's] perfectionism" (Lewis 96) was itself captured by the camera and conveyed to the screen. Each of his films records traces of the pro-filmic reality that he had produced: the performer chosen for a particular role; the scenes constructing the story he had developed, following the themes he wanted to examine—with those scenes edited and retaken to strengthen the arc of that story. Contextualizing each of these were the industrial factors that Thalberg had helped establish: the parameters of what could, or could not, be shown on the screen through the Production Code; the technical advancements of play-back recording in musicals. Perhaps most significant of all was Thalberg's abiding respect for the audience, manifested strikingly in the previews through which he gauged how successfully the films awoke that "peculiar closeness to reality and the no less peculiar suspension from reality" (28) of which Perez wrote. Or, more directly, the dream world described by Thalberg himself.

In this way, the abstract qualities of Thalberg's legacy—the myth of the Boy Wonder who reigned over classic Hollywood, the poignancy of the last tycoon who died too young—relate to the once-and-always source of his enduring attraction: the films themselves. To draw from Vivian Sobchack's observations on history, "we are now in a culture that does not have the time or desire to contemplate the past from a distance; we want to immerse ourselves sensually in it, to enliven and live it" through any number of reenactments or interactive exhibitions (2000: 310). As the following section will explore in detail, the medium of film is uniquely capable of fulfilling that longing for an immediate connection to a vanished age; bringing, in this case, audiences even closer to one of Hollywood's greatest figures. For it is not simply "the ghost of Irving" who continues to fascinate decades after his death, but the material ghosts of his motion pictures—haunting, now, any number of screens.

NEW CLASSICS

As with any figure who passed away too soon, there is an inevitable sense of pathos in discussing Thalberg's legacy and its accompanying questions of what could have been. But the mournfulness that features in these historical and fictional accounts is, as Perez maintains, all the more intrinsic to the cinematic medium itself. He writes of "the poignancy of what reaches us from the past with the urgency of the present" (35), noting that "the lifelike image is also the ghostlike image: the vivid harbors the vanished" (36). By this reckoning, cinema acknowledges the mortality of its subjects and the passing of time even as it brings that "vanished" past back to life; the material ghost awakens feelings of both loss and renewal. Though in these passages Perez takes the expressly "lifelike images" of Italian Neorealism and documentary filmmaking as points of consideration, his observations relate well to the Thalberg canon of studio-era Hollywood. Consider, for instance, *Grand Hotel*—a film that celebrates the persistence of human desire in the face of death, and exalts beauty both emotional and physical while acknowledging its transience. However "superlatively well-packaged [with] a high sheen" (269), to recall *Fortune*'s description, *Grand Hotel* is no less an existential drama; and its frames "harbor" the industrial conditions that Thalberg produced. As Perez would write, "The projector [. . .] brings the imprint of life"—whether captured in a Hollywood studio or the streets of Italy— "to new life on the screen" (28).

What changes, though, in that process of reanimation when audiences watch *Grand Hotel* not with a projector and movie screen, but streamed on an iPad or mobile phone? Laura Mulvey illuminates much about how new media has transformed cinema's elemental dialogue between mortality and rebirth. She notes that "the presence of the past in the cinema is also the presence of the body resurrected" (2006: 53), citing both the affect of early cinema (radical in its preservation and projection of pro-filmic reality) and the digital technologies that allow viewers to start and stop a film at will (36, 167). Such capacities enable new modes of viewing: possessive spectatorship, through which "like personal *objet trouvés* [. . .] scenes can be played and replayed" (167), and pensive spectatorship, evoked by the "fascination of time fossilized" in a still frame (187). Here, the material ghost encounters the contemporary spectator, who is not so much possessed *by* the film but seeks to possess *it*.

This interplay between modern-day agency and historical form defines the reception of studio-era Hollywood films. DVDs, online streaming, and cable networks like Turner Classic Movies offer primary access to classical cinema; Vieira has pointed out that "it is possible to go to a computer at any time of the day or night and track down a Thalberg film" (2008: 7). Incidentally, it is also possible to go to a computer and watch the Amazon Prime series of *The Last Tycoon*, in which Thalberg-as-Stahr returns as a hero—this time, for rather earnest perspectives on classic Hollywood.[11] Thinking more broadly about the modern-day acquisition of Thalberg films, the Warner Archive Collection—a subsidiary of Warner Bros. Studios—boasts a streaming site, a manufactured-on-demand (MOD) DVD-R service, and a YouTube channel that holds many of MGM's classic productions.[12] Here, we see the resurrection *and* manufacturing of cinematic bodies at the desire of the spectator—literally wherever he or she may be, on whatever device is most convenient. Moreover, the fact that a once-rival studio now owns the rights to MGM's classical canon signals still another disjuncture between historical context and present-day reception.

With all of this in mind, Thalberg's works have been effectively reborn through the digital moment. *He Who Gets Slapped* (1924), for instance, exists as both historical artefact of MGM's earliest days and an up-to-date source of entertainment (via DVD or clips on YouTube). And in 2013, the Warner Archive Collection released *The Merry Widow* on DVD "in a remastered edition with a much improved image and soundtrack" (Kehr 2013); the fact that the reviewer does not specify just what it has improved *from* suggests that digitization itself is enough to redeem a former box-office disappointment. Thalberg's canon provides only a few of the exhibits in what Barbara Klinger has eloquently termed an entire "cine-museum" of classic films curated by cable television channels and other home-viewing technologies (2006: 94). What distinguishes the Thalberg gallery, as it were, is the way that it sustains that juxtaposition of ubiquity and anonymity that defined his career in his lifetime: his films are virtually instantly accessible (in all senses of the phrase), but Thalberg the producer—as distinct from "the last tycoon"—remains comparatively elusive. *He Who Gets Slapped* is best remembered by silent-film aficionados as a Chaney film and/or a Victor Sjostrom work; the *New York Times* article cited above lauds Lubitsch, MacDonald, and Chevalier in *The Merry Widow*, but does not mention Thalberg at all.

Such, perhaps, is the quandary of the classic Hollywood producer more broadly. Where, for example, box-sets of golden-age stars and directors abound due to the dual allure of iconic images and *auteur*-ist personas, it is arguably harder to sell a producer. (Leaving aside, that is, the comparatively overdetermined trademark of figures like David O. Selznick and, today, Jerry Bruckheimer—who does have his own box-set.) From this perspective, Thalberg's belief that "credit you give yourself isn't worth having" (qtd. in Marx 1975: 30) did not just signal his resistance to rituals of ownership, but it also acknowledged the vagaries of public perception. To recall his own words in the 1929 USC lecture: "[C]hange is the life-blood of the art and this doesn't apply only to the form, but also to the people employed in the industry. The favorites of yesterday are gone and the favorites of tomorrow come up" (1977: 121). Thalberg has always been a "favorite" in popular culture, since his days at Universal; but given that perennial stardom, so easy to take for granted and relegate to golden-age nostalgia, it is all the more imperative to highlight his critical significance. That is, not only in the rigorous historical terms set out by recent scholars like Vieira, but in the theoretical context established in this book. What mattered to Thalberg was that the films endured; and because of that conceptual commitment to entertainment value, so does he.

One way to illuminate his abiding presence is to imagine an encounter between Thalberg and modern-day production practices. Such conjecture is always a risk—but a hypothetical meeting between Thalberg and new media has the makings of what he himself might have called a good yarn. In setting the scene for his definitive biography, Vieira posed the question:

> If you were to be transported from 2010 to 1930, what would you experience as you walked the studio streets leading to Thalberg's office? [. . .] What would you learn by sitting next to him in a story conference? (2010: xv)

By the same token, if Thalberg were to be transported from 1930 to the 2000s, what would *he* experience? The "studio streets leading to [his] office" are now owned by Sony Pictures Entertainment; on its website, the corporation provides a map of "the studio's storied structures" and cites its "commitment to preserving [the lot's] legacy while anticipating its future."[13] Though there is no mention of Thalberg's original office, the Thalberg Building features prominently on the virtual tour—the man himself might be amused to know that "Mayer had an office on the third floor and a private dining room on the fourth."[14] Once this Thalberg of the future accepted the industrial shifts—the fact that Warner Bros. now distributes his films and Sony Pictures "preserv[es] the legacy" of the lot he helped build—he would engage with more pressing questions of movie-making.

Given Thalberg's sensitivity to the movie-going public, he would likely first explore its contemporary relationship to film. In the 1920s and 1930s, Thalberg sat with his audiences to assume their collective subjectivity; he read preview cards and retook scenes in order to entertain the popular viewer most effectively. He would, then, recognize the more intensive iterations of these interactions: the use of social media as a mode of expression for spectators, descending from the preview card as an all-the-more immediate way to communicate responses to a production decision or completed film. Along the same lines, fans themselves may now carry on the tradition of the retake—manipulating footage of favorite films on YouTube, for example. Considering Thalberg's meticulous integration of distinct elements—story, star, scene—in a single production, he might be chagrined at such interventions, just as he would by the proliferation of Special Features that continually, compulsively, add *something* to a feature film (deleted scenes, voice-over commentaries, behind-the-scenes footage, alternate endings). As he stated in the meeting with Lord and Hays in the drafting of the Production Code, "Your purpose as producers in this industry is to comply with the wishes of the great public and give the people that which the public is demanding, *up to a certain point*, with a modicum of discretion."[15] Yet even as he might balk at the lack of "discretion" with which the industry and the public now communicate, Thalberg could perceive how he set the stage for such hypermediated encounters.

Just as he did, in fact, for the evolving nature of screens themselves. Thalberg's commitment to crafting one great scene in visual and narrative terms finds a counterpart in the contemporary parameters of great *screens*, with the continued popularity of IMAX technology and the resurgence of 3-D. This innate understanding of scale—expressed in statements like, "We deal in flesh and blood, not paper and ink. Ideas that register big on the typewritten page may not register at all on the screen" (1933: 85)—speaks to a fascination with how to heighten the relationship between viewer and film. By extension, then, the "flesh and blood" contact between viewer and miniature screen might appeal to Thalberg as much as the sensory pleni-tude of great screens. For Beugnet, the iPhone screen invites "an immer-sion in a miniature universe whose gate opens in the palm of one's hand" (206); for Gaudreault and Marion, the touch-screen provides a channel for reanimation. Through "a simple click or tactile contact," viewers now directly engage with the screen to see still images "brought to life": "No one today [. . .] is astonished at these screens' hypersensitive skins" (2015: 77). Both accounts of the screen's evolving impact capture how Thalberg's cinematic dream world of 1933 has transformed across the decades: where it was once the actor who "transport[ed] [their] audience" (1933: 85) into that suspended realm, now the sentient screen can offer a similarly moving experience (in both senses of the word).

In similar terms, the anthropomorphic language of these observations brings to mind the physical forms of the performers appearing on those screens, whether expansive or miniature—thus in turn recalling Thalberg's own attention to oblique casting. The historic versatility of Thalberg's stars parallels the variability of modern-day viewing platforms; now, the theory of oblique casting and its geometric connotations maps onto the dimensions of the screen itself. Star and screen share a polymorphic quality as they stretch themselves or minimize their presence to meet the demand for new ways of seeing films. Just as Thalberg cast a performer in an unexpected role or genre to develop the dimensionality of their persona, it is conceivable that he would today consider the screen on which that performer would be seen—moving actors between the Netflix and home-streaming trade, for instance, and the expanse of the great screen.

Of course, each Thalberg scholar would bring their own interpretation to this Twilight Zone scenario in which the theorist-producer of the studio era encoun-ters the contemporary mediascape. The *Fortune* article declared that "[t]he kind of pictures that MGM makes and the ways it makes them are Irving Thalberg's problems" (257); we can only imagine how he would have solved those problems today. Such conjectural exercises do more than attest to his allure ("once a star, always a star"), or to the legacy of his filmmaking style—as Sony succinctly state in their description of the Thalberg Building, he "introduced production prac-tices that have become standard today."[16] What these hypotheticals reveal is the resilience of his theories of filmmaking: they can be reframed, indeed retaken, to illuminate more about the mass appeal of the medium. Just as any theoretical perspective generates from a specific cultural or historical moment without being bound to it, Thalberg's conceptual approach to production endures in consider-ations of narrative cinema past, present, and future.

Thalberg maintained that "[t]he difference between something good and something bad is great, but the difference between something good and some-thing superior is often very small" (qtd. in Crowther 1957: 181). *Produced by*

Irving Thalberg has argued that in this case, his work as a film theorist—not "small" but cut short—helps to distinguish him as something superior even in an age of luminaries. In the tradition of Thalberg himself, these analyses have attempted to retake aspects of his long-established legacy by delving into the theories that he developed in an abbreviated, but utterly defining, period of innovation and creative ambition. In this way, the study has contributed to the discourse established by an entire genealogy of Thalberg scholarship: Shearer's desire for Hollywood to remember the best of her husband; Crowther, Marx, and Thomas's drive to record the challenges and triumphs of his vanished age; Vieira's honoring of these chronicles with his own landmark biography.

Thalberg intimately understood that the cinematic form has the propensity for evolution and renewal; so, too, does his body of theoretical work. There will always be more to say about his films and concepts of production. Taken together, they are another classic of the studio era—in the terms defined by Thalberg himself: "a work of beauty which has emerged victor over time" (1936: 1).

NOTES

1. As Vieira asks, "Who knows what Thalberg would have thought of the Andy Hardy films" (2010: 394).
2. For detailed discussion of MGM's output in this period, please see Balio 2018: 115–17, 118, 121, 127.
3. The only film that featured his name in his lifetime was the Universal production *The Dangerous Little Demon* (dir. Badger, 1922); he was listed as writer "I. R. Irving" (Vieira 2010: 11).
4. Available at <https://www.oscars.org/governors/thalberg> (last accessed October 24, 2019).
5. Ibid.
6. Ibid.
7. This is not strictly accurate—see Introduction (p. 8).
8. See conclusion of Chapter 3 in this book.
9. Wilder would win the Irving G. Thalberg Memorial Award in 1987.
10. Audiences would have also encountered the televised reminiscences of Thalberg-era stars like Groucho Marx, who spoke of Thalberg admiringly in appearances on the Dick Cavett Show in the early 1970s. See, for instance, this clip from a 1971 interview:<https://www.youtube.com/watch?v=ZzEflb-C8HU> (last accessed October 24, 2019).
11. According to actor Matt Bomer, who plays Stahr, "All these things that are coming to a head right now in our country—immigrants, sexism, the generational clash—are really big elements in our show. There are so many American ideals that Fitzgerald was wrestling with and that we're still struggling to perfect" (qtd. in Barnes 2017). Interestingly, in an effort to distance the series from the novel's historical context, producer Billy Ray included Irving Thalberg himself as a character in one episode: "We felt that it was really important to hang a lantern on the fact that Monroe Stahr is Monroe Stahr—that Monroe Stahr is not Irving Thalberg. And the best way to do that was to actually put Irving Thalberg in the piece" (qtd. in McNally 2017).

12. Please see <https://www.wbshop.com/collections/warner-archive-all-dvd> (last accessed October 24, 2019.

13. Available at <http://www.sonypicturesmuseum.com/studio/tour> (last accessed October 24, 2019).

14. Ibid.

15. Association of Motion Picture Producers [AMPP], "Discussion of the Production Code in Its Draft Form." MPPDA Digital Archive, Flinders University Library Special Collections. MPPDA Record 671, Record of Meeting. 8–1985 to 8–2132. Available at <https://mppda.flinders.edu.au/records/671> (last accessed 24 October, 2019), p. 89; emphasis added.

16. Available at <http://www.sonypicturesmuseum.com/studio/tour> (last accessed December 4, 2019).

Works Cited

ARCHIVAL SOURCES

MPPDA Digital Archive, Flinders University Library Special Collections

AMPP (Association of Motion Picture Producers), "Discussion of the Production Code in Its Draft Form." MPPDA Digital Archive, Flinders University Library Special Collections. MPPDA Record 671, Record of Meeting. 8-1985 to 8-2132. Available at <https://mppda.flinders.edu.au/records/671> (last accessed October 24, 2019).

Memo on *War Nurse*. MPPDA Digital Archive, Flinders University Library Special Collections. MPPDA Record 1240, Correspondence. 8-1726 to 8-1745. Available at <https://mppda.flinders.edu.au/records/1240> (last accessed October 25, 2019) .

Memo to Will H. Hays. MPPDA Digital Archive, Flinders University Library Special Collections. MPPDA Record 426, Memo. 4-2395 to 4-2396. Available at <https://mppda.flinders.edu.au/records/426> (last accessed October 24, 2019).

MPPDA (Committee on Public Relations, Sub-Committee on Eliminations). "Original Formulation of the Don'ts and Be Carefuls." MPPDA Digital Archive, Flinders University Library Special Collections. MPPDA Record 341, Report of Meeting. 3-1232 to 3-1234. Available at <https://mppda.flinders.edu.au/records/341 (last accessed October 24, 2019).

Margaret Herrick Library, Academy of Motion Picture Arts and Sciences

Hunt Stromberg Papers.
Irving G. Thalberg and Norma Shearer Papers.
Metro-Goldwyn-Mayer Legal Department collection.
Motion Picture Association of America, Production Code Administration records.

MGM Collection, University of Southern California

"Conference Notes, 'Mata Hari'." December 4, 1931. MGM Collection, University of Southern California.

BIBLIOGRAPHY

Affron, Charles. *Star Acting: Gish, Garbo, Davis*. New York: E. P. Dutton, 1977.

Altman, Rick. *The American Film Musical*. Bloomington: Indiana University Press, 1987.

Arnheim, Rudolf. *Film as Art*. Berkeley: University of California Press, 1957 [1933].

Balio, Tino. *Grand Design: Hollywood as a Modern Business Enterprise, 1930–1939*. Berkeley: University of California Press, 1993.

Balio, Tino. *MGM*. London: Routledge, 2018.

Barker, Jennifer M. *The Tactile Eye: Touch and the Cinematic Experience*. Berkeley: University of California Press, 2009.

Barnard, Timothy. "'The Whole Art of a Wooden Leg': King Vidor's Picturization of Laurence Stallings's 'Great Story'." In *The Problem Body: Projecting Disability on Film*, ed. Sally Chivers and Nicole Markotic. Columbus: Ohio State University Press, 2010, 23–41.

Barnes, Brooks. "Amazon Tackles Hollywood's F. Scott Fitzgerald Obsession." *New York Times* July 20, 2017. Available at <https://www.nytimes.com/2017/07/20/arts/television/f-scottfitzgerald-the-last-tycoon-amazon.html (last accessed October 24, 2019).

Baskette, Kirtley. "A Queen Comes Back." *Photoplay* July 1938: 20–22, 85–86.

Behlmer, Rudy. *Memo from David O. Selznick*. New York: The Modern Library, 2000 [1972].

Berke, Annie. "'Never Let the Camera Catch Me Acting': Lillian Gish as Actress, Star, and Theorist." *Historical Journal of Film, Radio and Television* 36.2 (2016): 175–189.

Bernstein, Matthew. *Walter Wanger: Hollywood Independent*. Minneapolis: University of Minnesota Press, 2000.

Bernstein, Matthew. "The Producer as Auteur." In *Auteurs and Authorship: A Film Reader*, ed. Barry Keith Grant. Oxford: Blackwell Publishing, 2008, 180–189.

Beugnet, Martine. "Miniature Pleasures: On Watching Films on an iPhone." In *Cinematicity in Media History*, ed. Jeffrey Geiger and Karin Littau. Edinburgh: Edinburgh University Press, 2015, 196–210.

"Big Last Minute Reviews." *Motion Picture* January 1936: 16.

"The Big Parade Wins *Photoplay* Medal for 1925." *Photoplay* December 1926: 40–41, 144.

Blake, Michael F. *A Thousand Faces: Lon Chaney's Unique Artistry in Motion Pictures*. Lanham, MD: Vestal Press, 1995.

Bordwell, David, Janet Staiger, and Kristin Thompson. *The Classical Hollywood Cinema: Film Style and Mode of Production to 1960*. Abingdon, Oxon: Routledge, 1988.

Braudy, Leo. "The Double Detachment of Ernst Lubitsch. *MLN (Modern Language Notes)* 98.5 (December 1983): 1071–1084.

"Brief Reviews of Current Pictures." *Photoplay* November 1932: 8, 10, 12, 129.

Brooks, Louise. *Lulu in Hollywood*. Minneapolis: University of Minnesota Press, 2000 [1982].

Calhoun, John. "Architecture: Unearthing a Rare Egyptian Artifact." *Entertainment Design: The Art and Technology of Show Business* 33.5 (May 1999): 34–27.

Canby, Vincent. "'Tycoon' Echoes '30s Hollywood." *New York Times* November 18, 1976: 59.

Chamberlain, Willard. "Are They Versatile?" *Picture Play* January 1930: 86–88, 113.

Christensen, Jerome. *America's Corporate Art: The Studio Authorship of Hollywood Motion Pictures*. Stanford, CA: Stanford University Press, 2011.

Clair, René. "The Art of Sound," in *Film Sound: Theory and Practice*, eds. Elizabeth Weis and John Bolton. New York: Columbia University Press, 1985, 92–95.

Coffee, Lenore. *Storyline: Recollections of a Hollywood Screenwriter*. London: Cassell and Company, 1973.

Cook, David A. *A History of Narrative Film*, 4th edn. New York: W. W. Norton and Company, 2004.

Crafton, Donald. *The Talkies: American Cinema's Transition to Sound 1926–1931*. Berkeley: University of California Press, 1997.

Crowther, Bosley. *The Lion's Share: The Story of an Entertainment Empire*. New York: E. P. Dutton and Co., 1957.

Crowther, Bosley. *Hollywood Rajah: The Life and Times of Louis B. Mayer*. New York: Henry Holt and Co., 1960.

"Current Pictures in Review." *Motion Picture* October 1928: 62.

"Current Pictures—Silent and Sound—in Review." *Motion Picture* May 1929: 62–63.

Davies, Marion. *The Times We Had: Life with William Randolph Hearst*. New York: Ballantine Books, 1975.

Day, Beth. *This Was Hollywood*. New York: Doubleday, 1960.

deCordova, Richard. *Picture Personalities: The Emergence of the Star System in America*. Urbana: University of Illinois Press, 2001.

Denbo, Doris. "The Phantom of Hollywood." *Picture Play* April 1925: 88–89, 100.

Doherty, Thomas. *Pre-Code Hollywood: Sex, Immorality, and Insurrection in American Cinema, 1930–1934*. New York: Columbia University Press, 1999.

Eames, John Douglas. *The MGM Story*. London: Octopus Books, 1982.

Eisenstein, Sergei. *Film Form: Essays in Film Theory*. Ed. and trans. Jay Leyda. San Diego: Harcourt, Inc., 1977 [1949].

Elsaesser, Thomas and Malte Hagener. *Film Theory: An Introduction through the Senses*, 2nd edn. New York: Routledge, 2015.

Evans, Robert. *The Kid Stays in the Picture*. London: Faber and Faber, 2003.

Evans, Robert. *The Fat Lady Sang*. London: IT Books, 2013.

Eyman, Scott. *The Speed of Sound: Hollywood and the Talkie Revolution 1926–1930*. New York: Simon and Schuster, 1997.

Feeley, Kathleen A. "'The Antithesis of the Film Magnate': Irving Thalberg and the Politics of Ethno-religious Identity in Early Hollywood." *Jewish Culture and History* 17.1–2 (2016): 45–58.

Feuer, Jane. *The Hollywood Musical*, 2nd edn. Bloomington: Indiana University Press, 1993.

Fischer, Lucy. "Greta Garbo and Silent Cinema: The Actress as Art Deco Icon." *Camera Obscura* 16.3 (2001): 83–110.

Fitzgerald, F. Scott. *The Love of the Last Tycoon: A Western*. Cambridge: Cambridge University Press, 1993 [1941].

Flamini, Roland. *Thalberg: The Last Tycoon and the World of MGM*. London: André Deutsch, 1994.

Florin, Bo. *Transition and Transformation: Victor Sjostrom in Hollywood, 1923–1930*. Amsterdam: Amsterdam University Press, 2013.

Fountain, Leatrice Gilbert. *Dark Star: The Meteoric Rise and Eclipse of John Gilbert*. London: Sidgwick and Jackson, 1985.

French, Philip. *The Movie Moguls: An Informal History of the Hollywood Tycoons*. London: Weidenfeld and Nicolson, 1969.

Friedrich, Otto. *City of Nets: A Portrait of Hollywood in the 1940s*. New York: Harper Perennial, 2014 [1986].

Gaudreault, André and Philippe Marion. *The End of Cinema?: A Medium in Crisis in the Digital Age*. New York: Columbia University Press, 2015.

Gebhart, Myrtle. "Just a Hard-woiking Goil!" *Picture Play*, August 1928: 52–53, 106.

Gish, Lillian. *The Movies, Mr. Griffith, and Me*. London: Columbus Books, 1969.

Golden, Eve. *John Gilbert: The Last of the Silent Film Stars*. Lexington: University of Kentucky Press, 2013.

Goodman, Ezra. *The Fifty-Year Decline and Fall of Hollywood*. New York: Simon and Schuster, 1961.

Greene, Jane M. "Manners Before Morals: Sophisticated Comedy and the Production Code, 1930–1934." *Quarterly Review of Film and Video* 28.3 (2011): 239–256.

Guiles, Fred Lawrence. *Marion Davies: A Biography*. London: W. H. Allen, 1973.

Gunning, Tom. "The Cinema of Attractions," in *Early Cinema: Space, Frame, Narrative*, ed. Thomas Elsaesser. London: BFI Publishing, 1990, 56–67.

Hall, Mordaunt. "Reflections and News of the Screen World." *New York Times* July 29, 1928: Section X, 3.

Hanssen, Eirik Frisvold. "How to Get a Personality: The Comedic Collaborations of King Vidor and Marion Davies, 1928–1930." *La Furia Umana* 20. Available at <http://www.lafuriaumana.it/index.php/48-archive/lfu-20> (last accessed December 9, 2019).

Haskell, Molly. *Frankly, My Dear: Gone With the Wind Revisited*. New Haven, CT: Yale University Press, 2009.

Herzog, Dorothy. "How to be a Producer." *Photoplay* April 1926: 66, 130–131.

Hopper, Hedda. *From Under My Hat*. Garden City, NY: Doubleday & Company, Inc., 1952.

Jacobs, Lea. *The Wages of Sin: Censorship and the Fallen Woman Film, 1928–1942*. Berkeley: University of California Press, 1997.

Jacobs, Lea. *The Decline of Sentiment: American Film in the 1920s*. Berkeley: University of California Press, 2008.

Jopp, Fred Gilman. "Making Up." *Screenland* March 1929: 72–73, 112.

Kehr, Dave. "That Lubitsch Touch, in Song." *New York Times* June 20, 2013: AR11. Available at <https://www.nytimes.com/2013/06/23/movies/warner-archive-restores-the-merry-widow.html> (last accessed December 11, 2019).

King, Homay. *Lost in Translation: Orientalism, Cinema, and the Enigmatic Signifier*. Durham, NC: Duke University Press, 2010.

Kingsley, Grace. "When Hollywood was a Pasture." *Photoplay* June 1927: 32–34, 140–144.

Klinger, Barbara. *Beyond the Multiplex: Cinema, New Technologies, and the Home*. Berkeley: University of California Press, 2006.

Klumph, Helen. "The Art and the Craft of the Motion-picture Actor." *Picture Play* April 1924: 21–23, 110.

Koszarski, Richard. *An Evening's Entertainment: The Age of the Silent Feature Picture, 1915–1928*. Berkeley: University of California Press, 1990.

Kracauer, Siegfried. *The Mass Ornament: Weimar Essays*. Cambridge, MA: Harvard University Press, 1995 [1963].

Lambert, Gavin. *On Cukor*. New York: Capricorn Books, 1973.

Lambert, Gavin. *Norma Shearer: A Life*. London: Hodder and Stoughton, 1990.

Lanckman, Lies. "'What Price Widowhood?': The Faded Stardom of Norma Shearer." In *Lasting Stars: Images that Fade and Personas that Endure*, ed. Lucy Bolton and Julie Lobalzo Wright. London: Palgrave Macmillan, 2016, 71–83.

Lane, Tamar. "That's Out." *Motion Picture* March 1924: 49–50, 84.

Lang, Harry. "Chaney Talks!" *Photoplay* May 1930: 75, 141.

Langdale, Alan (ed.). *Hugo Munsterberg on Film*. New York: Routledge, 2002.

Larkin, T. L. *In Search of Marie Antoinette in the 1930s: Stefan Zweig, Irving Thalberg, and Norma Shearer*. London: Palgrave Macmillan, 2019.

Leslie, Alice. "That Perfect Boss." *Motion Picture* May 1926: 56, 97.

Lev, Peter. *Twentieth-Century-Fox: The Zanuck-Skouras Years, 1935–1965*. Austin: University of Texas Press, 2013.

Lewis, David. *The Creative Producer*. Metuchen, NJ: The Scarecrow Press, 1993.

Lindsay, Vachel. *The Art of the Moving Picture*. New York: The Modern Library, 2000 [1915].

Loos, Anita. *Kiss Hollywood Good-bye*. London: W. H. Allen, 1974.

Maltby, Richard. "'Baby Face', or How Joe Breen Made Barbara Stanwyck Atone for Causing the Wall Street Crash." *Screen* 27.2 (1986): 22–46.

Maltby, Richard. "The Genesis of the Production Code." *Quarterly Review of Film and Video* 15.4 (1995): 5–32.

Maltby, Richard. *Hollywood Cinema*, 2nd edn. Oxford: Blackwell Publishing, 2003.

Manners, Dorothy. "The Boy Wonders." *Motion Picture* June 1929: 40, 94.

Marx, Samuel. "Dialogue by Thalberg." *The Hollywood Reporter* 70.31 (October 1942): section 2.

Marx, Samuel. "What Would Irving Do?" *The Hollywood Reporter* 90.24 (September 1946): section 2.

Marx, Samuel. *Mayer and Thalberg: The Make-Believe Saints*. New York: Random House, 1975.

Marx, Samuel. *A Gaudy Spree: Literary Hollywood When the West was Fun*. New York: Franklin Watts, 1987.

Marx, Samuel and Joyce Vanderveen. *Deadly Illusions: Jean Harlow and the Murder of Paul Bern*. New York: Random House, 1990.

McAllister, Anthony. "The Secret Behind Laughton's Acting." *Photoplay* February 1936: 36, 104.

McNally, Victoria. "Is Matt Bomer's 'The Last Tycoon' Character Based on a Real Person? He Resembles a True Hollywood Legend." *Bustle*. July 28, 2017. Available at <https://www.bustle.com/p/is-matt-bomers-the-last-tycoon-character-based-on-a-realperson-he-resembles-a-true-hollywood-legend-71673> (last accessed September 6, 2019).

"Metro-Goldwyn-Mayer." In *The American Film Industry*, ed. Tino Balio. Madison: The University of Wisconsin Press, 1976, 256–280.

Mulvey, Laura. *Death 24X a Second: Stillness and the Moving Image*. London: Reaktion Books, 2006.

Mulvey, Laura. "Visual Pleasure and Narrative Cinema" [1975]. In *Visual and Other Pleasures*, 2nd edn. London: Palgrave Macmillan, 2009, pp. 14–27.

Mulvey, Laura. "Thoughts on Marilyn Monroe: Emblem and Allegory." *Screen* 58.2 (Summer 2017): 202–209.

Nelson, Bradford. "Chaney Comes Back." *Screenland* May 1930: 33, 116–117.

Nemerov, Alexander. *Icons of Grief: Val Lewton and the Home Front*. Berkeley: University of California Press, 2005.

Oettinger, Malcom H. "Up from the Top." *Picture Play*, May 1930: 34–35.

Ohmer, Susan. "Jean Harlow: Tragic Blonde." In *Glamour in a Golden Age: Movie Stars of the 1930s*. Ed. Adrienne L. McLean. New Brunswick, NJ: Rutgers University Press, 2011, 174–195.

Perez, Gilberto. *The Material Ghost: Films and Their Medium*. Baltimore, MD: The Johns Hopkins University Press, 1998.

Pizzitola, Louis. *Hearst Over Hollywood*. New York: Columbia University Press, 2002.

"Plan Silent Versions of Metro Talkies." *New York Times* April 18, 1929: 32.

Platte, Nathan. *Making Music in Selznick's Hollywood*. New York: Oxford University Press, 2018.

Pravadelli, Veronica. *Lifestyles and Film Styles of American Cinema 1930–1960*. Trans. Michael Theodore Meadows. Urbana, IL: University of Chicago Press, 2015.

"A Producing Executive Describes the Gamut Run by Book or Play." *New York Times* December 20, 1925: Section X, p. 7.

Pudovkin, Vsevolod. "From *Film Technique* [1926]." In *Film Theory and Criticism*, 8th edition, ed. Leo Braudy and Marshall Cohen. Oxford: Oxford University Press, 2016, 6–11.

Quirk, James R. "The Enigma of the Screen." *Photoplay* March 1926: 63, 129–130.

Ramsey, Walter. "Strange as it May Seem." *Motion Picture* March 1930: 35, 92.

Randell, Karen. "Masking the Horror of Trauma: The Hysterical Body of Lon Chaney." *Screen* 44.2 (Summer 2003): 216–221.

Rapf, Joanna. "Classical Hollywood: 1928–1946." In *Producing*, ed. Jon Lewis. London: I. B. Tauris, 2016, 36–62.

Rittenhouse, Mignon. "What is an Epic Picture?" *Motion Picture* June 1926: 54–55, 74.

Rosenberg, Bernard and Harry Silverstein. *The Real Tinsel*. London: The Macmillan Company, 1970.

Rosten, Leo C. *Hollywood: The Movie Colony, the Movie Makers*. New York: Harcourt, Brace, and Co., 1941.

Salzberg, Ana. "Seduction Incarnate: Pre-Production Code Hollywood and Possessive Spectatorship." *Cinema: Journal of Philosophy and the Moving Image* 3 (2012): 39–61.

Salzberg, Ana. *Beyond the Looking Glass: Narcissism and Female Stardom in Studio-Era Hollywood*. New York: Berghahn Books, 2014.

Schatz, Thomas. *The Genius of the System: Hollywood Filmmaking in the Studio Era*. New York: Faber and Faber, 1996.

Schatz, Thomas. *Boom and Bust: American Cinema in the 1940s*. Berkeley: University of California Press, 1997.

Schulberg, Budd. *Moving Pictures: Memories of a Producing Prince*. London: Souvenir Press, 1981.

Schulberg, Budd. *What Makes Sammy Run?* New York: Ishi Press, 2011 [1941].

"The Shadow Stage." *Photoplay* April 1929: 52–55, 113–115.

"The Shadow Stage." *Photoplay* January 1936a: 48–52, 94.

"The Shadow Stage." *Photoplay* September 1936b: 52–55, 112.

"Silent Director of 'Big Parade' Got Results with Mental Telepathy." *New York Times* December 6, 1925: X9.

Silverman, Sid. "Broadway Melody." *Variety* February 12, 1929. Available at <https://variety.com/1929/film/reviews/broadway-melody-1200410242> (last accessed October 24, 2019).

Slide, Anthony. *Inside the Hollywood Fan Magazine*. Jackson: University of Mississippi Press, 2010.

Small, Frank. "Filming the World's Greatest Love Story." *Photoplay* September 1936: 46–48, 98–100.

Smedley, Nicholas. *A Divided World: Hollywood Cinema and Émigré Directors in the Era of Roosevelt and Hitler, 1933–1948*. Chicago: University of Chicago Press, 2011. E-book.

Spadoni, Robert. "Geniuses of the Systems: Authorship and Evidence in Classical Hollywood Cinema." *Film History* 7.4 (Winter 1995): 362–385.

Sobchack, Vivian. "'Surge and Splendor': A Phenomenology of the Hollywood Historical Epic." *Representations* 29 (Winter 1990): 24–49.

Sobchack, Vivian. *The Address of the Eye: A Phenomenology of Film Experience*. Princeton, NJ: Princeton University Press, 1992.

Sobchack, Vivian. "What is Film History?, or, The Riddle of the Sphinxes." In *Reinventing Film Studies*, ed. Christine Gledhill and Linda Williams. London: Arnold, 2000, 300–315.

Sobchack, Vivian. *Carnal Thoughts: Embodiment and Moving Image Culture*. Berkeley: University of California Press, 2004.

Spicer, Andrew, A. T. McKenna, and Christopher Meir (eds.). *Beyond the Bottom Line: The Producer in Film and Television Studies*. London: Bloomsbury, 2014.

Staiger, Janet. *Bad Women: Regulating Sexuality in Early American Cinema*. Minneapolis: University of Minnesota Press, 1995.

St. Johns, Adela Rogers. "An Impression of Marion Davies." *Photoplay* January 1925: 59, 104.

Studlar, Gaylyn. *This Mad Masquerade: Stardom and Masculinity in the Jazz Age*. New York: Columbia University Press, 1996.

Thalberg, Irving. "Footnote to the Filming of a Classic." In souvenir programme *Romeo and Juliet: A Metro-Goldwyn-Mayer Picture*. 1936.

Thalberg, Irving. "The Modern Photoplay." In *Introduction to the Photoplay 1929: A Contemporary Account of the Transition to Sound in Film*, ed. John C. Tibbetts. A National Film Society Publication, 1977, 111–132.

Thalberg, Irving and Hugh Weir. "Why Motion Pictures Cost So Much." *Saturday Evening Post* November 4, 1933: 10–11, 83–85.

Thalberg, Irving. "Technical Activities of the Motion Picture Arts and Sciences." *Journal of the Society of Motion Picture Engineers* 15.1 (July 1930): 3–16.

Thomas, Bob. *Thalberg: Life and Legend*. Garden City, NY: Doubleday, 1969.

Thomson, David. *The Whole Equation: A History of Hollywood*. London: Abacus, 2004.

Townsend, Leo. "Good News." *Modern Screen* August 1936: 20–23, 97–98, 100.

Tully, Jim. "Irving Thalberg." *Vanity Fair* October 1927: 71, 98.

Vertov, Dziga. "Selected Writings." In *The Avant-Garde Film: A Reader of Theory and Criticism*, ed. P. Adams Sitney. London: Anthology Film Archives, 1978.

Vertrees, Alan David. *Selznick's Vision: Gone with the Wind and Hollywood Filmmaking*. Austin: University of Texas Press, 1997.

Vidojkovic, Dario. "Early Representations of Wartime Violence in Films, 1914–1930." *Cultural History* 6.1 (2017): 37–56.

Vidor, King. *A Tree is a Tree*. London: Longmans, Green and Co., 1954.

Vieira, Mark A. *Greta Garbo: A Cinematic Legacy*. New York: Abrams, 2005.

Vieira, Mark A. *Hollywood Dreams Made Real: Irving Thalberg and the Rise of MGM*. New York: Abrams, 2008.

Vieira, Mark A. *Irving Thalberg: Boy Wonder to Producer Prince*. Berkeley: University of California Press, 2010.

Viviani, Christian. "The 'Foreign Woman' in Classical Hollywood Cinema." In *Journeys of Desire: European Actors in Hollywood*, ed. Ginette Vincendeau and Alistair Phillips. London: British Film Institute, 2006, 95–102.

Walker, Alexander. *Stardom: The Hollywood Phenomenon*. New York: Stein and Day, 1970.

Walker, Alexander. *The Shattered Silents: How the Talkies Came to Stay*. London: Harrap, 1978.

Waterbury, Ruth. "Close Ups and Long Shots." *Photoplay* November 1936: 11–12.

Weiss, Andrea. "'A Queer Feeling When I Look at You': Hollywood Stars and Lesbian Spectatorship in the 1930s." In *Stardom: Industry of Desire*, ed. Christine Gledhill. London: Routledge, 1991.

Whittaker, Alma. "Hit-Maker!" *Screenland* August 1932: 19.

Wilson, Leslie Kreiner. "The Education of Frances Marion and Irving Thalberg: Censorship, Development, and Distribution at MGM, 1927–1930." *Quarterly Review of Film and Video* 31 (2014): 123–135.

York, Cal. "Cal York's Gossip of Hollywood." *Photoplay* January 1937: 26–29, 86–88.

Zeitlin, Ida. "Norma Shearer Talks about *Romeo and Juliet*." *Motion Picture* October 1936, 32–33, 59, 61.

Index